W9-BYA-378

The Complete Idiot's Reference Card

Checklist for Building Great Interfaith Relationships

_____ 1. Recognize that interfaith relationships often spark negative reactions among participants, family members, and community members.

_____ 2. Understand that these feelings rarely vanish with time. In fact, they may intensify even when it seems that the religious issue has been settled.

_____ 3. Acknowledge that interfaith relationships introduce differences in many areas other than religion. These include food, clothing, non-religious behavior, even words and expressions.

_____ 4. Face the facts: Conflicts over interfaith relationships often require years of long, hard work to resolve.

_____ 5. Before you address conflicts over the role of religion in your relationship, you've got to decide what really matters to you as an individual.

_____ 6. Focus on your religious affiliation and degree of faith.

_____ 7. Learn as much as you can about your own religion and your sweetheart's religion.

_____ 8. Communicate with your sweetheart about your faith and the issues that matter to you.

_____ 9. Be ready to compromise on the minor issues.

_____ 10. If you have strong convictions on a specific issue, say so—or forever hold your peace.

_____ 11. Establish your identity as a couple by sticking together and making joint decisions.

_____ 12. Nip problems in the bud. Don't let differences swell to disagreements and then become cause for nuclear warfare.

_____ 13. You can be brutally honest with yourself, but don't be so quick to spread that honesty around. When in doubt, keep your mouth shut.

_____ 14. Decide what kind of religious faith you want your family to have. Then work with your spouse to create that spiritual identity.

_____ 15. Be proactive. Work to resolve differences in religious belief.

_____ 16. Develop a capacity for self-awareness.

_____ 17. Listen carefully, with empathy.

_____ 18. Keep your sense of humor..

_____ 19. Use common sense.

_____ 20. Recognize that a little tolerance buys a lot of goodwill.

alpha
books

Dealing with Interfaith Issues

If your sweetheart's family ...	Don't ...	Instead ...
Makes a mistake based on ignorance of your religious culture.	Be overly offended.	Educate them about your heritage.
Ignores you.	Assume that they know how you feel.	Explain how you feel in a straight-forward manner. Keep your cool.
Deliberately insults your religious beliefs.	Insult their spiritual beliefs.	Explain why you're hurt and state that their behavior isn't acceptable. Make sure your spouse backs your stance.
Dislikes you because of your faith.	Hate them in return.	Try to forge bonds through common interests and kindness.
Refuses to accept you.	Refuse to accept them.	Seriously consider whether this is the right relationship for you.
Tries to undermine the religious choices you and your spouse make.	Cut them off.	Present a united front with your spouse.

Sharpen Your Holiday Skills

How well interfaith couples manage during the holidays usually predicts how they deal with religious (and other) differences during the year. The skills interfaith families most need to navigate the holidays include the ability to ...

- ➤ *Listen effectively.*
- ➤ *Express yourself honestly.*
- ➤ *Keep your cool.*
- ➤ *Negotiate fairly.*
- ➤ *See the situation from your partner's viewpoint.*
- ➤ *Compromise.*
- ➤ *Resolve conflicts creatively.*
- ➤ *Keep your sense of humor.*

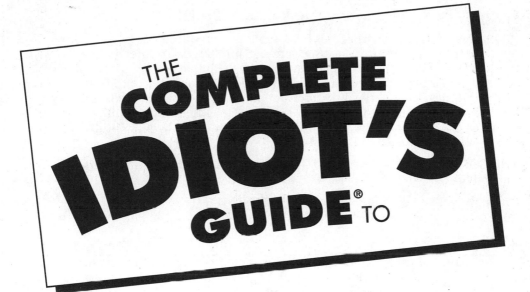

THE COMPLETE IDIOT'S GUIDE® TO

Interfaith Relationships

by Laurie Rozakis, Ph.D.

alpha books

Macmillan USA, Inc.
201 West 103rd Street
Indianapolis, IN 46290

A Pearson Education Company

Copyright © 2001 by Laurie Rozakis, Ph.D.

All rights reserved. No part of this book shall be reproduced, stored in a retrieval system, or transmitted by any means, electronic, mechanical, photocopying, recording, or otherwise, without written permission from the publisher. No patent liability is assumed with respect to the use of the information contained herein. Although every precaution has been taken in the preparation of this book, the publisher and author assume no responsibility for errors or omissions. Neither is any liability assumed for damages resulting from the use of information contained herein. For information, address Alpha Books, 201 West 103rd Street, Indianapolis, IN 46290.

THE COMPLETE IDIOT'S GUIDE TO and Design are registered trademarks of Macmillan USA, Inc.

International Standard Book Number: 0-02-863981-2
Library of Congress Catalog Card Number: Available from the Library of Congress.

03   02   01   8   7   6   5   4   3   2   1

Interpretation of the printing code: The rightmost number of the first series of numbers is the year of the book's printing; the rightmost number of the second series of numbers is the number of the book's printing. For example, a printing code of 01-1 shows that the first printing occurred in 2001.

Printed in the United States of America

Note: This publication contains the opinions and ideas of its author. It is intended to provide helpful and informative material on the subject matter covered. It is sold with the understanding that the author and publisher are not engaged in rendering professional services in the book. If the reader requires personal assistance or advice, a competent professional should be consulted.

The author and publisher specifically disclaim any responsibility for any liability, loss or risk, personal or otherwise, which is incurred as a consequence, directly or indirectly, of the use and application of any of the contents of this book.

Publisher
Marie Butler-Knight

Product Manager
Phil Kitchel

Managing Editor
Jennifer Chisholm

Acquisitions Editor
Randy Ladenheim-Gil

Development Editor
Michael Thomas

Production Editor
Billy Fields

Copy Editor
Amy Lepore

Illustrator
Jody P. Schaeffer

Cover Designers
Mike Freeland
Kevin Spear

Book Designers
Scott Cook and Amy Adams of DesignLab

Indexer
Angie Bess

Layout/Proofreading
Darin Crone
Mary Hunt

Contents at a Glance

Contents

Forewords

For countless generations, hearts have bonded, young love has blossomed, couples have been wed, and families have been born. In an idyllic world this is the way every relationship would work. However, as we all know—and, perhaps, as some of us have even spoken—words like "Love will conquer all!" are not always true.

Each person who has been in a romantic relationship knows well that even in the best of possible scenarios there are bound to be disagreements, arguments, periods of despair and, in all too many cases, separation or divorce. Add to the mix two people of different faiths and we find ingredients for a recipe which, when inadequately prepared, produces unpalatable results.

As a rabbi I am often asked to officiate at the marriage ceremonies of young couples, frequently couples of mixed faiths. While every rabbi handles these cases differently, my practice demands compassion and education, instructing these individuals about the challenges and disagreements they will inevitably face *because* they are of variant faith-traditions. The problems arise when the two individuals, because they are blinded by what is in their hearts and not considering what is in their heads, dismiss my advice and find that they must, in the end, tackle the eventual problems head-on.

It is for these people that I say, *"The Complete Idiot's Guide* series has done it again!" With the expertly researched data and resources collected by Dr. Laurie Rozakis, readers are introduced to an unbiased characterization of the realities of interfaith relationships. Throughout these pages readers are presented with answers and solutions to many of the primary questions asked by those involved in such relationships, their families and friends. While Laurie recognizes that there will always be issues and concerns unique to each couple, she provides us with explanations, statistics, and quizzes to help us better understand (and, for some, cope with) the trials and travails of dating and/or marrying someone outside of our own faith.

Dr. Rozakis, a veteran writer for *The Complete Idiot's Guide* series, has taken a very sensitive approach to a very challenging topic. As she points out in many places throughout the book, her goal is not to be judgmental; she claims no position other than one of "concerned facilitator." Recognizing that people are apt to follow their heart, Laurie presents a straightforward approach to appreciating that problems and obstacles in the interfaith relationship will likely develop, as well as directing those involved to potentially helpful resources.

Laurie skillfully leads readers to accept that what might be wrong for one might not be wrong for another. In fact, whether I—as the author of this Foreword—accept or deny the interfaith relationship as "good" or "bad" is entirely irrelevant. What matters here is how Laurie has so adeptly unlocked a door, allowing the communication between concerned parties to flow more freely.

I hope that this book will encourage couples to consult their clergy in order to address more specific issues related to their personal situations. Regardless of our stance on the issue of interfaith relationships, *The Complete Idiot's Guide to Interfaith Relationships* has offered us support for a topic not easily broached. Each one of us has something to gain from reading this volume.

—Rabbi Jeffrey Astrachan

Rabbi Jeffrey Astrachan is a graduate of the Hebrew Union College-Jewish Institute of Religion in Cincinnati, Ohio. Having earned a BA degree in Communication from the University of Hartford as well as a Master of Arts in Hebrew Letters degree and Rabbinic Ordination from HUC-JIR; he now serves as the spiritual leader of Temple Beth Elohim, a Reform congregation in Old Bethpage, New York.

Loving is primordial to our human experience, an expression of our faith and the method by which we share in the building of the kingdom of God. For the Christian, loving is the fulfillment of the call of Jesus to "love one another as I have loved you." Marriage, then, is a most sacred opportunity to live, express, and experience love.

What happens, though, when we fall in love and seek to marry someone outside our race, culture, or religion? If love comes from God, why are there obstacles to loving another who is created, like me, in the image and likeness of God? *The Complete Idiot's Guide to Interfaith Relationships* has come along, perhaps not to answer all these questions, but to help couples understand that these questions and many more are a necessary component to the life of an interfaith relationship.

In 1997, interfaith marriages accounted for 30 percent of all marriages blessed by the Catholic Church (Official Catholic Directory [OCD]). In our increasingly diverse culture, the number of those marriages will undoubtedly increase. An individual's preparation for marriage has always necessitated an important understanding of one's self. In *The Complete Idiot's Guide to Interfaith Relationships,* Dr. Laurie Rozakis assists the reader in recognizing that in today's society we are called to be more self-aware of our religious heritage, culture, and belief systems. The desire to share oneself in love must be accompanied by a willingness to understand and share one's own faith tradition as well as that of the beloved.

I am a recently ordained priest who has been serving the people of my diocese for just three years. In that time, though, I have had many opportunities to be with interfaith couples before and after marriage. I have become keenly aware of the need to assist couples in increasing their understanding of their individual faiths as well as making them aware of the various issues, challenges, and sometimes obstacles they will encounter. Some have asked and begun to answer many of the questions; others do not know where to begin. *The Complete Idiot's Guide to Interfaith Relationships* is an excellent starting point for couples who find themselves wandering in a maze of un-certainty as they begin an interfaith relationship. It is most helpful, too, for those whose relationship is further along.

Dr. Rozakis is a careful, respectful, and entertaining guide to an immensely challenging topic. Her well-researched work provides an opportunity to appreciate other faith traditions, illustrates a need for sensitivity, and exposes the challenges that await the reader. I know that her work here will continue to be a great resource to me and others who are charged with the responsibility of guiding in the ways of faith. I am confident that her efforts will encourage couples to allow their God-given gift of love for each other to be assisted by God's wisdom as well.

—Fr. Gerard Gentleman

Introduction

➤ How can I make my friends see that my religion is really a central part of who I am?

➤ Can you help me make my fundamentalist Christian girlfriend cope with my indifference to all religion?

➤ My fiancee is Indian. In her culture, a girl's parents have the final word as to whom she should marry. In mine that is not true. We intend to get married. How do we deal with this?

➤ My Asian wife's family hates me. I have broadened my horizons by learning her language and appreciating her culture, but they can't seem to get past the fact that I'm not Asian. How can I get my in-laws to accept me?

➤ My husband is from Pakistan, and I'm from India. Our daughter has had some questions about the tension between Pakistan and India over Kashmir. How should we deal with this?

➤ My ex and I still argue over religion—even though we're long divorced! What can I do to reduce the strife?

As these six opening anecdotes suggest, religious differences affect many different kinds of relationships:

➤ friendships

➤ casual lovers

➤ engaged couples

➤ married couples without kids

➤ married couples with kids

➤ divorced couples

In *The Complete Idiot's Guide to Interfaith Relationships*, I'll tell you how to cope with some of the most common—and distressing—situations you're likely to encounter when you date, marry, or divorce someone of a faith different from your own. This book is also designed for relatives and friends of those involved in interfaith relationships.

Today, having a successful relationship is more difficult than ever before, with divorce, nontraditional families, blended families, and step-parents, step-children, and step-everyone else. Add religious and cultural differences, and the situation becomes even more complex.

What You'll Learn in this Book

The Complete Idiot's Guide to Interfaith Relationships will give you the tools you need to decide if an interfaith relationship is right for you. And if you do decide to date or marry someone of a different faith (or are already in such a relationship), I'll help you develop strategies to make the relationship successful. You'll learn powerful ways to deal with the puzzling and painful issues that arise in mixed marriages. These same strategies work for the friends, siblings, and parents of offspring, too.

Being in an interfaith relationship takes a lot of hard work, but it can be well worth the effort. I can't promise you that if you become romantically involved with someone of a different religious background (or acquire a newcomer through someone else's marriage) you'll experience heaven on earth (that's a pint of rocky road, a down comforter, and a Ginger Rogers-Fred Astaire movie), but I *can* guarantee that by the time you finish this book, you'll have the skills you need to deal with the problems that arise.

How This Book Is Organized

This book is divided into six sections that take you through the process of developing healthy and fulfilling interfaith relationships. You'll learn how to probe your own values to discover if an interfaith relationship is right for you. Then I'll equip you with a full background in world religions, so you'll understand different belief systems. Next you'll learn how to deal with interfaith dating and marriage, as well as how to accept each other's differences. Most of all, you'll finish this book better equipped to create the kind of family that everyone wants—and deserves. Here's what you'll find in the six parts of this book:

Part 1: "Mixed Matches" introduces you to both the pleasure and pain of interfaith love. You'll also explore your own feelings about interfaith relationships to discover what hurdles you're likely to face. Finally, we'll discuss some solutions to help you improve your relationship right away.

Part 2: "Defender of the Faith" surveys the four main religions in the world—Judaism, Christianity, Islam, Hinduism—as well as Baha'i, Buddhism, Druze, Mennonite, Sikh, and Unitarianism. You'll learn what followers believe and also how each religion approaches intermarriage. The more you know about your beloved's religion, the more fully you will understand his or her values and beliefs. Then you can help replace ignorance with knowledge and empower people to work together to make the interfaith relationship strong.

Part 3: "Faith, Hope, and Charity: Interfaith Dating" provides a complete look at the situations that lovers face when they fall in love with someone from a different religious heritage. These issues include dealing with your honey's family and friends—as well as your own. This section of the book also concentrates on techniques for working through the problems you'll encounter with an interfaith romance. After you finish reading these chapters, you'll be ready to decide if an interfaith relationship is right for you; and if it is, how you can make it smoother from the get-go.

Part 4: "Celebrating Our Differences: Interfaith Marriages" shows you how to avoid a tempest in a tabernacle! Here, you'll learn all about the wedding ceremonies of many different religions as well as explore the issue of religious conversion.

Part 5: "And Baby Makes ..." a big family blow-up, unless an interfaith couple has decided on the child's religious upbringing first. These chapters explain ways to resolve religious issues when babykins is on the horizon as well as after he or she arrives. Baby names, first religious ceremonies (baptism, bris), holidays, and religious education are included here.

Part 6: "Untying the Knot" deals with divorce and death in interfaith families. Find out the funeral customs followed by Christians, Jews, and Hindus and see how to deal with the problems these differences can cause when a family dissolves through divorce or death.

The book concludes with a glossary of terms and a list of resources on interfaith relationships.

Dedication

To my daughter Samantha's friends, my great hope and faith for the future:

Jacky Allgier	Sean Bartlett	Sara Blackmore
Dawn Bodine	Betty Chan	Christine Curiel
Val Delaportas	Christine Dillon	Jillian Dorans
Jude Duffy	Christine Elliott	Lynn Ekstrand
Karl Ekstrand	Melissa Ferrarese	Lizzy Fink
Jill Fonda	Tracey Harris	Jade Ho
Ben Howell	Jessica Howell	Lauren Karp
Katie Keogh	Jeff Kessler	Alison Klein
Kristel Kubart	Tim Kubart	Laura LaCamera
Laura Lee	Rory Lyons	Chris McCoy
Carly Meyer	Brian Murphy	Heather Murphy
Nicole Padden	Andrea Plesica	Alison Schill
Stephanie Schiralli	Catie Star	Karl Siewertsen
Lee Sommers		

More For Your Money!

In addition to all the explanations and advice, this book contains even more of an "inside edge" when it comes to dealing with interfaith relationships. Here's how you can recognize these features.

Learn the Lingo

Every belief system has its own unique language. Here's where I explain important terms so you understand what your beloved is saying about faith.

Don't Go There

These warnings help you stay on track. They can make it easier for you to avoid the little goofs—and the major pitfalls—that can sink a relationship.

Family Matters

These hints help you deal with religious differences and keep your relationship growing.

Act of Faith

Here, I provide longer explanations of key religious customs and rites.

Did You Know?

These are interesting, useful bits of background information that give you even more help when it comes to dealing with different belief systems. You could skip these tidbits, but you wouldn't want to because they're much too useful!

A Word About the Stories in this Book

Because many of the people I interviewed didn't want to be identified, I have changed their names and altered some of the details of their stories. The exceptions are those people clearly identified by their professional titles, affiliations, or publications.

I wish to thank everyone who helped me by generously sharing their experiences and expertise, most especially Stephan (Gorilla Monsoon), Ro and Andy, Bob and Debbie, Angela, Diane E., Gudrun, Meish, Audrey and Alan, Jodi and Alex, Linda and Glenn, Nancy S., Mary Ellen, and Pat. To those whose names I changed, you know who you are, and you know you have my gratitude as well.

Special Thanks to ...

Robyn Smith, a generous friend.

Randy Ladenheim-Gil, my wonderful editor. Randy, thank you for supporting my idea for this book and for all the other help you have given me.

Michael Thomas, a superb editor whose fine work always makes me look good!

Billy Fields the production editor and Amy Lepore the copy editor.

I am very much indebted to my brilliant, generous, and gracious friend Diane B. Engel for her help with the Fundamentalist Christian section in Chapter 5.

I'd also like to acknowledge the knowledgeable and patient staff of Gutterman's Funeral Home in Woodbury, Long Island, for their assistance.

Part 1
Mixed Matches

My husband once claimed that we have a mixed marriage not because he's Greek Orthodox/Catholic and I'm Jewish, but because he's a man and I'm a woman. My husband is a smart man.

In effect, every marriage is mixed because we bring our own unique heritage and background to the table. But interfaith relationships still push hot buttons all over the world. As a result, these matches can be especially stressful for family and friends as well as the partners themselves.

In this section of the book, you'll explore some of the joys and sorrows of mixed matches. You'll also probe your own feelings about interfaith relationships. Finally, we'll discuss some solutions to help you improve your relationship right away.

Chapter 1

Keeping the Faith

In This Chapter

➤ Compare your interfaith romances to the ones described here

➤ Explore common characteristics of interfaith relationships

➤ See what some people say about mixed matches

➤ Learn about a new kind of revolution

➤ Discover a theory about faith and health

➤ Test your knowledge of believers

"Matters of religion should never be matters of controversy. We neither argue with a lover about his taste, nor condemn him, if we are just, for knowing so human a passion."

—George Santayana, *The Life of Reason: Reason in Religion* (1906)

Of course, the wise philosopher George Santayana is right: When someone is lucky enough to fall in love, we should celebrate his or her good fortune—even if the beloved follows a different faith. Other people, however, might say there's no cause for celebration at all; on the contrary, we should do everything in our power to break up the union.

Why does the issue of *interfaith relationships* evoke such violent emotions? There's no denying that the topic resonates powerfully. I've published more than a hundred books, and none has been as difficult to research and write as this one because none of the other topics has pushed so many hot buttons—including my own.

Interfaith relationships affect the individuals and their families intensely. These "mixed matches" also affect every local community and every house of worship. Participants in an interfaith relationship might be shunned by their fellow worshippers and might even be forced to leave the religious community. As a result, interfaith relationships are symbolic of many other things as well. Interfaith relationships are really powerful stuff.

In this chapter, you'll first explore the experiences of several interfaith couples. This will help you compare and contrast your experiences to those of others in interfaith affairs of the heart. Next you'll discover how some people feel about these relationships and what they say about them. You'll also see how people choose their mates and will explore one astonishing way in which religious faith may affect you.

Then you'll discover how much you know about faith in America and around the world today. Finally, I'll give you some statistics on religion and interfaith relationships.

Learn the Lingo

For our purposes here, an **interfaith relationship** is defined as one in which the lovers follow different religions or faiths.

Forbidden Fruit

A Jewish man recounted his experience of falling in love with a Catholic woman:

> "It was love at first sight, but custom dictated that it be love from afar. Why? Her name was Margaret Donohue, and mine is Marvin Goldstein. I had never gone out with a non-Jewish girl and knew that my parents would kill me if I did. I had an uncle who'd married a Protestant in 1940, and the whole family was still talking about it. It was a *shunde*, an embarrassment and shameful. This was 1990, but little had changed ….
>
> We began to date secretly. A few months later, I told my family about Maggie. Not unexpectedly, they were appalled and outraged. A Catholic! After what Christians had done to our people! 'Where did we go wrong?' they asked each other. My father laid down the law: No Irish Catholic *shikse* sluts for me. He took my car keys and went

Learn the Lingo

Shikse, from the Hebrew word meaning "abomination," is a pejorative term for a non-Jewish woman. **Shaygetz** is the male equivalent.

to his room in a rage, returning after a few moments to punch me in the face. My mother reminded me that he'd had a heart attack two years earlier and said I must never mention 'The Shikse' again.

Even though Maggie converted to Judaism shortly after we were married, my parents still don't consider her a 'real' Jew. She's never been accepted as a true member of the family. This has been a considerable source of pain for us."

—Marvin, age 40

An Asian-American friend recounted the following story of her love affair with a man from a very different background:

"I am a Japanese Buddhist, and my boyfriend Rick is an Anglo-American Baptist. After a few months, we were not getting along. Things just got worse and worse, so I finally confronted him. [Confronting someone] is not a very Japanese thing to do because it is considered very socially incorrect. It is extremely rude even to say 'no,' more so as a woman to a man. Everything is 'maybe' in order to pre-serve 'face' for the other person. Well, I had enough. I was not preserving face, but rather decided to get 'in his face.'

I couldn't believe that I was acting this way, but my family was even more shocked. They had not yet found a way to deal with my relationship with Rick, and here I was betraying my background and beliefs even more."

—Lin, age 25

What happened when a Catholic man fell in love with a Lutheran woman? In the man's own words:

"I am Mexican-American Catholic from Southern California. Anna, oh boy. Anna is every prom queen from every high school in history. Tall, blonde, and beautiful, Athena in bike shorts and a scrunchie. And not only that, she's a Midwestern Lutheran. Our love began as friendship when we met in a coffee bar in San Francisco.

But one day, I decided to seize the moment and ask her out. Other than our mutual ad-miration of high-priced coffee and maybe a zip code, we had nothing at all in common. Astonishingly, she accepted my invitation to date, and we began our relationship. We dis-covered that we had far more in common

Don't Go There

A successful relationship (inter-faith or otherwise) is *not* like football; there are no successful end-runs in this game. *Never* let your friends and family get in the middle of a relationship. And don't tolerate it if your beloved allows such interference.

5

than I would ever have predicted, but I never imagined the fierce opposition we would encounter from friends, family, and even co-workers over our different faiths. When we were dating a few months, people started telling us to break it off before we got too serious. After all, they said, our children would have problems with an interfaith household. Who's having children? We were just dating!"

—Juan, age 28

Top Ten Common Experiences in Interfaith Relationships

A Jewish/Catholic couple. A Buddhist/Baptist couple. A Catholic/Lutheran couple. On the surface, these three stories don't seem very common, but they all illustrate some common experiences that interfaith couples share.

Learn the Lingo

Religion can be defined as a way of life or belief based on a person's ultimate relation to the universe or God. As such, religion is often an integral part of a person's identity.

Below are 10 of these shared experiences. As you read, see how many of these experiences you've had:

10. One partner or both in an interfaith relationship may feel torn and confused over religious issues.

9. Interfaith relationships often spark surprisingly strong emotions among participants, family members, and community members. Often, these emotions are negative: disapproval, fear, and even panic.

8. These feelings rarely vanish with time. In fact, they may intensify even when it seems that the religious issue has been settled.

7. Outsiders often give unsolicited advice to lovers involved in interfaith relationships.

6. Interfaith relationships introduce differences in many areas other than religion. These include food, clothing, nonreligious behavior, even words and expressions.

5. Differences can be exciting, but they can also be threatening and even frightening.

4. Dating people from different backgrounds can change your behavior and self-image. This can threaten friends and family members very much.

3. People of different faiths who wish to get married often encounter significant obstacles, which go beyond the objections society raises. These obstacles include

powerful historic forces, ingrained religious beliefs, and undiscovered subconscious prejudices.

2. Interfaith relationships are often very challenging for everyone involved—the lovers as well as their friends and family.

And the most common experience among the partners in an interfaith relationship is ...

1. People in interfaith relationships tend to be unprepared for the roadblocks they'll encounter from each other, their families, and even themselves.

A Member of the Tribe

Remember the advice Anita gave to Maria in *West Side Story*?

> "A boy like that, he killed your brother.
> Forget that boy and find another.
> One of your own kind—
> Stick to your own kind."

How often have *you* heard that advice? Since people rarely sing it outside the movies, perhaps it was phrased in one of these ways:

➤ "She's not a member of the tribe."

➤ "He's not one of our kind."

➤ "You know what *they're* like."

➤ "You know that *I* don't care, but what will your Aunt Alice (Uncle Tomas, Auntie Jade, Cousin Guido, Grandpa Olotunu, and so on) say?"

➤ "What? A Jewish (Catholic, Muslim, Baptist, and so on) girl (boy) isn't good enough for you anymore?"

Did You Know?

The 1961 film adaptation of *West Side Story*, starring Natalie Wood and George Chakris, won 10 Academy Awards including Best Picture, Best Direction, Best Supporting Actor and Actress (George Chakris and Rita Moreno), Best Cinematography, Best Costumes, Best Art Direction/Set Direction, Best Editing, and Best Score. Jerome Robbins earned a special award for his choreography.

As the three anecdotes in this chapter and these comments reveal, people often oppose interfaith relationships. They fear outsiders and the different customs and culture they bring. As a result, you'd expect that few people would have the guts to enter into mixed matches and that even fewer people would continue with the relationship once they encounter opposition.

Just the opposite is true.

There's a major revolution taking place right under our noses. It's not as bloody as the French Revolution or as noisy as the Industrial Revolution, but it's every bit as earth-shaking. What *is* this revolution?

It's a social revolution, as millions of people are defying ancient taboos to form intimate relationships with partners from other religious backgrounds. Never before in the history of the world have so many people followed their hearts in defiance of the ancient traditions that govern love, marriage, and child rearing.

What I Did for Love

Take this quick quiz to see how much you know about the ultimate interfaith relationship—intermarriage. Just answer true or false to each question.

1. About one-quarter of all Jews born before 1930 marry someone of another faith.
2. Half of all Jews born after 1950 marry someone of another faith.
3. About one-quarter of all Catholics born before 1930 marry someone of another faith.
4. Half of all Catholics born after 1950 marry someone of another faith.
5. There is a higher rate of divorce among interfaith marriages than among marriages between people of the same faith.

Source: National Opinion Research Center's General Social Survey Qtd. in the Journal of Marriage & the Family

Gotcha. Every one of these sentences is true. The groundswell of interfaith relationships really is a revolution. It's gathering steam, too, if these statistics are any predictor. Even without a crystal ball, we can safely predict that more and more people are going to have relationships with others of different faiths.

Learn the Lingo

Among people from Hispanic backgrounds, it is good manners for friends to embrace and simultaneously pat each other on the back. This is called an **abrazo**.

Good and Good for You?

Freedom of choice is all fine and dandy since the Constitution guarantees us the right to "life, liberty, and the pursuit of happiness." The problem arises when we have to decide what to do about religious differences: yours, mine, ours, or nothing? Religion is a powerful force that affects us in many different ways. Believe it or not, it can even affect your health. Read on to see how!

Religion—Opiate or Antibiotic?

Some scientists believe that religious people are healthier than those who aren't religious. Both *The Washington Times* and *The New Republic* have recently published articles about this theory. The theory tests the faith of many nonbelievers, and sorting out the causes and effects hasn't made the task any easier.

The study quoted in the *Times* was certainly open to criticism. Originally appearing in *Demography* magazine, the survey of 21,000 adult Americans concluded that "those who never attend [church] exhibit 50 percent higher risks of [premature] mortality than those who attend most frequently." In other words, going to church can keep you from pushing up daisies before your time.

Unfortunately, without controlling for other factors, all we've got is smoke and mirrors. Take another analogy: People who work are healthier than those who don't, but that doesn't mean work makes you healthier. It may be, for example, that those who work are healthier to begin with. Furthermore, the study isn't large enough to knock the socks off those of us who can count; the statistical evidence just isn't strong enough to show cause and effect.

The results reported in *The New Republic* were more scrupulous. This study looked at surveys conducted by Duke University and one published in the *American Journal of Public Health* (*AJPH*). Surprisingly, they arrived at the same results: Religious worshipers were healthier than nonworshipers. In fact, the *AJPH* study concluded that believers "tended to start off in worse-than-average health and then gradually improve to superior outcomes." The Duke studies found equally good results for most forms of Christianity and for Judaism (there were too few followers of Islam surveyed to provide enough information about that faith), but some sects prove to have worse health than the general population. This would tend to work against a general notion that a religious attitude by itself promotes good health.

As *The New Republic* points out, "Every mainstream Western denomination encourages the flock to drink in moderation, shun drugs, stop smoking, live circumspectly, practice monogamy, get married, and stay married." The opposites of all of these behaviors are known health-risk factors.

Did You Know?

According to another recent study, prayer is a more powerful predictor of marital satisfaction than frequency of sexual intercourse. Hmmm ...

Learn the Lingo

Atheists are people who profess skepticism, disbelief, or are irreligious, including people opposed to all religion.

9

It may be that keeping the faith is the single best way to stay healthy. Aside from the health benefits (however unproven), most people follow their faith for more traditional reasons. Food for thought, readers.

Now, how many people actually consider themselves believers?

Who We Are, What We Believe

How much do you know about religion and its importance to people in America and around the world? Take this simple quiz to test your RQ (religious quotient). Select the item that best answers each question.

1. How many people in the world identify themselves as adherent to one religion or another?

   a. 1.5 million   **c.** 4.7 billion
   b. 4.7 million   **d.** 7.4 billion

2. What percentage of the world's population defines itself as religious?

   a. 25%   **c.** 75%
   b. 50%   **d.** 80%

3. In North America today, how many people identify themselves as Christians?

   a. About 100 million   **c.** About 500 million
   b. About 250 million   **d.** About 750 million

4. Of that figure, how many people identify themselves as Roman Catholics in North America today?

   a. About 1 million   **c.** About 50 million
   b. About 10 million   **d.** About 74 million

5. How many people belong to the Southern Baptist faith?

   a. 2 million   **c.** 10 million
   b. 5 million   **d.** 15.9 million

6. How many Southern Baptist congregations are there in North America?

   a. 42,000   **c.** 100,000
   b. 75,000   **d.** 1 million

7. In North America today, how many people identify themselves as Jews?

   a. About 1 million   **c.** About 6 million
   b. About 3 million   **d.** About 12 million

8. How many people identify themselves as Jews in the world today?

    a. About 5 million   **c.** About 50 million

    b. About 13 million   **d.** About 100 million

9. How many Buddhists are there in the world today?

    a. 35 million   **c.** 500 million

    b. 350 million   **d.** 1 billion

10. Where do most Buddhists live?

    a. Asia   **c.** Hoboken, New Jersey

    b. Africa   **d.** Europe

11. How many people practice the Hindu faith?

    a. About 75 million   **c.** About 750 million

    b. About 250 million   **d.** About 1 billion

12. Where do most Hindus live?

    a. Africa   **c.** Boca Raton, Florida

    b. Latin America   **d.** Asia

13. How many people practice the Muslim faith?

    a. Over 800 million   **c.** Over 5 billion

    b. Over 1 billion   **d.** Over 10 billion

14. Where do most Muslims live?

    a. Africa   **c.** Europe

    b. Asia   **d.** Cleveland, Ohio

15. What are the two most commonly followed religions in North America today?

    a. Baha'i and Confucianism

    b. Christianity and Judaism

    c. Hinduism and Sikhism

    d. Judaism and Jainism

Source: 1999 World Almanac and Book of Facts

Learn the Lingo

Adherents are people who follow a certain creed, sect, or religion.

Score Yourself

1. c	6. a	11. c
2. d	7. c	12. d
3. b	8. b	13. a
4. d	9. b	14. b
5. d	10. a	15. b

As you just learned, Christianity and Judaism are the two religions with the most followers in North America. However, in this book, we'll pay attention to mixed matches among people of other faiths as well.

The Least You Need to Know

➤ Interfaith relationships are often very challenging for everyone involved—the lovers as well as their friends and family.

➤ People of different faiths who wish to get married often encounter powerful obstacles.

➤ The number of interfaith relationships and marriages is increasing sharply.

➤ A strong religious faith may be good for your health.

➤ About 4.7 billion people around the world identify themselves as adherents of one religion or another.

➤ In North America, the two most commonly followed religions are Christianity and Judaism.

Well dad, whaddya think?

Chapter 2

Strangers to the Tribe

In This Chapter

➤ Examine how your background, religion, and culture shape your world view

➤ Define "normal" as you explore religious differences

➤ See what fears people have about mixed matches

➤ Learn eight emergency measures for fixing a broken interfaith relationship

➤ Make sure you practice what you preach

Way back when we were trying to figure out how to wrest our freedom from England, a visiting Frenchman named Hector St. John de Crevecoeur attempted to define an "American":

> "What, then, is this American, this new man? He is neither an European nor the descendant of an European; hence that strange mixture of blood, which you will find in no other country. I could point out to you a family whose grandfather was an Englishman, whose wife was Dutch, whose son married a French woman, and whose present four sons have now wives of different nations.
>
> He is an American, who, leaving behind him all his ancient prejudices and manners, receives new ones from the new mode of life he has embraced, the new government he obeys, and the new rank he holds. ... Here individuals of all nations are melted into a new race of men, whose labors and posterity will one day cause great changes in the world."

—*Letters from an American Farmer*

Crevecoeur was clearly on to something—America is the most democratic and unrestricted country that has ever existed. We have welcomed into our families people from scores of other nations, near and far, ancient and modern. This openness has given our country a richness and a strength unparalleled throughout the world (as well as some great music and excellent takeout).

As a result, we tend to pride ourselves on our acceptance, openness, and nonjudgmental attitudes. So why do we have such problems with interfaith relationships? That's what you'll learn in this chapter.

First you'll explore how your background, religion, and culture affect your world view. Next you'll take an easy quiz to see what you consider "normal." Then you'll trace the fears people have about interfaith relationships. I'll teach you eight ways to get your interfaith relationship on the right path, too. Finally, I'll help you review what you learned with a brief checklist.

Eyes Wide Shut

Stavros Aristides was 18 years old when he came to America from Athens, Greece. Soon after, most of his family followed and settled nearby. Stavros promptly changed his name to Steve and bought a diner. Since his English was flawless and his work ethic astonishing, the diner flourished. Steve employed most of his siblings as cooks, serving staff, and bookkeepers. His mother made the pastry for the diner; his father managed the rental properties that Steve owned. Steve was proud of his status as a successful American businessman and was eager to blend into the mainstream of American life, even though he was fiery in his Greek Orthodox religious beliefs.

He married Christine, a smart and well-educated American of Greek ancestry. "Steve thought he wanted a real American woman," she told me. "But what he really wanted was a Greek woman disguised as an American. My parents are third-generation Greek, and we weren't raised Greek Orthodox. I'm not that interested in learning the religion or culture," she concluded.

After the birth of their first child, Steve suddenly decided that Christine couldn't work outside the home. "A wife's place is in the home," he said. "Her job is to keep the house and raise our child to speak Greek and learn all about our people." Steve was astonished at the strength of his feelings. After all, he was an "American" now—wasn't he?

Background, religion, and culture are powerful stuff. Ingrained from birth, they shape the way we look at the world. That's because culture is a prism that reflects how we interpret someone's actions and emotions. Major cultural differences in a relationship can open a chasm as wide as the Grand Canyon, but even subtle religious variances between partners can lead to major misunderstandings. Steve and Christine shared the same faith but to very different degrees. Since they were so far apart in belief and background, they might as well have been of different faiths.

People who are not aware of the impact of religious and cultural differences—or choose to ignore them—will often have a hard time understanding their sweetheart. This lack of true communication extends to the sweetheart's family and friends as well.

Strangers in the Night

As you well know, little misunderstandings can balloon faster than a waistline at Thanksgiving dinner. Check out the following examples to see what I mean. As you read, compare these experiences with your own.

Don't Go There

Beware of making generalizations about people and their feelings based on their religion and culture. Remember: Everyone is an individual and evolves in his or her own way.

➤ **An Italian Catholic man dating a Protestant woman.** He sees himself as traditional and respectful of women; she sees him as a chauvinist who expects her to wait on him. When they discuss these differences, he sees himself as forceful and commanding; she sees him as verbally abusive.

➤ **A Lutheran woman in love with a Mormon man.** She can't understand why he is expected to go on an overseas mission for two years. Why can't he just attend church and leave the proselytizing to someone else?

➤ **An Episcopalian man engaged to a Jewish woman.** He sees himself as reserved and proper; she sees him as arrogant and cold. He feels she spends far too much time visiting her parents and wonders if such behavior is normal; she can't understand how he can go six months without calling his folks.

➤ **An Orthodox Christian man and a Muslim woman.** He has never washed a dish in his life and doesn't understand why he should be expected to do "woman's work" now. Both sets of parents agree with him and can't understand why his wife is making such a fuss about each partner's role.

➤ **A Jewish man married to a Catholic woman.** Since the Jewish man isn't religious, his Catholic wife was astonished when he refused to let her name their first child Christopher and have him baptized.

➤ **A Jewish woman married to a Polish Catholic man.** Her parents didn't come to the wedding because "Poles are the worst anti-Semites," they said. They can't forgive the Poles for their role in World War II, even though everyone in the family was born in America.

Each of these situations arose from long-held feelings and some cultural misunderstandings. All of us—whether intermarried or not—are caught between our need for continuity with tradition and the necessity of adapting to a rapidly changing world.

Did You Know?

In a number of Eastern countries, it's perfectly acceptable to eat dog. In recognition of the American taboo against eating Fido or his canine companions, during the 1988 Olympics, Korean restaurants in Seoul removed dog entrees from their menus.

As we each take up our own quest to search for a place where we belong and a partner to share in our life, we need to face these realities. We must learn how to recognize, understand, and deal with our religious and cultural differences.

One half of an interfaith couple may be shocked at what the other partner takes for granted because of religious differences. Even in the most secular and sophisticated environment, differences in religious training and background can astonish lovers. Let's start by defining what's "normal."

What, Me Worry?

How do you define "normal"? Take this quick quiz to see what behaviors you consider acceptable—and what behaviors seem stranger than Marilyn Manson. Just read each question and circle yes or no for your answer.

1. Is it normal to drink a milkshake with a hamburger?

   Yes   No

2. Is it normal to have a frosty beer at a ball game?

   Yes   No

3. Is it normal to chow down on pork sausage and peppers? (With a few onions for some zip, please.)

   Yes   No

4. Is it normal to have an open coffin at a funeral?

   Yes   No

5. Is it normal to shun shellfish (even when it's served with rivers of melted butter)?

   Yes   No

6. Is it normal for a woman to shake a man's hand at the end of a business deal?

   Yes   No

7. Is it normal for a woman to show her hair?

   Yes   No

8. Is it normal to enjoy a thick, juicy steak?

   Yes   No

9. Is it normal to fast for a solid month between sunup and sundown?

   Yes   No

10. Is it normal to hug and kiss your sweetie in public?

   Yes   No

11. Is it normal to kidnap your sweetie and force her to marry you?

   Yes   No

Answers

1. Not if you're an Orthodox Jew. Kosher laws forbid eating milk and meat products together. You'll learn more about this in Chapter 4.

2. Not if you're a Muslim, Hindu, Mormon, or member of specific Protestant sect—none of these people drink alcoholic beverages. These religious customs are explained in Chapters 5, 6, and 7.

3. Not if you're an Orthodox Jew or observant Muslim. People who belong to these faiths don't eat pork. See Chapters 4 and 5.

4. Not if you're Jewish. According to the tenets of this faith, the coffin is closed. You'll learn more about this in Chapter 4.

5. Yes, if you're Jewish or Muslim. See Chapters 4 and 6.

6. Not if you're an Orthodox Jewish woman or a very religious Muslim. In these two faiths, there's no touching between the sexes unless you're a married couple in the privacy of your own home. These customs are explained in Chapters 4 and 6.

7. Not if you're an Orthodox Jewish woman or a very religious Muslim. Orthodox Jewish women often wear wigs to cover their hair, while Orthodox Muslim women wear scarves or full-body garments called *chadors*. See Chapters 4 and 6.

8. Not if you're a Hindu or Seventh Day Adventist; people who belong to these religions do not eat beef. This is described in Chapters 5 and 7.

9. Yes, if you're a Muslim who observes the month-long holiday of Ramadan. See Chapter 6.

Don't Go There

According to one estimate, there may be twice as many Muslims as Episcopalians in America today. So never assume to know who's the majority and who's the minority.

Source: "Marketing in the Islamic Context," Sixth Annual Eastern University Michigan University Conference on Languages and Communication for World Business and the Professions, 1987.

10. Not always. Among Chinese people from Vietnam, for example, a man and a woman are discouraged from hugging or kissing if they are not married. Many Latinos, in contrast, expect body contact.

11. Some marriage customs that are illegal in America are customary in other cultures. Among the *Hmong*, marriage can take place when a young man takes a girl (often as young as 14) to his home and consummates the marriage. In exchange, the groom's family pays a "bride price" to the girl's family. This practice is called *zij poj niam*, "marriage by capture."

Learn the Lingo

The **Hmong** are a tribe of people from the hills of Laos, a country in Southeast Asia. Many Hmong escaped from their homeland after the end of the Vietnam War and settled in America.

Gimme That Old Time Religion

"Look up the word 'WASP' in the dictionary, and you'll find a picture of my in-laws. They're from the Midwest, the mayonnaise-and-white-bread Midwest. The women are blonde, blue-eyed, and demure; the men are all named Bud or Chip. And here I am, a Jewish girl from New York, with dark curly hair, brown eyes, and a big mouth. They don't know what to make of me. For a long time, they called me 'The New York Girl' in a way that my folks wouldn't appreciate. Even when I try to look and act like Donna Reed, I feel like Barbra Streisand."

—Beth, age 31

The freedom to worship as we please is one of the foundations of American life. Nonetheless, everyone knows that the law of the land is different from the law of the family. Most of the time, fuss about intermarriage develops out of a sincere concern for the family's unity and well being; other times, however, it's a result of fear and even prejudice. Whatever the reason for the friction among your family and friends when someone has a relationship outside the fold, their reactions can usually be explained by one of the following fears:

➤ **Fear of losing their child.** Fear aside, these parents have usually done a great job of raising independent children who feel secure enough to separate from the family and grow as individuals. Marrying out of the faith doesn't mean losing your child—unless someone does something that can't be undone. Don't let it be you.

➤ **Fear of the unknown.** These parents often worry that their child has joined a cult, but there are cults and then there are cults: It's often a matter of perception. A friend of mine who is a devout Catholic views the Methodists as a cult.

➤ **Fear of embarrassment.** Many relatives of an interfaith couple worry what their neighbors, friends, business associates, and others will think about their child and his or her sweetheart. We can say, "Who cares?" but people care about public appearances very much indeed. And don't kid yourself: John Q. Public does matter. Even today, what people perceive as an "inappropriate" pairing can stand in the way of a person's social acceptance in many places.

➤ **Fear of disobedience.** Some parents see an interfaith relationship as deliberate disloyalty to their heritage. Even though this is rarely the case, if it's what someone believes, then the issue must be addressed.

No matter what motivates a person's fear when someone they love is involved in a mixed match, social pressure rarely resolves the issue to anyone's satisfaction.

Emergency Rx

While it may not be the primary cause of all family feuds, religion ranks in the top five reasons for family friction and the crumbling of relationships. What can you do if you find yourself to be half of an interfaith couple in the middle of a family conflict? How can you demonstrate that you're more than whom you pray to?

Below are some ways to get the relationship off to a good start (or to correct a bad start, if that's the case). In Chapters 9, 10, and 11, I discuss each of these methods and many more in detail.

1. **United we stand, divided we fall.** First of all, it's essential that you and your sweetheart present a united front. You and your beloved must explain to your families, in private, that you chose your mate. Cat got your tongue? Try this line: "If you love and respect me, you'll need to respect my choice and my mate."

2. **Show interest in your sweetheart's faith.** For example, if you're Catholic and your sweetie's parents are Jewish, attend their *Passover seder* if you are invited.

Did You Know?

The United States now has 1,100 mosques and Islamic centers, 1,500 Buddhist centers, and 800 Hindu centers.

Source: "Harvard Tracking Religious Diversity."

Hold On!

Don't Go There

Never degrade yourself or your beliefs—no matter how different they may be from what your sweetie believes.

Learn the Lingo

The **Passover seder** is the ritual meal that observant Jews celebrate to commemorate the exodus of the Israelites from Egypt and their safe flight across the Red Sea. This flight, described in the book of Exodus, was led by Moses.

Learn the Lingo

A **matzoth** (or **matzo**) is the unleavened bread eaten by observant Jews during Passover. It recalls the unleavened bread eaten by the Israelites during their flight from Egypt because they didn't have time to let their bread rise. Matzoth is made from flour and water and tastes like a cracker.

(Watch the *matzoth* balls; a bad matzoth ball makes a good paperweight. They repeat like episodes of *I Dream of Jeannie*.) Chapters 4–8 describe the religious celebrations you'll most likely encounter in different faiths and what to expect at each one.

3. **Invite your sweetheart's family to learn more about your religion.** Difference is scary; knowledge decreases fear. When your sweetie and his or her family see that you don't handle snakes or sacrifice raccoons, they're likely to feel less threatened by your religious beliefs. (Unless you *do* handle snakes and sacrifice raccoons. Thanks for not sharing.)

   Whatever you believe, recognize that none of your sweetheart's family or friends are under any obligation to worship as you do. They have to *respect* your beliefs, not follow them. So share and share alike, but don't insist that yours is the one true faith. No proselytizing, please—no earnest sermons or tracts on pillows.

4. **Try to avoid confrontations.** Religious beliefs are a funny thing; you either have them or you don't. And if you do, nobody's going to sway what you deeply hold to be true. You won't get anywhere by antagonizing your sweetie's family and friends and discussing red flags. Stay away from abortion, euthanasia, and other similar hot topics that are sure to offend.

5. **Consider compromise.** One couple I know was married in a Unitarian church because, being Jewish and Episcopalian, they sought to find some middle ground of civilization where family members on both sides were less likely to kill themselves or each other. (They selected that particular Unitarian church because, on the day they checked out the church, it was dedicating a pew to a cat.)

   Compromise works well for some couples, but it's a disaster for others. It's been my experience that compromise works best when one partner has a strong faith but the other does not. If both partners are very devout, there may not be any room for compromise. Don't beat yourself up about this, and don't try to force your sweetie to walk your walk and talk your talk.

6. **Find a support group.** The Web is a wonderful place to find support groups. In Appendix B, "Resources on Interfaith Relationships," you'll find different resources including Web sites with message boards. You might want to use these sites to meet people and share experiences with interfaith relationships.

7. **Be patient.** Be patient with your partner. Be patient with family and friends. It's not uncommon for couples to spend months secretly trying to come to terms with their differences, yet then expect family and friends to react positively when they announce their relationship. Give your family and friends time to get to know your partner and answer their questions the best you can.

8. **Try a little humor.** As you've probably figured out by now, I think a little humor goes a long way to defuse tough and touchy situations. But keep the humor light and playful, never snide or sarcastic. And never make one of your sweetie's friends or family members the butt of a joke—no matter how much they deserve it.

Give Peace a Chance

Each of us grows up in a religious (or nonreligious) culture that provides patterns of acceptable —and unacceptable   behavior and beliefs. Understanding the culture of your sweetheart is crucial if you want to avoid blowing the lid off the relationship.

Family Matters

Remember that how you and your partner view your differences is key to your happiness and the longevity of your relationship.

Act of Faith

Unitarians (Unitarianism is a type of Christianity) deny the doctrine of the Trinity, believing instead that God exists in one person only. They also reject the deity of Jesus Christ, the doctrine of original sin, and everlasting punishment, regarding these beliefs as unscriptural and unnatural. They celebrate the Eucharist as a commemoration of Jesus' death and to show spiritual communion with him. In general, members are tolerant and welcoming of differences.

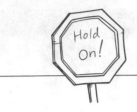

Don't Go There

Never assume that your partner can read your mind. Unless you're communicating with Carnak the Magnificent, spell out your meaning clearly—especially when it comes to key issues of religious faith.

You need to make the effort to learn your sweetheart's religious heritage and to share your own with his or her family. Use the following checklist to make the task a little easier.

Am I …

_____ 1. aware of my sweetheart's religious values and beliefs?

_____ 2. sensitive to religious and cultural differences among my beloved's family?

_____ 3. aware that my preferred values and behaviors are influenced by my religion and culture and are not necessarily "right"?

_____ 4. flexible and open to differences of opinion?

_____ 5. sensitive to nonverbal as well as verbal cues?

If you answered "yes" to most of these questions, you may be well on your way to peaceful coexistence.

The Least You Need to Know

➤ Background, religion, and culture, all ingrained from birth, shape the way we look at the world.

➤ What we consider "normal" is a cultural construct.

➤ Keep your interfaith relationship healthy by presenting a united front with your sweetheart, showing interest in your sweetheart's faith, and inviting your sweetheart's family to learn more about your religion.

➤ Try to avoid confrontations, consider compromise, and find a support group.

➤ To thine own self be true, but respect others' beliefs.

➤ Be patient, too. Consider trying a little humor and looking on the positive side.

Chapter 3

Present Your ID, Please

In This Chapter

➤ Explore your identity

➤ See what roles you play

➤ Use poetry as a means of self-exploration

➤ Keep a journal to see what matters most to you

➤ Find out what values you cherish

➤ Apply your self-knowledge to your interfaith relationship

"O Romeo, Romeo, wherefore art thou Romeo?
Deny thy father and refuse thy name;
Or if thou wilt not, be but sworn my love,
And I'll no longer be a Capulet."

—William Shakespeare's *Romeo and Juliet,* II, ii, 33–36

The world's most famous star-crossed lovers grappled with a family feud, not religious differences, but you know as well as I do that fights over religious differences can often explode into family feuds. And it's not pretty.

In this chapter, you'll explore your values so you can begin to decide what role each one has in your life. Which values are most important to you? Least important? Probing your identity can help you decide how to best resolve issues in interfaith love affairs, relationships, and marriage.

The Name Game

As Romeo stays hidden in the bushes below the balcony, Juliet considers her problem and comes up with a solution: If Romeo would only change his name, all their problems would vanish. What she's really asking him to do, however, is reject his family, and Juliet sweetens the pot by offering herself as the prize. Here's how she puts it:

> "'Tis but thy name that is my enemy;
> Thou art thyself, though not a Montague.
> What's a Montague? It is not hand nor foot,
> Nor arm nor face, nor any other part
> Belonging to a man. O, be some other name!
> What's in a name? That which we call a rose
> By any other name would smell as sweet;
> So Romeo would, were he not Romeo call'd,
> Retain that dear perfection which he owes
> Without that title. Romeo, doff thy name,
> And for thy name, which is no part of thee,
> Take all myself."

> —*Romeo and Juliet,* II, ii, 37–48

Juliet has a simple solution to a complex problem. We'll give her some wiggle-room here because she is only a child. (Besides, sometimes easy fixes do indeed work.) But in the real world, thorny problems are rarely solved with such simple strokes.

You're older; you know the score. Difficult problems such as conflicts over interfaith relationships often require years of long, hard work to resolve.

Before you can begin to address conflicts with your lover over the role of religion in your relationship, you've got to decide what really matters to you as an individual. Crystallizing your identity and figuring out what matters most to you will help you to …

➤ Enter into an interfaith relationship with your eyes wide open, knowing what to expect.

➤ More easily resolve issues within the relationship if you are already in love with someone of a different faith.

Let's start at the very beginning by seeing how you define yourself.

Act of Faith

According to most scholars, Shakespeare wrote the tragedy of *Romeo and Juliet* around 1595, but the story is much older. The use of a sleeping potion as a way out of an unwelcome marriage goes back to the *Ephesiaca* of the Greek novelist Xenophon in the fourth century C.E. Masuccio of Salerno uses the same plot device, together with a tale of star-crossed lovers, in *Il Novellino* (1476). Around 1530, Luigi da Porto placed the action in Verona and named the feuding families the Montecchi and the Cappellatti. There was a French version of the same story in 1542, an Italian poem in 1553, and an Italian play in 1578. The timeless history of this story demonstrates the impact that family can have on the success—or failure—of a love affair.

Who Are You?

"Who are you?" is a wonderful question that has been asked since ancient times. Looked at from a philosophical perspective, it stimulates us to delve deeply into ourselves, into our true identity. As humans, we wear masks, but when the mask is removed, we see that there is far more to who we are than the mask suggests. We are the identities with which we face the world, yet we are so much more.

"Who are you?" As I write this, I have just returned from the funeral of a wonderful woman I knew for more than 35 years. Her daughter felt that, with her mother's passing, she had lost her identity. "I am a daughter," she said. "That is my identity." "Yes," I replied, "but you are so much more as well. You are a wife, a mother, and a friend." But who is she *really?* Only she can determine that.

Role Playing

"Who are you?" How do you define yourself? Start by reading the following list of roles that people assume. Add any I've omitted. Then select the ones that, in your view, best describe you. Arrange your roles from most to least inclusive.

➤ Catholic, Jew, and so on [name your religion]
➤ Employee [name your job]
➤ Employer [name your job]
➤ Daughter
➤ Son
➤ Sister

➤ Brother

➤ Wife

➤ Husband

➤ Mother

➤ Father

I am best described as a(n) …

1. _____

2. _____

3. _____

4. _____

5. _____

Don't Go There

Remember that we describe ourselves by the roles we play in society, but we are not limited to those roles. Don't let labels stand in the way of true, complete self-definition.

Now show the list to someone close to you: a parent, sibling, or lover. See if he or she agrees with the way you define yourself. Make any changes you think are necessary to the list.

Are you surprised at the wide range of roles you play? Everyone is, but identifying yourself in so many ways gives life its richness and depth. However, wearing many hats also complicates our relationships. In every relationship, you're acting—and reacting—in different ways. For example, when your child falls in love with someone of a different faith, are you acting in this situation as a mother concerned for her child? As a wife reacting to the strains in her own marriage? As a child thinking about her parents' marriage? By analyzing your reactions and teasing out the reasons for them, you'll be better equipped to deal with the strains of interfaith relationships—your own as well as others'.

Poetry, the International Language

Now that I've got you thinking about who you really are behind the mask you present to the world, let's explore the issue from a different slant—as poets.

Poetry is a type of literature in which words are selected for their beauty, sound, and power to express feelings. It's a kind of language that says *more* and says it *more intensely* than does ordinary language. As a result, poetry is as universal as language and is almost as ancient.

"I'm not a poet," you might protest. Maybe not, but I'll bet you can write a simple poem to probe your identity. Below are the directions. Read them through from start to finish. Then, on a separate sheet of paper, write your identity poem. Why not give it a shot? Hey, it's only 11 lines long!

Identity Poem

Line 1:   Your first name

Line 2:   Four traits that describe you

Line 3:   Lover of (or sibling of, father of, mother of …)

Line 4:   Admirer of (name three ideas)

Line 5:   Who feels (name three words)

Line 6:   Who needs (name three words)

Line 7:   Who gives (name three words)

Line 8:   Who fears (name three words)

Line 9:   Who would like to see (name three words)

Line 10:   Resident of (give your address)

Line 11:   Your last name

What new slant does this identity poem reveal about the way you define yourself?

Act of Faith

Probing your identity often leads to an interest in mapping your heritage. If you find yourself interested in family genealogy, the Web is a great place to start. The following are some general Web sites to get you started. (A $ symbol indicates a fee for access or membership.)

Ancestry.com (www.ancestry.com) $ This site includes a link to the Social Security Death Index, which has more than 60 million death–benefit payment records.

Broderbund (www.genealogy.com)

Cyndi's List (www.cyndislist.com)

Federation of Genealogical Societies (www.fgs.org) $

Genweb Project (www.usgenweb.org)

National Genealogical Society (www.ngsgenealogy.org) $

Rootsweb (www.rootsweb.com) The Internet's oldest genealogy site, Rootsweb lets you see who is looking for the same last names as you are.

Write This Way: Journaling

Still having trouble trying to decide what really matters most to you? If so, you're clearly an intelligent and thoughtful person. It's not at all easy to pin yourself down, slap on a label, and call yourself finished.

Working out your identity is an ongoing process since your personality and character change as you mature. That's one important reason why having a successful interfaith relationship can be so difficult: You are not the same person at 40 that you were at 20—and neither is your partner! In part, that's because your experiences mold you in unique ways. Further, you can never predict how a specific experience will affect you, now or in the future.

Words to Live By

When you're trying to decide whether you should embark on a relationship with someone of a different belief system, you may torment yourself by turning the unresolved and confusing issues over and over in your mind. Writing promotes self-understanding. As a result, a journal is a powerful tool to help you discover who you are, what you want, and what you're willing to do to get it.

A journal is ...

➤ A personal dialogue.

➤ An objective extension of your thought process, a way to take ideas out of your head and put them on paper.

➤ A means of getting in touch with your deepest feelings.

➤ A method for dealing with hurt.

➤ A personal expression, meant for your eyes only.

A journal isn't ...

➤ A diary.

➤ A date book.

➤ Something to share.

➤ A shortcut for working through a relationship.

➤ A substitute for action.

Voyage of Self-Discovery

If you decide to keep a journal for self-discovery, try these suggestions:

1. Use your journal as a tool for self-definition. Writing in a journal is an effective way to help you define the values that really matter to you, now and in the future. To get started on your path, ask yourself questions like these:

   ➤ Would I describe myself as a religious person? Why or why not?

   ➤ What aspects of my religion are especially important to me? Why?

   ➤ How has my religion shaped me?

   ➤ If I could change one thing about myself, what would it be? Why?

   ➤ If I could change one thing about my partner, what would it be? Why?

   ➤ Why is religion an issue in this relationship?

2. Look inside yourself and probe your feelings. As you write, ask yourself questions such as these:

   ➤ How do I feel about my religion? What emotions does it evoke in me?

   ➤ How do I feel about the religious differences between my partner and myself?

   ➤ What makes me feel this way?

   ➤ Have my feelings changed in the past month? The past year? The past several years? If so, how?

   ➤ How do other people make me feel about our relationship?

   ➤ Do I feel that my mixed match is the biggest source of conflict in my life? Why or why not?

Family Matters

It can sometimes be easier to communicate sensitive issues with your partner in writing rather than orally. You might decide to share your journal with your partner to convey issues that are hard to talk about.

Hold On!

Don't Go There

Never, never write your personal journal on your office computer. According to recent court decisions, anything you write on office time on office equipment becomes the company's property.

3. As you write in your journal, make discoveries about yourself by looking through the eyes of others. In this case, you can ask yourself questions such as these:

   ➤ Would other people describe me as religious? Why or why not?

   ➤ What do other people think about my mixed match?

   ➤ Which outside opinions do I value most? Why?

   ➤ How do I want people to regard me? My companion?

   ➤ Have people's opinions about me changed as a result of my interfaith relationship?

   ➤ If so, how can I tell that they regard me differently?

4. You might also look for parallels between what you see in other interfaith relationships and how you perceive your own relationship. Here are some issues to consider:

   ➤ Which of my friends and relatives have *successful* interfaith relationships?

   ➤ What makes these particular mixed matches work?

   ➤ Which of my friends and relatives have *unsuccessful* interfaith relationships?

   ➤ What makes these particular mixed matches less than satisfactory?

   ➤ How do my friends involved in interfaith relationships handle religious observations and other holiday celebrations?

   ➤ Which customs can my partner and I adopt for our own?

Value Packed

A friend passed along this story. See what it says about different values.

> "My ex-husband and I were both Catholics, but he was much more Catholic than I—kind of a Fundamentalist, super Catholic. I, on the other hand, believe in a tolerant, come-day-go-day deity who blesses those of us who don't make others uncomfortable with undue piety. No one considered ours an interfaith marriage—after all, we *are* both Catholics—but I was never comfortable with his extreme views. A wide range of belief/faith within a religion can be as big a problem as having completely different religions."

As this story illustrates, religion itself may not be the issue; rather, the *degree* of faith becomes the pivot point. That's because faith is a value and values are emotional rather than rational. You can argue with someone's actions, but not with their values.

Your *values* give life its meaning. Knowing in your heart what matters most can help you make successful choices in interfaith relationships, romance, and life.

Your values often direct your life and define you as a person. They help make you who you are. As you did earlier in this chapter with roles, follow these three easy steps:

1. Read the following list of values.

2. Add any values that I've left out.

3. Select the values that matter to you most.

> **Learn the Lingo**
>
> Your **values** are your moral touchstones, the ideals and customs that spark emotional responses.

➤ A good reputation	➤ Awards
➤ A fancy car	➤ Charity work
➤ Children	➤ Fame
➤ Family	➤ A big house
➤ A happy marriage	➤ A big salary
➤ Public service	➤ Religion
➤ Status	➤ Personal appearance

Now, select 10 values from your list. Arrange them on the following lines from most to least important.

most important   1. _____

     2. _____

     3. _____

     4. _____

important   5. _____

     6. _____

     7. _____

     8. _____

     9. _____

least important   10. _____

Did You Know?

The divorce rate for the general population ranges from 37 percent to 50 percent, depending on whose figures are used.

After you've completed this list, see what it reveals about your values. What *really* matters to you? What is less important? When you select a partner, find someone whose values mirror your own. All relationships have a better chance of succeeding if partners share the same values and goals. Similar values are especially crucial in interfaith relationships, however, because they provide the bedrock for building a lasting love in the absence of shared religious traditions.

The Main Event

You've explored your identity by looking at the roles you fulfill and the values you cherish. The one area we've only touched on, however, is the importance of religion in your life. Let's look at religion now.

Complete the following survey to see what importance you place on religion. You may want to make a copy of this page and invite your sweetheart to complete it as well. Sharing responses can help you open up a dialogue about religion and the role it plays in your life.

1. Maternal grandparents' religion(s)

   _____

2. Paternal grandparents' religion(s)

   _____

3. Father's religion

   _____

4. Mother's religion

   _____

5. Religion in which I was raised

   _____

6. Religions I have tried

   _____

7. Religion I consider myself

   _____

8. My subdivision of the religion (Reform Jew, Conservative Jew, Orthodox Jew, for example)

   _____

9. I would rate myself (circle one):

   Very knowledgeable about my religion

   Somewhat knowledgeable about my religion

   Not at all knowledgeable about my religion

10. I would rate myself (circle one):

   Very religious

   Moderately religious

   Not religious

Based on this survey, what role do you think religion plays in your life? Be honest now. No fudging!

Now that you've examined your values and decided what really matters to you, apply what you've learned to picking a mate. Building a relationship is hard work under ideal circumstances, but it's even more difficult when partners have a fundamentally different way of looking at the world. Finding someone whose values match yours significantly increases your chances of lasting happiness. And I'd like you to be happy; after all, you deserve it!

The Least You Need to Know

➤ Conflicts over interfaith relationships often require years of long, hard work to resolve them.

➤ Before you address conflicts over the role of religion in your relationship, you've got to decide what really matters to you as an individual.

➤ Crystallize your identity by exploring the roles you play, writing an identity poem, and journaling.

➤ Focusing on your values can help you define who you are spiritually and equip you for the challenges of interfaith relationships.

Part 2
Defender of the Faith

Four religions—Christianity, Islam, Hinduism, and Buddhism—claim 4.2 billion adherents, or 72 percent of the world's population. This section of the book describes the major religions of the world, including their basic beliefs, scriptures, school, sects, and history.

Knowledge is power. The more you know about your beloved's religion, the more fully you will understand his or her values and beliefs. Then you can help replace ignorance with knowledge and empower people to work together to make their interfaith relationship strong.

An interfaith family can help others find bridges between two-faith communities. A willingness to explore the traditions, beliefs, history, and community of a sweetheart's faith can bring shared growth to all.

Judaism

A woman sent this query to an advice columnist:

> "Our son writes that he is taking Judo. Why would a boy who was raised in a good Christian home turn against his own?"

Interesting question, silly woman. But on the odd chance that her son is converting to Judaism rather than taking up the martial arts, this chapter will help her understand his belief system.

If your sweetie or spouse is Jewish, this chapter will work for you, too. How? Learning about your beloved's religion will help you understand your mate's heritage and deal with stress points in your relationship. The more you learn, the better equipped you'll be to cope with difficulties and misunderstandings that arise.

And you don't even have to learn judo.

Origins of Judaism

Judaism is the oldest of the world's three major *monotheistic* religions and is a forerunner of Christianity and Islam. Judaism originated in the land of Israel (also known as Palestine) in the Middle East.

Learn the Lingo

Monotheistic religions are based on the belief that there is only one God.

The Hebrew Bible recounts the story of the world and humankind from creation, through the flood, to the work of the patriarch Abraham, who brought his people from Mesopotamia to Canaan, the Promised Land. His descendants were enslaved in Egypt until Moses led them out of captivity. During the Exodus, God gave Moses the Ten Commandments that form the bedrock of Jewish law. Here's how the Bible states it:

> "And he gave unto Moses, when he had made an end of communing with him upon Mount Sinai, two tables of testimony, tables of stone, written with the finger of God."
>
> —Exodus 31:18

Two different versions of the Ten Commandments are given in Exodus 20:1–17 and Deuteronomy 5:6–21, but the substance in both is the same. In Jewish tradition, the commandments are organized as follows:

1. I am the Lord thy God, which have brought thee out of the land of Egypt, out of the house of bondage. Thou shalt have no other gods before me.

2. Thou shalt not make unto thee any graven images. You shall not bow down to them or serve them.

3. Thou shalt not take the name of the Lord your God in vain.

4. Remember the Sabbath day and keep it holy.

5. Honor thy father and mother.

6. Thou shalt not kill.

7. Thou shalt not commit adultery.

8. Thou shalt not steal.

9. Thou shalt not bear false witness against your neighbor.

10. Thou shalt not covet.

Jewish custom and law further evolved from the tenth century B.C.E. and the conquest of Canaan to the destruction of Jerusalem by the Romans in 70 C.E.

At present, the total world Jewish population is about 12.8 million, of which about 6 million live in America, more than 3.9 million in Israel, and nearly 1.2 million in Russia, the three largest centers of Jewish settlement. About 1.2 million Jews live in the rest of Europe, most of them in France and Great Britain. About 356,700 live in the rest of North America and 32,700 in Asia other than Israel. About 433,400 Jews live in Central and South America and about 148,700 in Africa.

What Do Jews Believe?

Central to Jewish belief is the idea of a single God—called *Yahweh*—who created the universe and continues to govern it.

Jewish people also hold these beliefs:

➤ Yahweh made a *covenant* with his chosen people that he would protect them and provide for them if they acknowledged his rule and obeyed his laws.

➤ Yahweh shapes history and imposes his will on humankind: He saves and he judges.

➤ Nothing that humanity experiences is capricious; everything ultimately has meaning.

➤ All humans have divine and spiritual essences within them and around them. This is our connection to the spiritual worlds.

Act of Faith

Most Protestant, Anglican, and Orthodox Christians follow Jewish tradition, which considers the introduction ("I am the Lord ...") to be the first commandment and makes the prohibition against graven images the second commandment. Roman Catholic and Lutheran traditions follow a division used by St. Augustine that combines the first and second commandments and splits the last one into two that separately prohibit coveting a neighbor's wife and his goods. This arrangement alters the numbering of the other commandments by one.

Learn the Lingo

A **covenant** is an agreement or a contract.

While Yahweh guides Jewish destiny, humanity is defined by a person's ability to make ethical choices in keeping with his law. As a result, there is a direct link between human behavior and human destiny. The failure to act according to Yahweh's law is sin. A basic tenet of Jewish faith is that sin is a willful act; so, too, is returning to God.

Yahweh is revealed in the holy book called the *Torah* ("revealed instruction"), and his will for humankind is expressed in commandments (*mizvoth*) by which individuals interact with one another and with God.

The book of Isaiah explains that God would send His Messiah, a divine ruler descended from the house of David, to redeem the Jewish people and return them to Israel. The Messiah will be restored to the throne of David and bring peace to the world. By studying and following God's commandments, each person could accelerate the Messiah's arrival. Each individual's action thus assumed a cosmic importance.

Types of Judaism

Judaism in America today is divided into three main movements: *Reform Judaism, Conservative Judaism,* and *Orthodox Judaism.* Some people also include a fourth movement, the *Reconstructionist* movement, although it is substantially smaller than the other three. Orthodox and sometimes Conservative Judaism are described as "traditional" movements. Reform, Reconstructionist, and sometimes Conservative are described as "liberal" or "modern" movements. The descriptions depend on who's doing the describing: the Orthodox Jews consider the Conservatives to be more liberal, while the Reform Jews consider it more traditional. Here's what they're all about.

Don't Go There

Contrary to popular belief, Judaism does not maintain that Jews are better than other people. Although Jews refer to themselves as God's chosen people, they do not believe that God chose the Jews because of any inherent superiority.

Reform Judaism

In general, Reform Judaism is liberal and nonauthoritarian. Reform Jews believe that the Bible was written by separate sources, not by God. Reform Jews retain much of the values and ethics of Judaism, along with some of the practices and the culture. Men and women pray side by side, and much of the service is in English. The religious service is shorter than that found in Conservative or Orthodox congregations.

There are about 800 Reform synagogues in America with approximately 2 million members. (For more information about Reform Judaism, you can contact The Union of American Hebrew Congregations.)

Conservative Judaism

The Conservative movement respects traditional Jewish law and practice while advocating a flexible approach.

Conservative Judaism, formally organized as the United Synagogue of Conservative Judaism in 1913, maintains that the truths found in Jewish scriptures and other

Jewish writings come from God but were transmitted by humans and contain a human component. Conservative Jews follow Jewish laws but believe that the law should change and adapt, absorbing aspects of the predominant culture while remaining true to Judaism's values.

There is a great deal of variation among Conservative synagogues. Some seem just like Reform congregations except that they use more Hebrew; others are practically Orthodox except that men and women sit together. There are an estimated 800 Conservative synagogues in America today with approximately 1.3 million members.

Orthodox Judaism

Orthodox Judaism is actually made up of several different groups. It includes the modern Orthodox, who have largely integrated into modern society while maintaining observance of Jewish Law; the *Chasidim,* who live separately and dress distinctively; and the *Yeshivish* Orthodox, who are neither Chasidic nor modern.

The Orthodox movements all believe that the Torah is true and has come down intact and unchanged. Men and women do not sit together at prayer, and the service is nearly all in Hebrew. Orthodox Jews follow traditional customs such as lighting the Sabbath candles, limiting their activities on the Sabbath, and observing special food laws. These customs are rare among American Reform Jews.

It has been estimated that there are 1,200 Orthodox synagogues in America today with a total of approximately 1 million members.

Orthodoxy is the only movement that is formally and legally recognized in Israel. Until very recently, only Orthodox Jews could serve on religious councils in Israel. The Orthodox rabbinate in Israel controls matters of personal status such as marriage, conversion, and divorce. Israel is very important for nearly all American Jews; it is seen as a touchstone and guarantee that Judaism will survive.

Learn the Lingo

The most commonly used word for a non-Jew is **goy.** The word, which means "nation," refers to the fact that **goyim** are members of nations other than the Children of Israel. There is nothing inherently insulting about the word "goy," although it has adopted a slight disparaging edge.

Did You Know?

To observant Jews, God's name is considered too sacred to write out. Instead, it is written G-d.

Reconstructionist Judaism

An offshoot of the Conservative movement, Reconstructive Jews believe that Judaism is an evolving religious civilization. They don't believe in a personified deity that is active in history or that God chose the Jewish people.

From this, you might assume that Reconstructionism is to the left of Reform; however, Reconstructionism stresses traditional Jewish observance much more than Reform Judaism. Although Reconstructionism is a very small movement—it contains only about 60,000 members—it gets a lot of press. This is probably because many Reconstructionist rabbis serve Jewish-college student organizations and Jewish community centers.

Who Is a Jew?

A Jew is any person whose mother was a Jew or any person who has gone through the formal process of conversion to Judaism.

Being a Jew has nothing to do with what you believe or what you do. In this sense, Judaism is more like a culture than a religion, and being Jewish is like a citizenship.

Here are three ways that Judaism is defined:

➤ A person born to a Jewish mother is Jewish. Even if that person is an atheist and never practices the Jewish religion, he or she is still a Jew. This is true even in the eyes of the ultra-Orthodox.

➤ A person who converts to Judaism is Jewish. Once a person has converted to Judaism, he or she is as much a Jew as anyone born Jewish.

➤ A person born to non-Jewish parents who has not converted is not a Jew. Even if he or she believes everything that Orthodox Jews believe and observes every law and custom of Judaism, he or she is still not considered Jewish.

Not So Fast ...

Although all Jewish movements agree on these general principles for defining a Jewish identity, there are occasional disputes as to whether a particular individual is a Jew. Most of these disputes fall into one of two categories.

First, traditional Judaism maintains that a person is a Jew if his mother is a Jew, regardless of who his father is. The liberal movements, on the other hand, consider a person to be Jewish if either of his parents was Jewish and he was raised Jewish. Thus, if the child of a Jewish father and a Christian mother is raised Jewish, the child is a Jew according to the Reform movement but not according to the Orthodox movement. On the other hand, if the child of a Christian father and a Jewish mother is not raised Jewish, the child is a Jew according to the Orthodox movement but not according to the Reform movement.

Second, the more traditional movements don't always acknowledge the validity of conversions accepted by the more liberal movements. In addition, Orthodoxy doesn't accept the authority of Conservative, Reform, and Reconstructionist rabbis to perform conversions. The Conservative movement has debated whether to accept the authority of Reform rabbis.

Ashkenazic and Sephardic Jews

American Jews fall into two main divisions, categorized according to their heritage.

➤ **Ashkenazic Jews** are descended from Jews who emigrated from Germany and Eastern Europe in the mid 1800s. Some speak Yiddish, a language based on German and Hebrew.

➤ **Sephardic Jews** are descended from Spaniards. Some speak Ladino, which is based on Spanish and Hebrew.

Both Jewish cultures exist in the world today, although Ashkenazic Jews are more common in America.

Family Matters

Yemenite Jews, Ethiopian Jews (also known as Beta Israel and sometimes called Falashas), and Oriental Jews also have some distinct customs and traditions. These groups, however, are relatively small and are virtually unknown in America.

Conversion

In general, Jews don't try to convert non-Jews to Judaism. According to Jewish law, rabbis are supposed to make three vigorous attempts to dissuade a person who wants to convert to Judaism.

If a person does decide to convert, he or she must learn Jewish religion, law, and customs and begin to observe them. This takes at least a year because the prospective convert must experience each of the Jewish holidays; however, the actual amount of study required varies from person to person, and is determined by the rabbi.

After the teaching is complete, the person is brought before a rabbinical court that determines whether he or she is ready to become a Jew. If the person passes this oral examination, the rituals of conversion are performed. If the convert is male, he is circumcised (or, if he was already circumcised, a pinprick of blood is drawn for a symbolic circumcision). Both male and female converts are immersed in a ritual bath. The convert is given a Jewish name and is then introduced into the Jewish community.

House of Worship

The synagogue is the center of the Jewish religious community: a place of prayer, study and education, social and charitable work, and a social center. Jews of different movements use various terms for the synagogue:

➤ The Orthodox and Chasidim typically use the word "shul," which is Yiddish.

➤ Reform Jews use the word "temple" or "synagogue."

In America, individual synagogues do not answer to any central authority. Synagogues are generally run by a board of directors composed of lay people. They manage and maintain the synagogue and its activities and hire a rabbi for the community. A synagogue can exist without a rabbi: Religious services can be, and often are, conducted by lay people. It is not unusual for a synagogue to be without a rabbi, at least temporarily. However, the rabbi is a valuable member of the community, providing leadership, guidance, and education.

Synagogues do not pass around collection plates during services, as many churches do. Instead, synagogues are financed through membership dues paid annually, voluntary donations, and the purchase of reserved seats for services on Rosh Hashanah and Yom Kippur (the holidays when the synagogue is most crowded). You do not have to be a member of a synagogue to worship there.

Act of Faith

Originally, Yiddish was spoken mainly by Jewish people in Europe, but many Yiddish expressions have become part of the everyday language in large American cities. Here are some of the most common Yiddish words and expressions:

chutzpah (Khoot' spah)   nerve, real gall

kibitzer (kib' its ruhr)   a spectator, especially someone at a card game who gives unwanted advice

mazel tov (ma' zel tov)   good luck

nebbish (neb' ish)   a drab, insignificant person

mensch (mensh)   a decent, mature, sincere person

nudnik (nood' nik)   a pest

oy (oi)   an expression for pain or annoyance

schlepp (shlep)   to lug something heavy around

schlock (shlok)   a cheap, shoddy article

schmooz (shmooz)   gossip

Ritual Items in the Synagogue

Prayer services are performed in the synagogue's sanctuary on the Sabbath (Friday night) and Saturday before sundown. Here's what you'll find in the sanctuary:

➤ **The Ark.** The most important part of the sanctuary is the Ark, a cabinet in the wall that holds the Torah scrolls.

➤ **The Eternal Lamp.** Located above the Ark, the Lamp symbolizes the commandment to keep a light burning in the tabernacle.

➤ **The menorah.** The menorah is a candelabrum.

➤ **The bimah.** The pedestal in the center of the room; it's used to lead services and as a stand for the Torah.

➤ **A women's section.** Orthodox synagogues have a separate section where the women sit.

Attending Services

Non-Jews are welcome to attend services in a synagogue. Here are some questions I often get about attending synagogue (and their answers!):

➤ **What should I wear in a synagogue?** Men are required to wear a yarmulke (skullcap) as a sign of respect. *Yarmulkes* are available at the entrance for those who do not have one. In some synagogues, married women should wear a head covering such as a piece of lace or a scarf. Many Jews also wear a prayer shawl, but non-Jews should not wear one.

Dress conservatively—no shorts, sandals, or tight clothing. In an Orthodox synagogue, women must have their arms and shoulders covered.

➤ **What should I do during religious services?** As a sign of respect, stand whenever the Ark is open and when the Torah is removed from the Ark. At any other time when worshippers stand, non-Jews may stand or sit. Feel free to follow along with the service.

Did You Know?

Every culture has its traditions about the evil eye. In Yiddish, some people utter the magical phrase *kine-ahora* to ward off the evil eye.

Family Matters

Gifts to charity, Jewish weddings, and bar and bat mitzvahs (coming-of-age ceremonies) are routinely given in multiples of 18, the numeric value of the word "chai."

Five Symbols of Jewish Faith

There are five symbols commonly associated with Judaism: the chai, mezuzah, menorah, Star of David (Magen David), and yarmulke. You've probably seen these symbols many times. Here's what each one represents:

Family Matters

Chanukah is also spelled "Hanukkah" or "Hanukah." Don't obsess over the spelling—you should really worry about all the calories in the scrumptious potato pancakes (called "latkes") served to commemorate the rededication of the Temple of Jerusalem by Judas Maccabee after it had been profaned by the King of Syria. According to talmudic tradition, only one small vial of oil could be found, but it miraculously burned for eight days. Today, candles are lit on the menorah for eight days and foods with oil are eaten to celebrate this miracle. Children receive small gifts, one per night. The joyous holiday falls in the winter.

➤ **Chai.** This symbol, commonly seen on jewelry, is the Hebrew word for "life." It looks a lot like the mathematical symbol for pi.

➤ **Mezuzah.** A *mezuzah* is a small case attached to the doorposts of traditional Jewish homes. It serves as a reminder of God, not as a good-luck charm. Jews touch the mezuzah and then kiss their fingers to express love and respect for God.

➤ **Menorah.** The menorah, a seven-branched candelabrum, can be found in synagogues and is used during a holiday called Chanukah.

➤ **Star of David (Magen David).** This six-pointed star is the symbol most commonly associated with Judaism today. It appears on Israel's flag as well as many other items.

➤ **Yarmulke.** The yarmulke is worn by Jewish men as they pray and by non-Jewish men in a synagogue as a sign of respect.

Three Major Jewish Holidays

The three most important Jewish holidays are *Yom Kippur, Rosh Hashanah,* and *Passover*. These are the holidays you are most likely to be invited to celebrate with your sweetheart's family. Here's what each holiday entails.

Yom Kippur

Yom Kippur, the Day of Atonement, is the most important holiday of the Jewish year. Many Jews who do not observe any other Jewish custom will refrain from work, fast, and attend synagogue services on this day.

On Yom Kippur, observant Jews atone for the sins of the past year by demonstrating repentance and making amends. Most of the holiday is spent praying in the synagogue. Services end at nightfall with the blowing of the *shofar,* the ram's horn. The holiday takes place in the fall.

Rosh Hashanah

Rosh Hashanah, the Jewish New Year, culminates in Yom Kippur. It's a time of introspection when observant Jews look back at the mistakes of the past year and plan changes to make in the new year. People don't fast, but they do spend the day praying in the synagogue. Apples dipped in honey are often eaten to symbolize a sweet new year.

Passover

Passover (Pesach) is an eight-day holiday that celebrates the Jewish Exodus from Egypt after generations of slavery. It refers to the fact that God "passed over" the houses of the Jews when he was slaying the firstborn of Egypt. The holiday falls in March or April.

Observant Jews remove any leavened bread from their homes to commemorate the fact that the Jews leaving Egypt were in a hurry, so they did not have time to let their bread rise. Homes are scrubbed from top to bottom to remove any leftover crumbs.

Jews who observe the holiday do not eat any leavened foods for its duration. Instead, they eat unleavened bread called *matzoth*. A special meal, called a *seder,* is held on the first night of Passover (on the first two nights for more observant Jews). The ritual meal involves special foods served in a set order, prayers, and songs.

Jews and Interfaith Relationships

An acquaintance who isn't Jewish once told me that Jews don't like Gentiles. "And how did you reach this conclusion?" I asked.

"I'm dating a Jewish man, and his family doesn't approve of me," she said. "Therefore, Jews don't like non-Jews."

Family Matters

All Jewish holidays begin the evening before the date specified. This is because a Jewish "day" begins and ends at sunset.

Did You Know?

A doctor was upset when his patient, an Orthodox Jew, bled profusely and then died. The doctor was shocked, however, when the patient's in-laws demanded his blood-covered medical scrubs. When buried, Orthodox Jews must have everything containing their bodily fluids interred with the body. This includes bandages, fluids from tubes, and any and all amputated limbs.

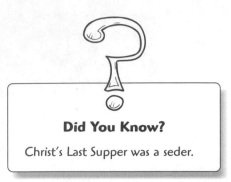

Did You Know?

Christ's Last Supper was a seder.

I explained that her sweetheart's family didn't disapprove of her because she was Christian; they disapproved of her because she was *a Christian dating a Jew*, which is another kettle of fish altogether.

Traditional Judaism doesn't permit interfaith marriages. The Torah states that the children of such marriages would be lost to Judaism (Deut. 7:3–4), and experience has shown that this is often the case. Children of intermarriage are rarely raised Jewish; they are normally raised Christian or nonreligious.

This may reflect the fact that Jews who intermarry are not deeply committed to their religion in the first place. Regardless, the statistics on interfaith marriages alarm the Jewish community.

One Orthodox Jew actually stated that intermarriage is accomplishing what Hitler could not: the destruction of the Jewish people. Although this is an extreme view, it clearly illustrates how seriously many Jews take the issue of intermarriage.

Jewish intermarriage will be discussed in great detail later in the book. See Part 4, "Celebrating Our Differences: Interfaith Weddings."

The world's oldest religion, Judaism can seem daunting to newcomers because the traditions are so time-honored. Don't be intimidated. If you're dating a Jewish man or woman, learn as much as you can about the religion so you understand where your honey's coming from.

The Least You Need to Know

➤ Central to Jewish belief is the idea of a single God—called Yahweh—who created the universe and continues to govern it.

➤ Reform, Conservative, and Orthodox Judaism are the three main types of Judaism in America. Some people also include the small Reconstructionist movement.

➤ A Jew is any person whose mother was a Jew or any person who has gone through the formal process of conversion to Judaism.

➤ Being a Jew has nothing to do with what you believe or what you do. Judaism is more like a culture than a religion.

➤ The synagogue is the center of the Jewish religious community.

➤ The three most important Jewish holidays are Yom Kippur, Rosh Hashanah, and Passover.

➤ Judaism doesn't sanction interfaith marriages.

Christianity

The Apostles' Creed

I believe in God, the Father almighty,
creator of heaven and earth.
I believe in Jesus Christ, God's only Son, our Lord,
who was conceived by the Holy Spirit,
born of the Virgin Mary,
suffered under Pontius Pilate,
was crucified, died, and was buried;
he descended to the dead.
On the third day he rose again;
he ascended into heaven,
he is seated at the right hand of the Father,
and he will come again to judge the living and the dead.
I believe in the Holy Spirit,
the holy Catholic Church,

the communion of saints,
the forgiveness of sins,
the resurrection of the body,
and the life everlasting.

The Apostles' Creed may have been the first widely recognized summary of what Christians believe; it certainly wasn't the last. Indeed, when you look at the scope and range of such statements of Christian faith, you can see that Christianity is like an umbrella that shelters a great variety of people who hold different views on Christ and worship.

Family Matters

The Apostles' Creed was traditionally attributed to the 12 apostles. Now, however, it is widely agreed that the Apostles' Creed was developed around 215 C.E. as the baptismal confession of faith. A form identical with what is now called the Apostles' Creed emerged early in the eighth century, in the writings of St. Pirminius.

Learn the Lingo

Messiah is the Greek word for "Christ," or "the anointed one."

In this chapter, you'll explore the major Christian denominations in America, from the Adventists to the United Church of Christ. This chapter also discusses the issue of Christianity and interfaith relationships. Finally, I'll explain two major Christian holidays to make it easier at religious gatherings where you're apt to meet a good chunk of your sweetheart's family while you're passing the mashed potatoes. If you're dating a Christian, are engaged to a Christian, or have married a Christian, you'll want to know all about this religion.

Origins of Christianity

Christianity, the most widely distributed of the world's religions, is based on the acts and sayings of Jesus Christ as related by his followers and apostles.

> "Now the birth of Jesus Christ was on this wise: When his mother Mary was espoused to Joseph, before they came together, she was found with child of the Holy Ghost."

—Matthew 1:18

According to this passage from the Bible, Jesus' birth was the result of an immaculate conception. We know that Jesus was born in Bethlehem about 4 B.C.E. Details about Jesus' childhood and adolescence are sparse. When he was in his early 30s, Jesus was baptized by John the Baptist, whose ministry prophesied the coming judgment of God and acknowledged Jesus as the *Messiah*.

Jesus' ministry, mainly among the poor and dispossessed, lasted only a few years before the Romans crucified him.

> "And they crucified him, and parted his garments, casting lots: that it might be fulfilled which was spoken by the prophet .... And set up over his head his accusation written, THIS IS JESUS THE KING OF THE JEWS."

—Matthew 27:35–37

According to Christian belief, Jesus rose from the dead three days after his crucifixion. Forty days later, he ascended to heaven to sit at the right hand of God.

The Gospels

The central portion of the Bible's New Testament consists of the Four Gospels, which describe Jesus and his life. Each Gospel is attributed to one of Christ's early followers: Matthew, Mark, Luke, and John. Although each Gospel tells the story of Christ's life, death, and resurrection, they differ in details. The story of the spread of Christianity in the first century is told in the Acts of the Apostles and the *Epistles* of St. Paul.

Learn the Lingo

An **epistle** is a letter.

Christianity Spreads

At the time of his death, Jesus had only a handful of followers among the Jews. His teachings were not widely accepted among the greater Jewish community, so his followers preached to non-Jewish people throughout the Roman Empire. The message spread quickly, but Christians were widely persecuted until the Emperor Constantine legalized the religion in 313 C.E.. In 380 C.E., Christianity became the official religion of the Roman Empire.

Did You Know?

Today, there are more Christians in Africa (360 million, nearly half the population) and Asia (303 million) than in North America (255 million).

European explorers, colonists, and missionaries spread Christianity to the Americas, Asia, and Africa. The Spanish and Portuguese brought Catholicism to Latin America. Many Protestants settled in North America beginning in the early 1600s.

What Do Christians Believe?

Christians believe that, by his death on the cross, Jesus Christ made a covenant for the redemption of humanity. Each denomination differs about the precise meaning of this covenant: Some believe that Christ's voluntary sacrifice redeemed all; others contend that only those who earn their redemption by faith alone, or by faith and good works, will be saved.

Believing in Jesus as the resurrected Son of God, Christianity rests on three basic principles:

➤ **Incarnation.** Christ was the human embodiment of God.

➤ **Atonement.** Humankind was reconciled to God through Christ.

➤ **The Trinity.** God has three natures: God the Father, God the Son (Jesus), and God the Holy Spirit.

Christians also hold these beliefs:

1. Christianity contains the one eternal truth and is the one universal salvation.

2. God is almighty over heaven and earth, righteous in judgment over good and evil.

3. God is love, and he created the world and the human race as manifestations of his love.

4. Every person is worthy because he or she has been created in God's image.

5. Human life is sacred. Therefore, marriage and the family are sacred.

Don't Go There

The Seven Deadly Sins in the Christian tradition are pride, covetousness, lust, anger, gluttony, envy, and sloth. Watch it, now!

The Bible is the basic sourcebook for all Christians. While some take it to be the literal word of God, others see it as a source of inspiration and enlightenment that may or may not be factually correct in every detail.

Types of Christianity

Christians are organized into congregations, and they worship in churches led by priests or ministers who administer the sacraments. Most denominations set aside Sunday as the Sabbath.

Christianity can be divided into three major branches: Eastern Orthodoxy, Roman Catholicism, and Protestantism. The division between Eastern Orthodoxy and Roman Catholicism came in 1054 C.E.. Protestantism came about in the sixteenth century when reform-minded priests broke with Rome.

Let's look at the most popular denominations in America, in alphabetical order.

Adventists

Adventists belong to Protestant denominations that stress the imminent Second Coming of Christ. Adventism became codified under the leadership of the American Baptist preacher William Miller in the mid-nineteenth century.

After the failure of the world to end on October 22, 1844, as Miller had predicted, many Adventists lost faith and returned to their former churches. Those remaining split into three main bodies: the *Seventh-Day Adventists, Advent Christian Church,* and *The Church of God of the Abrahamic Faith.*

Seventh-Day Adventists

By far the largest group is the Seventh-Day Adventists, with about 5.5 million members worldwide. The church was formally organized in 1863.

Seventh-Day Adventists hold the following beliefs:

1. Christ will return to earth soon, even though the exact time cannot be determined.
2. The Bible is the sole religious authority.
3. Grace alone is sufficient for salvation.
4. The wicked will be destroyed at the Second Coming.
5. The just (including the living and the resurrected dead) will be granted everlasting life.

Since they believe that the body is the temple of the Holy Spirit, Seventh-Day Adventists put great stress on health and avoid eating meat and using narcotics and stimulants. The Sabbath is observed on Saturday. Dancing and theatergoing are forbidden, and baptism is by immersion.

Advent Christian Church

First organized in 1860 in Salem, Massachusetts, the Advent Christian Church preaches a doctrine of "conditional immortality," according to which the dead remain in an unconscious state until the Resurrection, which will take place at the Second Coming after the millennium. Baptism is by immersion. The Advent Christian Church has about 27,000 members in America and Canada.

The Church of God of the Abrahamic Faith

Unified in 1921, this denomination is also called the Church of God General Conference. Members hold the following beliefs:

1. The Bible is the supreme standard, resulting in a literal interpretation.
2. The return of Christ will precede the millennial kingdom of God predicted in Revelation 20:1–6.

3. The dead are merely asleep; at the time of the Second Coming, the righteous will be resurrected on earth, and the wicked will be destroyed.

Baptism by immersion is required for admission to the church. The individual churches are autonomous; about 4,100 people belong. In general, followers of the Church of God of the Abrahamic Faith do not support interfaith unions.

Baptists

The Baptist movement began in 1609 with demands for separation of church and state and objections to infant baptism. Early founders included John Smyth (1609) and Roger Williams (1638).

Baptists believe that the New Testament is God's authority for all matters of faith and conduct. In the South, some Baptists interpret the Bible literally.

Baptists also hold that …

➤ Christians are reborn through faith in God and his work.

➤ No authority can stand between the believer and God.

Did You Know?

The Primitive Advent Church, a small offshoot of early Adventism, claims about 350 members, all in West Virginia.

Learn the Lingo

The Catholic Church is called **Roman** because its spiritual leader, the pope, is based in Rome.

Special rites include total immersion baptism, usually performed when a believer is a teenager. Some congregations are opposed to alcohol and tobacco. Followers of this branch of Christianity do not support mixed-faith unions.

Catholics

The largest body of Christians in the world belongs to the Roman Catholic Church. Catholics believe that Jesus Christ established the Church under the leadership of Peter, his disciple.

Catholics accept the seven sacraments:

1. Baptism, the sacrament that frees humankind from original sin and personal guilt, that makes him or her a member of the Christ and His church.

2. Confirmation, the sacrament of maturity and coming of age. It completes the sacrament of baptism.

3. Holy Matrimony, marriage.

4. Holy Orders, priestly vows.

5. Anointing of the Sick, given to strengthen the sick and prepare them for a happy passage to the hereafter.

6. Reconciliation (or Confession), the forgiving of sins. The believer is thus reconciled to God.

7. The Eucharist (or Holy Communion), the sacramental offering and consumption of bread and wine representing the body and blood of Christ.

At the head of the Roman Catholic Church is the pope, who has final authority in all religious matters. Then come the cardinals, appointed by the pope. There are about 160 cardinals today. When the pope dies, the cardinals elect his successor.

The pope appoints bishops to dioceses and then transfers them to others. The main unit of organization in the Roman Catholic Church is the diocese, headed by a bishop. In America today, the Roman Catholic Church has about 1,880 dioceses and about 520 archdioceses. The major church in a diocese is the cathedral, where the bishop presides at worship and other ceremonies.

Directly under the bishop are the clergy, both secular and religious. Secular clergy, who may marry and work outside the church, generally serve as deacons with limited duties. Religious clergy, in contrast, must remain celibate and are committed to their orders or congregations.

Did You Know?

The Church teaches that the seven sacraments were instituted by Christ and given to the church to administer. The vehicles of grace which they convey, the sacraments are necessary for salvation.

Learn the Lingo

Catholic men ordained to serve as religious clergy are called **priests.** Catholic women bound to a religious order are called **nuns** or **sisters;** their male counterparts are called **monks, friars,** or **brothers.**

Roman Catholics celebrate their faith in a service called Mass. Observant Catholics attend Mass on Sundays and on major feasts during the year. Mass is also celebrated daily in most churches and is the essential element of the service at marriages, funerals, and other Catholic observances.

Mass consists of several parts, of which the longest and most important are the *Liturgy* of the Word and the Liturgy of the Eucharist, during which Holy Communion is distributed. Within this structure, music, pageantry, and other elements are varied to suit the occasion.

Learn the Lingo

Liturgy is the religious ritual, the particular arrangement of services.

Learn the Lingo

The **rosary** is a way of praying. The worshipper holds a strand of beads, divided in five sets of ten, with one bead between each set. The worshipper says specific prayers at each set of beads.

Don't Go There

The Catholic Church does not allow divorce and remarriage, but annulments are sometimes granted. Annulments state that the marriage never took place in the eyes of the church; divorces dissolve the marriage.

Catholics express piety in many ways in addition to Mass and sacraments. These include …

➤ Saying the *rosary* of the Virgin Mary.

➤ Keeping fast days and abstaining from meat on certain days. (This is now optional but is still observed by many Catholics.)

➤ Educating children in Catholic schools, elementary through university.

The Roman Catholic Church has been a fierce opponent of liberalized abortion laws and has inspired political resistance to such legislation in several Western countries. Although the Church permits women under certain circumstances to administer the Eucharist and perform some other ministries, it does not allow them to be ordained priests or deacons. Priests are forbidden to marry.

Interfaith couples can marry within the Church. Catholic priests may marry a Catholic to a non-Catholic without requiring conversion.

All couples who marry within in the Catholic Church (interfaith or not) are required to undergo premarital counseling. Further, Catholics who marry non-Catholics must promise that they will raise any children who result from the union as Catholics. This promise has been of great concern to many Jewish families whose children have married Catholics. The Jewish families see their grandchildren losing the Jewish faith.

Church of Christ

"Where the Scriptures speak, we speak; where the Scriptures are silent, we are silent."

Begun in Kentucky and Pennsylvania in the early part of the nineteenth century, the Church of Christ was formally organized in 1832. These Christians adhere closely to the New Testament and avoid any elaboration not firmly based in scripture. Special rites include adult baptism and weekly Lord's Supper. Church of Christ followers tend to be highly tolerant in doctrinal and religious matters and strongly supportive of education. In general, this denomination is not tolerant of interfaith relationships.

Episcopalians

Reach way back to high school history and you'll no doubt remember that King Henry VIII of Great Britain wanted nothing more than a male heir. (Actually, he wanted a whole lot more, but he wanted a son most of all.) When Henry's wife Catherine of Aragon produced only a daughter (Mary) and proved too old to have another child, Henry decided it was time to trade her in for a newer, more fertile model.

The problem? Trade-ins weren't allowed because the Roman Catholic Church—of which Henry and his wife were members—does not allow divorce. What to do? Henry decided to split from the Roman Catholic Church in 1534 and set up his own church. He called it the Church of England and made himself the head. (And yes, divorce is allowed.)

The Episcopalian Church was established in America in 1789.

Not surprisingly, Episcopalians believe in many of the same rites as the Roman Catholics, including:

➤ Infant baptism

➤ The Eucharist

➤ The Apostles' Creed

The admission of women to holy order during the 1970s brought considerable division in the church, as did the church's position on matters relating to sexuality. The church is relatively tolerant of interfaith relationships.

Learn the Lingo

In England, the Church of England is also called the Anglican (English) Church; in America, it's called the Episcopalian Church.

Did You Know?

Fundamentalist Christians today often display a fish symbol to show their faith. This is not just because the Bible calls the Apostles fishers of men. It is also because the letters of the Greek word for fish, *ichthus*, match up with the Greek word for Jesus Christ, Son of God, Savior. From the second century on, the fish appears as a symbol of Christ and the newly baptized.

Fundamentalist Christians

Fundamentalist Christians are not an organized denomination like Methodists or Southern Baptists. Fundamentalism is more a viewpoint that runs through many churches, and some denominations may be largely made up of Fundamentalists.

Fundamentalist Christians take their name from their belief that the Bible truly is the Word of God and that it is to be interpreted literally. They believe that no one is or ever will be good enough to reach God by his or her own effort. To reach God, it takes an admission of need (that is, a recognition that one has sinned and thus has a need to be forgiven by God) coupled with the belief that it was Jesus' death on the cross that provided payment for sin.

Followers also believe that ...

➤ Jesus took the punishment for all sin.

➤ Deliverance from that punishment (and a place in heaven) will come if the individual lives by faith in Christ.

Learn the Lingo

Fundamentalist Christians often prefer to call themselves **evangelical Christians**—*evangelical* referring to a belief in the Gospel, the Christian message of the New Testament—because the term "fundamentalist" is often used in a derogatory way.

Learn the Lingo

Jehovah is the name of the God of the Hebrew people, incorrectly translated from the Hebrew text.

Fundamentalists do not approve of interfaith marriages. Jews look to God's commands to the Israelites not to intermarry with the unbelieving Gentiles among whom they lived, along with verses such as Amos 3:3 ("Can two walk together, except they be agreed?"). Fundamentalists agree with this principle and reinforce it with some New Testament teaching. Perhaps the most pointed passage in this regard is found in 2 Corinthians 6, in which the apostle Paul writes, "Be ye not unequally yoked together with unbelievers; for what fellowship hath righteousness with unrighteousness? And what communion hath light with darkness?"

That being said, interfaith marriages are represented in most fundamentalist churches. The congregation usually is supportive of such families but also prays that the spouse who has rejected the faith will have a change of heart.

Jehovah's Witnesses

You may have encountered a member of the *Jehovah's Witnesses* preaching door to door or distributing literature on street corners. Or perhaps you visited a service conducted in Kingdom Hall, as the meeting places are called.

Established in 1870 in Pennsylvania, Jehovah's Witnesses believe in the Second Coming of Christ and consider each Witness (member) a minister. The religion teaches that Christ began His invisible reign as king in 1914. They believe that soon the forces of good (led by Christ) will defeat the forces of evil (led by Satan) at the battle of Armageddon. Thereafter, Christ will rule the world for a thousand years. The dead will rise again, and everyone will have a second chance for salvation. Perfect humanity will enjoy perfect life on earth.

Since Witnesses acknowledge allegiance only to the kingdom of Jesus Christ, they refuse to …

➤ Salute any flag.

➤ Vote.

➤ Perform military service.

Latter Day Saints (Mormons)

In the early 1800s, the Mormon religion came to Joseph Smith in a vision of a book written in a hieroglyphic script on golden plates. He published his vision as *The Book of Mormon* in 1830.

Although Mormons acknowledge that all religions contain elements of truth, the Mormon Church sees itself as "the only true and living church upon the earth"—the only church authorized by God. Based in Salt Lake City, Utah, the Mormons are well known for a powerful missionary program.

Doctrine comes from four sources:

1. The Bible

2. *The Book of Mormon*

3. *The Doctrine and Covenants* (issued by Smith, 1830-1840) This is a supplementary text written by Smith.

4. *The Pearl of Great Price* (1842)

While Mormons follow many basic tenets of Christianity, they diverge in several key points:

➤ A belief in the prenatal existence of human souls

➤ A conviction that the Trinity is three separate individuals

➤ The belief that humans can attain the status of godhood

Mormons do not sanction intermarriage.

Don't Go There

Mormons came under great hostility for practicing polygamy, the custom of one man having multiple wives. Although Mormons claim to have abolished the practice, which is illegal in America, *The New York Times* recently claimed that it is still being practiced among some members. You may wish to check this out in more detail if you're considering marrying a Mormon man.

Lutherans

"Salvation by faith alone."

—Martin Luther

Lutheranism, a Protestant denomination that originated as a sixteenth-century movement headed by Martin Luther, affirms the ultimate word of the Bible and emphasizes Christ as the key to understanding the Bible.

According to Lutheran doctrine, everyone is a sinner due to original sin and is in bondage to the powers of evil. Salvation is God's gift, not dependent on worthiness or merit.

Lutherans follow two of the original seven sacraments: infant baptism and the Eucharist. Many Lutherans are of German and Swedish extraction. They tend to be tolerant of interfaith relationships.

Learn the Lingo

Predestination is the belief that God has foreordained ("predestined") salvation for the elect, his chosen people.

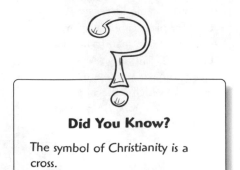

Did You Know?

The symbol of Christianity is a cross.

Methodists

This branch of Protestantism began in 1729 when a group of students at Oxford University in England met for worship. Among the group was John Wesley (considered the founder of Methodism) and his brother, Charles. Together they brought about a spiritual revolution, rejecting the Calvinist emphasis on *predestination*. They sparked a religious revival, especially among the poor.

Methodists believe in …

➤ Personal salvation through faith.

➤ Christian perfection.

Methodists follow two of the original seven sacraments: baptism (as infants or adults) and the Eucharist. Unlike Roman Catholics, Methodist ministers are not members of a priestly order. They hold office (for life, if they wish) and can marry and have a family. Methodists are well known for their social consciousness and good works. In general, they are tolerant of interfaith relationships.

Orthodox Christianity

The Eastern Rite churches, including the Maronite, Chaldean, Ruthenian, and Ukrainian denominations, adhere to their own centuries-old traditions rather than the Roman Catholic rites.

The liturgy, for example, is very traditional. Icons are venerated, and emphasis is placed on Christ's resurrection rather than on His crucifixion. Most important for our purposes, these churches tend to be tolerant in their ethics. For instance, divorce and remarriage are permitted in some cases. The same is true of interfaith relationships.

Act of Faith

The Anglican, Eastern, and Roman Catholic churches celebrate Epiphany on January 6; in the Eastern Church, the feast is recognized as the anniversary of Christ's baptism. In the Western Churches, Epiphany marks the coming of the Three Wise Men and the revelation of Jesus Christ as the Savior. The eve of Epiphany is called Twelfth Night. In the Eastern Church, holy water is blessed on Epiphany; the same rite takes place on Holy Saturday (the day before Easter) in the Roman Catholic Church.

Pentecostal

Originally a movement rather than a formal organization, the Pentecostal denomination stresses Scripture and the teachings of the Holy Spirit (Christ). Leaders are highly charismatic.

In the beginning, these groups were labeled "Holy Rollers" for their vigorous prayer and their practice of speaking in tongues, faith healing, and exorcism. Recently, however, Pentecostalism has begun to appear in mainline churches and has established middle-class congregations. On the whole, the Pentecostal church takes the same stand as fundamentalists on the issue of interfaith marriage: They do not support it.

Presbyterian

As with the Lutherans and Episcopalians (Anglicans), the Presbyterians emerged from the Protestant Reformation of the 1500s. In the beginning, the religion stressed the authority of scripture and predestination; the former remains, but the latter is no longer a central element.

Presbyterians retain infant baptism and Eucharist. Religious services tend to be simple and somber with the sermon as the focal point. Members tend to be strict about church and self-discipline but are otherwise tolerant.

The Presbyterian Church suggests that ...

> "A noncoercive, nonmanipulative family environment is important for spiritual well-being. Striving for conversion of one spouse to the other's faith does not encourage harmony. While a Christian may believe that the Spirit of God is preparing the heart of the partner for faith in Jesus Christ, it is important that any conversion be an individual's personal response to God."

United Church of Christ

A Protestant denomination, the United Church of Christ was organized in Cleveland, Ohio, in 1957, when the General Council of the Congregational Christian Churches and the Evangelical and Reformed Churches combined. As such, it's the first major union in American Protestantism to have different historical and cultural backgrounds and mixed forms of worship. Not surprisingly, there's a wide latitude of religious interpretation.

The organization is tolerant in general, with an emphasis on some social action. Members tend to be open-minded toward interfaith couples.

Act of Faith

Some of the most famous sayings in English come from the Bible, especially from the Old Testament. For instance, the word "scapegoat" was coined by the sixteenth-century scholar William Tyndale in his translation of the Old Testament. It comes from Leviticus 16 and refers to a goat that was ritually laden with the sins of the community. Other famous sayings from the Old Testament include "[Can] the leopard change its spots?" (Jer. 13:23), "Pride goeth before ... a fall" (Prov. 16:18), "I am holier than thou" (Isa. 65:5), "the apple of his eye" (Deut. 32:10), and "a still small voice" (1 Kings 19:12).

Two Major Christian Holidays

Christmas and Easter are the two major holidays in the Christian faith. Although Christmas has become increasingly secular, make no mistake: It is still a religious holiday. Easter is equally religious but less commercial. (Although my husband is disconcerted by the Easter lights—bunny- and egg-shaped, no less—he now sees festooning many homes.)

Christmas

Celebrated on December 25, Christmas commemorates the birth of Jesus Christ. Although celebrations vary from family to family, many Christians erect a Christmas tree, decorate outside their house with garlands of lights, attend Mass, exchange cards and gifts, and have a large, festive meal. Italian families might have a feast with many fish on Christmas Eve; others celebrate on Christmas Day itself.

Easter

Celebrated on varying dates between March 22 and April 25, Easter commemorates the resurrection of Christ. Easter is preceded by a 40-day period of penance called Lent, beginning on Ash Wednesday and concluding at midnight on Holy Saturday (the day before Easter Sunday).

Even though all Christians believe in Christ, don't make the mistake of seeing Christianity as a monolith. Just the opposite is true: different denominations—even different congregations—hold their own beliefs. As a result, learn as much as you can about your sweetie's faith without assuming that he or she follows general Christian teachings.

Did You Know?

Charles Dickens's 1843 classic tale *A Christmas Carol* describes how the heartless and despised Ebenezer Scrooge accepts the Christmas spirit to become benevolent, cheerful, and loving. Scrooge recalls three past Christmas celebrations—when he was a school boy, a young lover, and an apprentice—and reaches out to his employee and the employee's crippled son, Tiny Tim.

The Least You Need to Know

➤ Christianity is like a tent that shelters a great variety of people who hold different views on Christ and worship.

➤ In general, Christians believe that, by his death on the cross, Jesus Christ made a covenant for the redemption of humanity.

➤ Christianity is divided into many denominations, each with different views on interfaith relationships. Roman Catholics, for example, allow interfaith couples to marry in the church; Fundamentalist Christians, in contrast, strongly disapprove of interfaith marriages.

➤ Speak to your religious leader and your sweetheart's religious leader to see where they stand on this issue.

➤ The two major Christian holidays are Christmas and Easter.

Chapter 6

Islam

In This Chapter

➤ A quick language lesson

➤ The origins of Islam

➤ Who is Muslim?

➤ What Muslims believe

➤ The Five Pillars of Faith

➤ Muslims and intermarriage

With 1.1 billion adherents in 184 countries, Islam is the second-largest religion in the world. It is the dominant religion throughout the Middle East, North Africa, Central Asia, Afghanistan, Pakistan, and Indonesia. There are 104 million Muslims (followers of Islam) in India alone—11 percent of the population. Islam has several million followers in North America, too.

As these statistics show, one fifth of the world's population belongs to the Islamic faith. It's surprising, then, that Islam is still unfamiliar to many Americans, despite intermarriage. In this chapter, you'll learn all about Islam. I'll start by teaching you three key terms you need to know. Then we'll explore the origins of Islam and its belief system. Finally, we'll see how Muslims feel about intermarriage.

Learn the Lingo

In Arabic, the word **Islam** means "surrender" or "submission" to the will of God. **Muslim** means "one who surrenders to God."

Origins of Islam

Let's start with the basics:

➤ *Islam* is the religion.

➤ A follower of Islam is called a *Muslim*

➤ Muslims worship *Allah.*

➤ The symbol of Islam is a crescent and star.

All discussion of Islam begins with Muhammad, the founding prophet.

The crescent and star, the symbol of Islam.

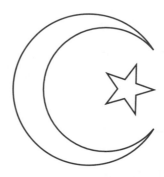

The Prophet Muhammad

Muhammad was born around 570 C.E. in Mecca in western Saudi Arabia. Raised by his uncle, at the age of 25, Muhammad became a trader and married his employer, the widow Khadija.

Family Matters

The Islamic Centre of Long Island can be reached on the Web at http://muslimsonline.com/icli.

In 610, the archangel Gabriel appeared to him in a vision and ordered him to proclaim the word of God. Understandably, Muhammad first kept this vision and subsequent ones close to his vest, sharing his revelations only with family and friends. After four years, however, he began to preach openly in his hometown.

Reviled by his neighbors, in 622, Muhammad left Mecca and traveled to Medina, a pilgrimage called the *Hegira.* From this date, the Islamic calendar begins. At Medina, Muhammad was soon recognized as a prophet and lawgiver. Eight years later, Muhammad returned to Mecca. By the time of Muhammad's death in 632, most Arabs were Muslims, and Muhammad was the leader of a rapidly growing Arab state.

Islam Spreads

Within two centuries, Islam spread into Syria, Egypt, North Africa, Spain, Persia, India, and eastward. In the following centuries, Islam also spread into Anatolia and the Balkans to the north and sub-Saharan Africa to the south.

In the twentieth century, some traditional Islamic countries such as Turkey became more secular states, while others such as Saudi Arabia and Iran came under strict Islamic Fundamentalist rule.

Who Is a Muslim?

Today, Islam is the fastest-growing religion in the world. One of the reasons for this growth is the Muslim community's openness to new members. Children born to Muslim parents are automatically considered Muslim. At any time, a non-Muslim can convert to Islam by declaring him- or herself to be a Muslim. A person's declaration of faith is sufficient evidence of conversion to Islam, and it need not be confirmed by others or by religious authorities.

Muslims belong to two different sects: Sunnites and Shi'ites. The division reflects differences in opinion about who should have succeeded Muhammad.

➤ **Sunnites.** Most Muslims (83 percent) identify themselves as Sunnites or "traditionalists."

➤ **Shi'ites.** About 16 percent of all Muslims belong to the Shi'ite or "partisan" sect.

What Do Muslims Believe?

Along with Judaism and Christianity, Islam is one of the three major world religions that preach a belief in a single God who created the universe.

Islam has clear links to Judaism and Christianity. For example, Muslims believe that Muhammad was the last and most important in a series of prophets including Moses (the Hebrew prophet

Don't Go There

Muslims resent being called *Muhammadans* because it implies a personal cult of Muhammad, which is forbidden in Islam. They also object to the spelling "Moslem" as a distortion of "Muslim."

Family Matters

We all tend to replay childhood memories, especially in times of stress. This often sparks a desire for a partner to return to previous lifestyles and attitudes. As a result, partners in interfaith relationships must be on their guard not to revert to childhood patterns unthinkingly. Consider why you're reacting as you are—is your response based on ingrained religious beliefs?

and lawgiver) and Jesus (whom Christians believe to be the Son of God). The Koran recounts the virgin birth of Jesus but does not accept his divinity.

The Koran includes stories of Abraham and Isaac as well as Moses and the Ten Commandments. Unlike Jews, who trace their descent from Abraham through Isaac (the son of Sarah), Muslims trace their descent through Ishmael, Abraham's son by Hagar.

Islam teaches that all Muslims are equal before God. Thus, all Muslims belong to one community, the *umma*, no matter what their ethnic or national background may be.

The Holy Books

The two main sources of Islamic doctrine are the Koran (*Qur'an*), the holy book of Islam, and the *Sunna,* the exemplary conduct of the prophet Muhammad.

Learn the Lingo

The **Koran** (or **Qur'an**) is the holy book of Islam.

➤ **The Koran.** Muslims regard the Koran as God's direct speech to Muhammad, mediated by Gabriel (the angel of revelation). As a result, the Koran is considered to be infallible. It was transcribed by Muhammad's followers over the course of 23 years. The Koran has 114 chapters, roughly organized in order of length, beginning with the longest and ending with the shortest chapters. With few exceptions, the verses do not follow a story line.

➤ **The Sunna.** The Sunna is made known through the *Hadith,* the body of traditions based on what Muhammad did or said. Unlike the Koran, the Hadith is considered to be fallible because it has come down through the oral tradition.

Further Guidelines

Islam has strict dietary laws and prohibitions:

1. Pork is not eaten.
2. Only animals specifically slaughtered for food can be eaten.
3. Liquor and intoxicants are forbidden.
4. Promiscuity is forbidden.
5. Theft is forbidden.
6. Gambling is forbidden.
7. Lying is forbidden.
8. Living creatures cannot be portrayed in art. As a result, Muslim art often shows texts from the Koran or a plan of the Great Mosque in Mecca, for example.

Since Islam does not recognize any spiritual inter-mediary between humans and Allah, there is no religious clerical hierarchy. Scholars—always male—are often hired or volunteer to become clergy, called *Imaam.*

The Five Pillars

A Muslim's relations to God are regulated by the Five Pillars of Faith, the essential religious duties required of every adult Muslim who is mentally able. They constitute the core practices of the Islamic faith.

The Five Pillars of Faith are ...

1. Profession of faith
2. Five daily prayers
3. Charity to the poor
4. Fasting during the holy month of Ramadan
5. A pilgrimage to Mecca

Let's look at each pillar of faith in detail.

Act of Faith

Arabs today still use the language of the prophet Muhammad, more than 1,300 years after his death. Modern written Arabic, and the spoken language of ed-ucated Arabs, is not significantly different from classical Arabic, the language on which the Koran is based. Modern collo-quial Arabic, however, has di-verged from the written language. Therefore, even though Muhammad would be able to converse today with edu-cated Arabs, he would probably need an interpreter to talk to unschooled ones.

Profession of Faith

As you have already read, the focus of Islamic piety is Allah, the supreme deity. The profession of faith is therefore essential for membership in the Muslim community. Every day, an observant Muslim will repeat the profession, "I bear witness that there is no god but Allah and that Muhammad is his prophet." The profession of faith can be said anywhere, at any time.

Reciting the profession of faith shows that the person belongs to the Muslim commu-nity and believes in the religion.

The Five Daily Prayers

All adult Muslims are supposed to perform five prayers every day, after a ritual clean-ing of the body. The prayers are offered at dawn, noon, midafternoon, sunset, and evening. Muslims face Mecca when they give the daily prayers. In Muslim countries, worshippers are called to prayer on public announcement systems by a *muezzin* (crier) from a mosque.

The worshiper stands, bows, kneels, and then prostrates himself while reciting verses from the Koran as well as other prayers.

In addition to the five required daily prayers, Muslims can pray anytime they wish. Weekly, the primary worship is Friday at midday.

Learn the Lingo

An **imam** is a prayer leader.

Family Matters

The month of Ramadan is sacred because the first revelation of the Koran occurred then.

Learn the Lingo

The profession of faith is **shahada,** prayer is **salat,** alms-giving is **zakat,** fasting is **sawm,** and the pilgrimage is the **hajj.**

Charity to the Poor

Giving charity to the poor shows devotion to God. It also offers a way for a Muslim to attain salvation. The money collected can be used not only to help the poor but also to assist orphans and widows.

Since the Koran doesn't specify the exact amount that should be given to charity, the formula has been the subject of elaborate discussions among Muslim legal experts. At this time, observant Muslims pay 2.5 percent of their assets yearly.

Fasting During the Holy Month of Ramadan

For the entire month of Ramadan, Muslims fast from daybreak to sunset by refraining from eating, drinking, and sexual intercourse. Menstruating women, travelers, and sick people are exempted from fasting but have to make up the days they miss at a later date.

The fasting is believed to create physical and spiritual discipline, remind the rich of the misfortunes of the poor, and foster unity among Muslims. After the fasting ends, the holiday of breaking the fast begins, lasting for three days.

Fasting is also required as a compensation for various offenses and violations of the law. Many Muslims also perform voluntary fasts at different times to show devotion and spiritual discipline. However, such additional fasting is not required by Islamic law.

A Pilgrimage to Mecca

The fifth pillar requires that Muslims perform a pilgrimage, or *hajj,* to Mecca at least once in a lifetime.

The hajj must take place during the twelfth lunar month of the year, known as *Dhu al-Hijja.* It involves a specific, detailed sequence of rituals that are completed over several days.

House of Worship

The *mosque* is the Muslim house of worship. Here's what you can expect to see outside a mosque:

➤ Mosques usually have one or more *minarets* from which the Muslims are called to prayer five times a day.

➤ Most mosques also have a dome.

➤ The building will be oriented toward Mecca.

Here's what you can expect to see inside a mosque:

➤ There isn't any furniture.

➤ The floors are covered in carpets and mats.

➤ There is usually a separate section for women.

➤ There is usually a separate area for performing ritual ablutions.

➤ Columns are often used to mark the way for worshipers to line up during prayer.

Visitors are welcome inside the mosque but must be clothed modestly and fully: Shoulders and legs must be covered, and women must wear a scarf on their heads. Everyone must remove his or her shoes before entering the worship area.

Learn the Lingo

A **minaret** is a tower on a mosque.

Family Matters

Many Muslims also take a pilgrimage to Jerusalem, the third sacred city for Islam. Muslims believe that Muhammad was carried to Jerusalem in a vision. The Dome of the Rock houses the stone from which Muhammad is believed to have ascended to heaven and Allah. There are no standard prescribed rituals for these pilgrimages nor are they treated as obligatory acts of worship.

Muslims and Interfaith Relationships

Since there are so many Muslims spread out all over the world, there is great political and ethnic diversity among the faithful. The radically different political, economic, and cultural conditions under which contemporary Muslims live make it difficult to identify what constitutes standard Islamic practice in the modern world. However, the Koran specifically forbids intermarriage.

How do the following two experiences compare to your own?

"I am Christian. When I first met Ahmed, a Muslim, I didn't know much about his culture or his religion—Islam. When I told my parents that I was going to

Learn the Lingo

The Arabic name for God, **Allah,** refers to the same God worshipped by Jews and Christians.

Don't Go There

In Islam, the children are raised in the religion of the father. The children are the property of the father—regardless of what American law says.

marry a Muslim, the response I received was worse than I would have ever imagined!

My father said I was dead to him if I married Ahmed. My mother was sympathetic, but she wouldn't go against my father. Anguished, I cried for nights over what I should do. When I told Ahmed what my parents said, he said that the marriage was my decision, and he would accept whatever I thought best. I prayed many nights and felt assured that I should marry Ahmed.

For six months I did not speak to my father, and my mother had to call me when my dad wasn't home. Finally, my family decided to visit us. After spending two weeks with us, my father admitted that he had made a mistake about Ahmed and that he understood why I married him. Ahmed had morals, loved me, and treated my children [from my first marriage] like they were his own. In fact, Ahmed encouraged me to go to church consistently or not go at all because it was sending a mixed message for the girls."

—Nanci, age 26

"My husband and I visited his home country of Egypt shortly after we married in America. My husband's parents were furious with my husband 'for marrying a non-Muslim. They said I was *kafir*—religionless and bound for hell. The whole trip I was miserable because they wouldn't have anything to do with me and argued the whole time with my husband over marrying out of his faith. This has put a great strain on our marriage.

Now he's planning to move back home. He refuses to take me with him because he plans to marry a Muslim woman and win his family's approval. I was shocked because my husband is American-educated and has lived in America for over a decade."

—Christa, age 28

Since Arab society emphasizes the group over the individual, people see themselves as extensions of the *hamula* (kinship group). As a result, collective principles prevail over individual desires. The Arab family is the source of economic, social, and emotional support, so a person who rejects traditional values may face complete ostracism. Honor is inextricably connected to all aspects of life.

In traditional Islamic culture ...

➤ You don't choose your spouse—the group does.

➤ Pre-engagement courtship is brief and strictly chaperoned.

➤ Arranged marriages are common. Family connections, prestige, status, and health are considerations.

➤ Exchange marriages are often common, whereby a man agrees to marry another man's sister on the condition that the other man marries his sister.

➤ Individuals may fall in love, but the decision to marry is always made after close consultation with the family.

If the beloved practices a different religion or is deemed unacceptable by the family, the individual will either follow family expectations and end the relationship or continue with the relationship and be cast out. These guidelines apply only to strictly observant Muslims. Remember that each individual and family is different.

The Least You Need to Know

➤ Islam is the second-largest and fastest-growing religion in the world.

➤ Islam is the religion, followers of Islam are called Muslims, and Muslims worship Allah.

➤ Muhammad is the founding prophet of Islam.

➤ Children born to Muslim parents are automatically considered Muslim. At any time, a non-Muslim can convert to Islam by declaring him- or herself to be a Muslim.

➤ Muslims believe in a single God—Allah—who created the universe. The holy book is the Koran; worship is conducted in a mosque.

➤ Islam has strict dietary laws and prohibitions. Muslims must follow the Five Pillars of Islam.

➤ The Koran forbids intermarriage. In general, non-Islamic partners are expected to conform to Islam's ways.

Hinduism

"... see my forms
in hundreds and thousands;
diverse, divine,
of many colors and shapes.
See the sun gods, gods of light,
Howling storm gods, twin gods of dawn
and gods of wind ...
wondrous forms not seen before.
... see all the universe,
animate and inanimate,
and whatever else you wish to see;
all stands here as one in my body."

—Bhagavad Gita

As this passage from the Hindu holy book the *Bhagavad Gita* shows, Hindus believe in many different gods that take many different forms. Learn this—and so much more about Hinduism—in this chapter.

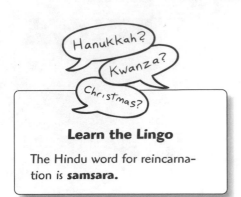

Learn the Lingo

The Hindu word for reincarnation *is* **samsara.**

In the first half of this chapter, you'll learn how Hinduism got started and what observant Hindus believe. I'll explain how Hindus worship, too. In the second half of the chapter, you'll learn how Hindus feel about interfaith relationships. That way, you'll be prepared if your sweetheart takes you home to meet mom and dad—and they happen to be Hindus.

Origins of Hinduism

Hinduism is a major world religion, not only because of its many followers—about 793 million people around the globe—but also because of its deep influence on many other religions during its long history, which dates from about 1500 B.C.E.

The religion began in India, where it is still followed by most of the country's inhabitants. Indians who have emigrated to East Africa, South Africa, Southeast Asia, the East Indies, England, and America also follow this religion. Important for our purposes here, Hinduism is a culture as well as a religion.

What Do Hindus Believe?

Hinduism is rooted in the belief that the individual should connect his or her self (*Atman*) with Brahman (or Godhead), the spiritual source of the universe.

> "As a man discards
> worn-out clothes
> to put on new
> and different ones,
> so the embodied self
> discards
> its worn-out bodies
> to take on other new ones."
>
> —Bhagavad Gita

Hindus also believe in reincarnation; your subsequent status depends on your actions—*karma*—and duties—*dharma*—in this life. The cycle of reincarnation is broken when the individual attains liberation (*moksha*) from the temporal world through self-discovery, the union of the self with the Godhead, *Atman-Brahman.*

There are four paths to union with Brahman:

➤ **Jnana yoga,** based on knowledge

➤ **Bhakti yoga,** based on service to God

➤ **Karma yoga,** based on work for God (as opposed to work for yourself)

➤ **Raja yoga,** based on psychophysical exercise

Cult of the Gods

Although all Hindus acknowledge the existence and importance of a number of gods and demigods, most individual worshipers are primarily devoted to a single god or goddess. The religion has three primary traditions that have developed around the cult of gods:

➤ Brahman is the creator.

➤ Shiva (or Siva) is both protective and destructive. Shiva is the creator, preserver, and destroyer of the universe.

➤ Vishnu is the loving god incarnated as Krishna.

Most Hindus worship Shiva, Vishnu, or the goddess Devi, but they also worship hundreds of additional minor deities that are peculiar to a particular village or even to a particular family.

Learn the lingo

Dharma is a code of moral and religious conduct followed by the devout.

Different, Yet Alike

Although very few practices or beliefs are shared by all Hindus, some common threads can be seen. Almost all Hindus ...

1. Have a deep respect for all living things.

2. Honor and protect cows.

3. Do not eat meat in any form.

4. Marry within their caste.

Learn the Lingo

Saktism is a form of worship dedicated to the female consorts of Vishnu and Siva.

The Caste System

Traditional Hinduism observes a complex system of divisions within society involving four main (and thousands of subsidiary) *castes*. These are defined by occupation and social standing. The four main castes are:

➤ **Brahmins** (leaders, philosophers, artists)

➤ **Kshatriyas** (princes, soldiers, and administrators)

➤ **Vaishyas** (merchants and landowners)

➤ **Shudras** (laborers)

Learn the Lingo

Hindu society is divided into so-cial strata called **castes.** Traditionally, observant Hindus would never date or marry out-side their caste, much less their religion.

Beyond the caste system are the *Untouchables,* the out-casts. India's modern constitution outlawed the caste system, but many people still cling to their traditional identities.

The caste system developed from the belief that each person is born to perform a specific job, marry a spe-cific person, eat certain food, and create children to do likewise. Further, it is considered better to fulfill your own role than anyone else's role. This is true even if your own role is low or objectionable, such as that of the Untouchables, whose very presence was once considered polluting to other castes.

The Holy Books

The *Vedas* are the Hindu holy books. Different Hindu sects rely on different Vedas, but common to the majority are the Vedic *Upanishads*. The *Svetasvatara Upanishads* describe Shiva.

Sources for Hindu mythology include the *Mahabharata, Ramayana* (concerning Rama, incarnation of the great god Vishnu), and *Puraranas*. The *Mahabharata* (Great Epic of the Bharata Dynasty) is India's greatest epic. It contains about 100,000 Sanskrit cou-plets, which makes it about four times longer than the *Odyssey* and *Iliad* combined.

Act of Faith

The *Bhagavad Gita* has influenced many people around the world. Robert Oppenheimer (1902–1967), the director of the Manhattan Project, which built the world's first atomic bomb, recited a passage from the *Bhagavad Gita* after the first successful test of the bomb: "... I am become Death / The shatterer of worlds ...." The quote described the dual nature of creation and destruction. American writer Henry David Thoreau (1817–1862) took the *Gita* with him to his retreat at Walden Pond; the *Gita* also was the inspiring force in the life and thought of the eminent modern Indian leader Mahatma Gandhi (1869–1948).

The *Bhagavad Gita* ("Song of the Lord") is a dialogue between Krishna (another incarnation of the god Vishnu) and Prince Arjuna that contains a description of the three paths to union with god. The poem contains about 700 verses. It is just one section of the *Mahabharata*.

How Hindus Worship

Unlike Islam, which involves group worship, Hindu worship is largely an individual and family matter. Hindus worship in temples devoted to a particular god or group of gods. Observers pray and make offerings to the gods. The rituals are designed to bring the worshipper closer to the god.

As in many religions, rites of passage are important in Hinduism. Some of these rites include the birth of a child, the first time a child eats solid food, a boy's first haircut, marriage, and the blessings upon a pregnancy. Last is the funeral ceremony (cremation and, if possible, sprinkling the ashes in a holy river such as the Ganges). There is also a yearly offering to dead ancestors.

Hindus have many pilgrimage sites including seven sacred cities. Several famous temples are located on the banks of the Ganges River, which is sacred to Hindus. Thousands and even millions of Hindus worship at annual festivals. Important festivals include

Learn the Lingo

The Hindu place of worship is called a **temple**.

Did You Know?

A flock of self-proclaimed Indian religious teachers have come to America, where they have inspired large followings. Some, such as the Hare Krishna sect founded by Bhaktivedanta, claim to be based on classical Hindu practices.

➤ **Dipavali** (or Diwali), "festival of lights," which is sacred to Lakshmi, goddess of prosperity. The festival takes place in early winter.

➤ **Holi**, a spring festival when members of all castes mingle and sprinkle one another with cascades of red powder and liquid.

➤ **Dashara**, a harvest festival.

Hindus and Intermarriage

Meena came from a happy home and was raised in the Hindu faith. She was 24 when she met Hamid at the accounting firm where they worked. He considered himself a "progressive Muslim," and she liked his open-mindedness. Three years later, Hamid asked Meena to marry him. She said yes. That's when the trouble started.

"His parents were more than willing to accommodate some of our culture, but mine were opposed. My father was aghast. The more I tried to talk with him, the harder he was on me. My mother stopped talking to me altogether. Staying home became traumatic. The last straw was when I came home one evening and my father said that a doctor was coming to ask for my hand in marriage. I argued, cried, and pleaded, but he had made up his mind. I decided to leave home. I stayed with friends and four months later I was married. On my side, only four people turned up for the wedding; they were my friends.

Just before the wedding, Hamid and I went to see my family. Except for my siblings, no one else spoke to us. We've been married for two years. My father still doesn't talk to me. Hamid and I still go to visit my parents' home. We chat in the kitchen. My mother doesn't say much. We're planning on having a baby. My in-laws tell me that, when a baby comes, ties get renewed.

I hope it's true."

—Meena, 24

On the other hand, not all Hindu interfaith experiences are difficult. An Indian woman we'll call Mrs. Malhotra from Houston, Texas, is the proud mother-in-law of a white Christian girl. Her son Sanji married Jennifer after they met at a hospital in Indianapolis where they were training. Says Mrs. Malhotra, "I didn't have any opposition to my son marrying an American girl. My children have been raised in this country, so I don't expect them to marry a Hindu." Asked if there was any opposition from the Hindu community, Mrs. Malhotra replied, "No one said anything to me. Interreligious marriages are quite common now." Happily married for four years, Sanji and Jennifer have successfully integrated Hindu and American culture.

Family Matters

Many conflicts and interpersonal tensions result from differences in cultural backgrounds rather than religious issues. Families should take care to distinguish cultural issues from religious issues and deal with them appropriately.

Tradition Tempered with Reason

How concerned are Hindu parents about their sons and daughters finding interreligious partners? "They are very concerned," says Bina Parekh, a volunteer at a hotline and counseling center serving the Indian community. "We hold forums for both parents and teenagers about dating, interfaith marriages, and so on," she says.

My Hindu neighbor Namita Chablani, the mother of a daughter and a son, echoes Bina's concern. "Hindus are strongly opposed to intermarriage," she says. In India, such couples would be shunned, she notes, because in rural India especially, intermarriage is still taboo. Outside India, most people are getting used to it, however.

According to Mrs. Chablani, "Arranged marriages are still the preferred option for helping to ensure the future happiness of one's adult children. However, you cannot force your children into marriage with someone you have chosen." Further, because it's hard to find people from the same social, educational, and economic background, less orthodox families are prepared to be more flexible.

Veena Ramachandran, a student in Washington, D.C., feels that interfaith dating and marriage are still quite foreign to her parents' generation. Veena says, "Their marriages were arranged with other Indians and were mostly successful, so they cling instinctively to the logic that 'If it worked for us, it will work for you.'" She adds, "I think this happens in every society—parents worrying about love, race, and religion. We shouldn't think that this happens only among the Hindu community."

Words to the Wise

Since interfaith marriages among Hindus are increasingly common in America, here are some guidelines:

➤ Interfaith couples can still get married in the temple (as long as one partner is Hindu).

➤ Interfaith ceremonies can be arranged. Usually, each religious ceremony is performed on its own day. For example, a Catholic-Hindu couple might have the Hindu wedding ceremony on Saturday and the Catholic wedding ceremony on Sunday. Mrs. Chablani and her family have attended several such weddings.

➤ Children born from an interfaith union do not have to be raised Hindu to be welcome in the Hindu community.

The Least You Need to Know

➤ Hindus believe in many different gods that take many different forms.

➤ Hinduism is rooted in the belief that the individual should connect with Brahman (God).

➤ Observant Hindus also believe in reincarnation, respect all living things, and do not eat meat.

➤ Hindus worship in temples devoted to a particular god or group of gods.

➤ Traditional Hindus are strongly opposed to intermarriage. In India and among the observant in America, arranged marriages are still the preferred option.

Other Organized Religions

A colleague shared this story:

> "My father is Indian/Hindu and my mother is Japanese, Buddhist/Shinto with shades of Christianity. I married a Presbyterian American. As a person with a rich, varied heritage, I can't emphasize enough the importance of understanding people of different backgrounds and finding your own identity."

—Sunni, age 34

In this chapter, you'll learn about some other religions whose members you are likely to meet (and perhaps marry!) in America today. We'll start with the Baha'i and then discuss Buddhism, the Druze, Mennonites (as well as the Amish), Sikhs, and Unitarians.

After a discussion of each religion, I'll explain its official stance and general attitude toward interfaith relationships. Of course, each individual is different, and members are under no obligation to toe the party line. Never assume that people hold the same religious beliefs just because they identify themselves with the same label.

That said, it's only when we understand other faiths that we can begin to build bridges between them.

The Baha'i Faith

I found this story especially interesting:

> "I'm a Christian of British descent, and my wife is a Baha'i. We have faced many difficulties because of our different faiths. My attitude towards things has changed in some cases; in other instances, I was forced to think about and justify to myself how I think about things. The Baha'i faith has acted as a unifying force in our relationship. We were aware when we married that intermarriage was encouraged in the Baha'i faith, despite the recognized difficulties. The faith has also given us some common ground on such vital matters as worship and the direction we want our joint lives to head."
>
> —Richard, age 51

Founded by Baha'Ullah ("glory of God") in Iran in 1844, Baha'i teaches that the revealed religions of the world are in agreement. Since the founders of all religions are believed to be manifestations of the same God, they must all have taught the same faith. Each religion has adapted its belief system to meet the needs of a particular culture and a particular period in history. Therefore, each prophet-founder revealed the will of God at a particular place and time in history.

About 6 million people follow the Baha'i faith. The religion is now based in Israel, and there is a major temple in Wilmette, Illinois.

Followers of Baha'i believe that today's problems began in the imbalance between the spiritual and material aspects of human life. As a result, people need to rediscover a spiritual purpose and direction in their lives—before society can find its own direction.

Baha'i principles emphasize the following:

1. The oneness of humankind, which will lead to world unity
2. Independent investigation of truth
3. The common foundation of all religions
4. The essential harmony of science and religion
5. Equality of men and women
6. Elimination of prejudice of all kinds

7. Universal compulsory education

8. A spiritual solution to economic problems

9. A universal auxiliary language

10. Universal peace upheld by a world government

The Baha'i faith has no priesthood or clergy. The Baha'i followers of each city elect nine of their members annually to form a Spiritual Assembly for the administration of local affairs. An annual convention elects a National Spiritual Assembly.

Given these guidelines, it's not surprising that the Baha'i faith is friendly toward interfaith relationships including interfaith marriage.

Buddhism Begins

Buddhism was established in northeastern India and is based on the teachings of Siddhartha Gautama, known as the *Buddha,* or Enlightened One. The number of Buddhists worldwide has been estimated at between 150 million and 300 million in 92 countries.

According to legend, Siddhartha Gautama was born in 563 B.C.E. near the India-Nepal border. Raised in opulence, Buddha married and had a child. When he was 29 years old, Buddha renounced earthly attachments and embarked on a quest for peace and enlightenment. He reached enlightenment after sitting under a bodhi tree near Patna. After 49 days of rapture (and withstanding the temptations of the devil Mara), Buddha inspired an order of monks and went forth to teach his philosophy for 45 years before passing to nirvana.

Learn the Lingo

In Buddhism, **nirvana** is freedom from the endless cycle of reincarnations, each with its own form of suffering. In Hinduism, **nirvana** is salvation through the union of Atman (the individual's self) with Brahman (the Godhead).

Buddhism Spreads

Buddhism spread rapidly throughout the land of its birth. Missionaries introduced the religion to southern India, the northwest part of the subcontinent, and Sri Lanka. It was adopted by the Thai people between the 1100s and 1300s and then moved into Laos and Cambodia. From Central Asia, Buddhism entered China. Buddhism also expanded into Vietnam, Korea, and Japan.

Buddhist Scripture

The Buddhist holy books are the *Tripitaka,* oral beliefs written down after Buddha's death. The Tripitaka has three parts:

➤ The story of Buddha's life

➤ Buddha's laws for personal conduct (*Dharma*)

➤ Guidelines for the monks (*Sangha*)

What Buddhists Believe

Unlike the adherents of most major religions, Buddhists do not believe in an all-powerful God, nor do they accept the existence of an individual soul. As with Hindus, Buddhists believe in a cycle of reincarnation.

Buddha's teachings are based on the Four Noble Truths:

1. Life is impermanent and produces suffering (or *dukkha*), which continues through the cycles of life, death, and rebirth.

2. Suffering is caused by ignorance of reality and the craving, attachment, and grasping that result.

3. Suffering can be ended by overcoming ignorance and attachment.

4. The way to end suffering is the Eightfold Path, which consists of right views, right intention, right speech, right action, right livelihood, right effort, right-mindedness, and right contemplation.

Family Matters

Theravada Buddhists have traditionally considered the Tripitaka to be the remembered words of Siddhartha Gautama. Mahayana Buddhists have never bound themselves to a closed canon of sacred writings.

Main Sects

Buddhism today is divided into three major branches:

➤ **Theravada** (or Hinayana), the Way of the Elders, most common in Sri Lanka, Myanmar, and Thailand. This sect is closest to the beliefs of early Buddhist sects.

➤ **Mahayana**, the Great Vehicle, most common in Japan, Korea, and China. This group of followers stresses compassion for others. Mahayana Buddhists account for 56 percent of all Buddhists, about 168 million people. *Zen Buddhism*, a subdivision of Mahayana, stresses enlightenment through meditation.

➤ **Tantric Buddhism** (Vajrayana), most common in Tibet and Mongolia, relies on chants, hand gestures, and visible icons to help its followers reach nirvana.

Buddhist Worship

The hallmark of Buddhist practice is the monastic order, in which monks withdraw from the everyday world and live simple lives devoted to meditation. Monks can devote their entire lives to the monastery or can withdraw for a few years at a time. In some Buddhist sects, teenagers spend time in a monastery as a rite of passage into adulthood.

Buddhist houses of worship are called *temples*. They are mainly for individual meditation. Collective rituals are not a focal point.

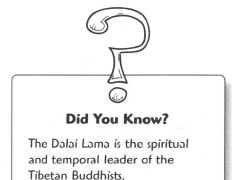

Did You Know?

The Dalai Lama is the spiritual and temporal leader of the Tibetan Buddhists.

Buddhists and Intermarriage

Jim, an American married to a Buddhist, recounted his experiences as follows:

> "I was studying Japanese culture when Nami and I became pen pals. Later, I took on a trip to Japan, met Nami's father, and he invited me to visit. Eventually Nami and I got married. My father was a Baptist minister and didn't approve, but I chose my own path."

Did You Know?

The dot in the middle of Buddha's head symbolizes the third eye of enlightenment.

His wife, Nami, had this to say:

> "My father is a Buddhist Singhalese but also a Shiva devotee with a shrine for both Buddha and Shiva. He is a vegetarian. My father was happy when I married Jim because he is a good man but also because Jim is a vegetarian!"

In general, Buddhists are tolerant of differences in belief systems. As with Hindus, traditional Buddhists prefer that their children marry within the fold, but they recognize that life in America presents new challenges and customs.

The Druze Faith

The Druze (or Druse) are members of a Middle Eastern sect who live mainly in mountainous regions of Lebanon and southern Syria. The Druze believe that, at various times, God has been divinely incarnated in a living person; his final incarnation was in the person of al-Hakim (985–1021).

Although an outgrowth of Islam, the Druze religion contains elements of Judaism and Christianity. The Druze abstain from alcohol, tobacco, profanity, and obscenity.

Numbering about 1 million worldwide, the Druze do not permit religious conversion or intermarriage.

The Mennonites

The Mennonites are named after Menno Simons (1496–1561), a Dutch Anabaptist leader. The Amish began as a sect of the Swiss Mennonites during the late seventeenth century.

Did You Know?

The Amish do not take photographs. This is based on the prohibition in Exodus 20:4 that reads: "Thou shalt not make unto thee any graven image, or any likeness of anything that ... is in the earth."

As a result of William Penn's "holy experiment" in religious tolerance, many Amish started settling in Lancaster County, Pennsylvania, during the 1720s. Other groups settled in the Midwest, notably in Illinois, Indiana, Iowa, Missouri, and Ohio.

The Mennonites and the Amish are determined to preserve the elements of late-seventeenth-century European rural culture. As a result, they reject most of the developments of modern society. Members do not own or use automobiles, electricity, radios, or TV sets. Children are encouraged to leave school after Grade 8 to work full time on the family farms. The Old Order Amish is the most conservative of the different sects.

Mennonites do not release census figures, but the Amish claim about 100,000 members in 22 states. There are about 1,500 Amish in Ontario, Canada.

Amish Beliefs

The Amish are a very conservative Christian faith group. Many of their beliefs are identical to those of fundamentalist and other evangelical churches, including baptism and a literal interpretation of the Bible. Differences include ...

➤ Their determination to remain separate from the world.

➤ Their rejection of the military and warfare.

➤ Their lack of a central authority; each district is self-governing.

➤ They usually do not seek converts. Recently, however, some Amish groups have become active in evangelization.

Amish men usually dress in plain, dark-colored suits. Amish women usually wear plain-colored dresses with long sleeves, bonnets, and aprons. Women wear a white prayer covering if married, black if single. Religious services are held biweekly on Sunday in the homes of members. They meet in a different home each week.

The Issue of Intermarriage

Mennonites and the Amish have strict rules against interfaith relationships. Conversion is almost nonexistent.

Marriages outside the faith are not allowed, and the rule is enforced. A member who does not conform (in any way) is shunned; the community terminates all contact with him or her.

Sikhism

Founded by Guru Nanak in the early sixteenth century, the *Sikh* religion is a combination of Hindu and Islamic beliefs. The religion advocates a search for eternal truth, rejects the Hindu caste system, and stresses the equality of all men and women. Sikhs believe in reincarnation but reject the notion of divine incarnation.

Sikhism has very few doctrines. Its principal message can be summarized as follows:

➤ Follow your religious tradition and not meaningless rituals.

➤ Lead an honest and truthful life in thought, words, and actions.

➤ Meditate on God.

➤ Serve God by leading a normal family life.

➤ Share with the needy whatever you can spare.

➤ Treat all people as equals.

Sikhs follow the sacred text known as *Guru Granth Singh* ("collection of sacred wisdom").

Act of Faith

Because they do not marry outsiders and few outsiders have joined the order, the Amish community has been essentially a closed genetic population for more than 12 generations. Thus, the Amish have a high rate of certain genetic mutations that were present in the initial genetic pool (as there are in any population), making the Amish host to several inherited disorders. These include dwarfism, mental retardation, and a large group of metabolic disorders.

Learn the Lingo

Sikh means disciple, one who seeks the truth.

There are more than 19 million Sikhs in the world, based in the Punjab region of India. One million Sikhs live outside India, primarily in America and Canada.

You may have noticed male Sikhs because they wear turbans and have beards. Most of these men belong to the *Khalsa,* a group of Sikhs who commit themselves by an initiation ceremony to a life of religious purity. Khalsa men receive the surname Singh (lion), women the surname Kaur (princess).

Khalsa Sikh males wear five items of prescribed dress, often referred to as the five Ks:

1. *Kesh* (uncut hair and beard; the turban covers the hair). This represents moderation and compromise.

2. *Kangha* (a wooden comb to hold the hair together).

3. *Kara* (a steel bracelet worn on the right wrist). This represents moral restraint and chastity.

4. *Kirpan* (a miniature sword). This represents a readiness to take up arms in defense of the faith.

5. *Kachh* (knee-length underwear). This also represents moral restraint and chastity.

Worship

The Guru Granth Singh is kept under a canopy in the house of worship, called the *Gurdwara.* People entering the Gurdwara remove their shoes and show reverence to the scripture by covering their heads and touching the ground with their foreheads before sitting down in the congregation. Non-Sikhs are invited to participate in worship services (usually on Sunday mornings), which consist of the reading and singing of the hymns from the scripture. The worship service is followed by a free community meal in another part of the Gurdwara, the *Langar* (common kitchen).

Sikhs and Intermarriage

As Sikhs do not believe in it, intermarriage is very rare in America and abroad. However, with more and more Sikhs immigrating to America, issues of interfaith dating and marriage are likely to arise.

Unitarianism

Unitarian roots reach back to the Reformation, but the religion took hold in America in 1796 when the King's Chapel in Boston officially adopted Unitarianism and left the Episcopal Church.

Unitarians deny the doctrine of the Trinity, believing instead that God exists in one person only. They also reject the deity of Jesus Christ, the doctrine of original sin, and everlasting punishment, regarding these beliefs as unscriptural and unnatural. They celebrate the Eucharist as a commemoration of Jesus' death and to show spiritual communion with him. In general, members are tolerant and welcoming of differences.

Unitarians are a liberal group. As a result, it is not uncommon for interfaith couples to compromise by getting married in the Unitarian church. Although this doesn't go over well with observant Jewish and Muslim families, it has proven to be a workable compromise for many couples of less observant but still different religious backgrounds.

The Least You Need to Know

➤ Baha'i teaches that the revealed religions of the world are in agreement. Baha'i followers are friendly toward interfaith relationships including interfaith marriage.

➤ Buddhists do not believe in an all-powerful God, nor do they accept the existence of an individual soul.

➤ Traditional Buddhists prefer that their children marry within the fold, but they recognize that life in America presents new challenges and customs.

➤ The Druze, a Middle Eastern sect, do not permit religious conversion or intermarriage.

➤ The Mennonites and the Amish, as very conservative Christians, do not allow interfaith relationships. Conversion is almost nonexistent.

➤ Sikhism, a combination of Hindu and Islamic beliefs, has so far seen few interfaith relationships.

➤ It is not uncommon for interfaith couples to compromise by getting married in the Unitarian Church.

Part 3

Faith, Hope, and Charity: Interfaith Dating

The various religions are like different roads converging on the same point. What difference does it make if we follow different routes, providing we arrive at the same destination.

—*Mahatma Gandhi,* Autobiography *(1924)*

In this part, you'll learn strategies for helping you and your honey arrive at the same destination—even if you travel different routes to get there.

The Dating Game

I received this e-mail as I was researching this book:

> "My girlfriend is Jewish, and I am Christian. The problem is her parents, who believe that she should only date Jewish men. Because of their attitude, she and I avoid doing 'couple' things at her parents' house or family gatherings. What can we do to change the way her parents think?"

> —Gregory, age 22

Here's my answer:

> "Dear Gregory: Nothing, and don't get caught trying. They have their opinion of interfaith dating, which they've probably held since long before you graced the earth, and they are entitled to their opinion. What you *can* affect is their opinion of you. If you're good to their daughter, as well as honest and respectful, they might warm to you. Then the issue of religion recedes from center stage."

When you're dating someone of another faith, the ball is in *your* court. That's because your attitude and behavior can make or break the relationship. If you make a good impression on your sweetheart and his or her parents, the odds are strong that they will come to like you as a person. The issue of religion then becomes easier to deal with, which is especially important if dating leads to marriage … and children.

In this chapter, I'll teach you ways to get your relationship with your sweetheart's parents off to a good start. You'll learn the importance of body language as well as words. Finally, we'll discuss warning signs that a relationship may not be worth saving.

Saturday Night Fever

Worse nightmare, male version: It's the first time you're picking up your girlfriend at her house. Even though you've been dating only a short time, she seems to be The One you want to spend eternity with. You quickly wipe your clammy hand on your jeans before you shake hands with your beloved's father. So what if he's glowering like a bull under a red flag, staring at the cross around your neck? So what if he's bigger than the national debt—and just as out of control? "We raised our precious daughter to respect the ways of our faith," he growls.

Family Matters

I have an astonishingly wise 15-year-old daughter. Her solution for uncomfortable or baffling situations: "Smile and nod." If you're put on the spot, this strategy buys you enough time to figure out how to respond—if at all.

Meanwhile, your beloved's mother looks like she just escaped from the stake at Salem. Nonetheless, you make a stab at conviviality with this witty suck-up: "I really like Jewish food, Mrs. Nudelbaum." She shoots you a look that would curdle milk. You dive for cover under the sofa.

Worse nightmare, female version: It's the first time you're having dinner at your boyfriend's house. Even though you've only been dating a short time, he seems to be The One you want to spend eternity with. You quickly wipe your clammy hand on your designer jeans before you shake hands with your beloved's father. So what if he's glowering like a bull under a red flag, staring at the Jewish star around your neck? So what if he's bigger than the national debt—and just as out of control? "We raised our precious son to respect the ways of our faith," he growls.

Meanwhile, your beloved's mother looks like she just escaped from the stake at Salem. Nonetheless, you make a stab at conviviality with this witty suck-up: "I love Catholic food, Mrs. O'Connor." She shoots you a look that would curdle milk. You dive for cover under the sofa.

Ever been there? And you lived to tell the tale?

Did You Know?

A woman's definition of an ideal date changes with time. For example:

Age	Definition
17	Tall, dark, and handsome
25	Tall, dark, and handsome with money
35	Tall, dark, and handsome with money and a brain
48	A man with hair
66	A man

Hey, Look Me Over

That first meeting with your date's parents usually takes place long before anyone thinks seriously of walking down the aisle. In most cases, you meet your prospective in-laws for the first time when you and your intended are still dating. First contact usually takes place so early in the relationship that neither party really believes that this is It.

Below are the reasons why it's so important that you always make nice to your date's parents, siblings, and assorted kinfolk.

➤ **First impressions are made fast.** Studies have shown that most people form an impression of someone in less than five minutes. It usually takes longer to get a burger than it does to form a first impression. That being the case, you don't have a lot of wiggle room to impress someone with your strength of character.

➤ **First impressions can be lasting impressions.** Most people are stubborn. (I know, tell me something I don't know.) People may describe themselves as resolute, steadfast, or unwavering, but it's really just plain ornery. No one likes to be proven wrong. This can work in your favor if you create a good first impression. If things go well, you can glide on that goodwill for years.

➤ **Religious strife can break up even the strongest relationships.** We all believe that we can make our sweetheart see the light, the one truth faith. We can't. Don't try to change your partner and vice versa. If you go into the relationship thinking you can change him or her, it won't work. You can only change yourself.

Don't Go There

Never proselytize at the dinner table or anywhere else for that matter. Religion is an intensely personal matter, and attempts to sway another person's beliefs are never appreciated.

Family Matters

Among the most frequently cited reasons for a poor first impression are bad hygiene and perceived rudeness. So wash and be nice.

And even if we could change someone's long-held beliefs, we don't have the right—a person's beliefs may be different from our own, but that doesn't give us the right to judge them. We *do* have the right to convince others that we're a perfect partner for them, however.

➤ **Dating is easier without family strife.** Who needs another layer of aggravation? Even if a particular relationship isn't going to lead to a lifetime commitment, a relationship is far more pleasant if you're getting along with your sweet-heart's family while you're dating. Dating is difficult enough without having to cope with constant sniping and strife over religious differences.

➤ **Romantic relationships can lead to lifelong friendships.** Many dates make better friends than lovers. I'm still friends with my 10th grade boyfriend and my date to the 11th grade prom. Both have proven to be staunch friends for far longer than I'm willing to admit.

Face Off

That being the case, it's vital for you to make a great first impression on your beloved's family. Below are 12 tips to make that process less painful. (I've tried them all myself!)

Dress for success.

Guys, put on clean underwear. I know this may be tough because some of you are very attached to your undies, but work with me here. How can you tell it's time to change your dainties?

➤ When your boxers have turned the color of a dead whale and have developed new holes so large that you're not sure which ones were originally intended for your legs.

➤ When your BVDs are down to eight loosely connected underwear molecules and have to be handled with tweezers.

Girls, the Brittany Spears look, hip as it may be, doesn't play in the heartland. Whether you're an innie or an outie, no one wants to see your belly button at the dinner table. (Ditto on other body parts better left unidentified as well as covered.) Difficult as it may seem, even RuPaul is a little over the edge for some folks. Consult the following chart for some role models to emulate when you meet your sweetie's family for the first time:

Yes	No
Marilyn Monroe	Marilyn Manson
Bo Derek	Bozo the Clown
Debbie Gibson	Debbie Does Dallas
Oprah	Orca (the Killer Whale)
Mary Queen of Scots	Typhoid Mary
Betty Crocker	Joe Cocker
Madonna (classic style)	Madonna (zesty Italian)

Remember that you're not just representing yourself; you're representing all the members of your faith. Especially if your beloved's parents have never met anyone of your faith, they're going to judge all (Jews/Catholics/Muslims/Hindus/ …) on you and your behavior.

Now this certainly doesn't mean that you have to make yourself over to suit your sweetie's family. It *does* mean that you don't have to deliberately offend.

Think carefully about wearing religious symbols.

This is not the time to start wearing religious jewelry so they know your faith; trust me here—they know your faith already and have spent the last few months trying to deal with it. If you already sport a sign, only you can decide if you want to tuck it in for the night. If people are already looking for a reason to dislike you, a large piece of religious jewelry in the center of your chest might be just the ticket.

Avoid charged situations.

Set the first meeting on a nonoccasion—*never* on a religious holiday. Pick an ordinary Tuesday night so you can all sit around and watch reruns of *The Honeymooners* on TV as you chow down on those cute little cocktail franks.

> **Hold On!**
>
> **Don't Go There**
>
> Don't park in the family's driveway. That spot is usually reserved for someone who lives there, pays the rent, and is just itching to find something wrong with you.

Keep it intimate.

If at all possible, try to make the first meeting a small one. Just have the usual suspects: Mom, Dad, and any resident children. It's tense enough having to meet just immediate family, but add cousin Gomer, Uncle Albert, Aunt Edna, and their 16 children ... well, let's not go *there*.

Just Desserts

Instead of going to dinner at your beloved's house or having him or her to your house, you might want to make the encounter shorter by meeting for just coffee and cake. The shorter the encounter, the less chance people have to say something they'll regret later.

Family Matters

If you have people for dessert, always provide a showy no-sugar dessert for dieters and diabetics. I serve ornate no-sugar Jell-O molds, expensive no-sugar ice cream/frozen yogurt, and no-sugar pudding pies. You'll get extra points for consideration ... and the leftovers aren't fattening!

I'm a big fan of meeting the folks over dessert because you're less likely to run into religious-based food preferences. Few people serve pork-and-beans ice cream, lobster parfaits, or hummus cheesecake, for example.

If you're planning the menu, stick with the basics: some fresh fruit, a pound cake, and a pie. Round it off with coffee and tea, and you're home free.

In tense situations, consider meeting on neutral ground.

If you know you're going to be uncomfortable in your sweetheart's house because it's decorated in Early Religion (and it's *not* your religion), meet for the first time in a de-militarized zone such as a restaurant, a bowling alley, or a county fair. Other possibilities include ...

➤ A park on a beautiful day.

➤ A flea market or swap meet.

➤ A public garden.

➤ A museum.

➤ A concert. (Bonus: There's little chance for a lot of conversation)

➤ The lake or beach boardwalk.

➤ Downtown at the gazebo or town square.

➤ The mall food court.

Remember your manners.

A little consideration goes a long way toward making a good impression. You know the basics:

➤ Say please and thank you.
➤ Don't make any strange noises.
➤ Put the seat down.

If you're coming for a visit, bring a hostess gift.

When we were dating, my husband-to-be beat my mother into submission with frequent gifts of elaborate desserts. Although she railed that the lemon meringue was runny, the linzer tortes dry, and the seven-layer cakes a layer short, she ate every crumb. Afterward, she was even civil to him. This was a major accomplishment since he is Catholic/Greek Orthodox and I'm Jewish. Besides, she was trying to staple my feet to the carpet so I would live with her forever.

Treat the sibs well.

Hey, you never know. Your sweetheart's brothers and sisters can be potent allies in the battle to win the family over to your side. And if the relationship endures, you've made some life-long friends.

Avoid controversial topics.

This is not the time to debate the issue of land mines in Bosnia, the situation on the West Bank, or the relative merits of I Can't Believe It's Not Butter.

Don't rise to the bait.

Some people just can't stop going at you with bigoted, biased remarks. You know the kind: You want to smack them upside their heads with a two-by-four to beat some sense into their cement craniums. No matter what insults someone hurls at you, stay cool. Repeat this mantra silently to yourself: "This too shall pass." If you find the comments simply too insulting to bear, get up and leave. Thank your hostess for the hospitality and get out of there.

Did You Know?

A friend of mine whose child is dating someone of a different religion assured me that her problems with her child's intended are not about religion. "Oh, this is harder than religion," she said. "This is family."

Family Matters

What can you do if you get trapped in a sticky conversation? For example, what happens if someone asks you to explain why Jews get circumcised or why Catholics believe Christ died for their sins? Smile, nod, and change the subject—fast.

Under no circumstances should you take the offender to task, even if he or she is from your side of the family. The last thing you want to do is call further attention to the idiot's comments. Everyone knows the person's acting like a jerk, so it doesn't need to be pointed out. And if the person doesn't know it, you're surely not going to convince him or her by saying, "Uncle Bozo, must you always act like such a clown?"

Above all, be yourself.

Former president Calvin Coolidge once invited friends from his hometown to dine at the White House. Worried about their table manners, the guests decided to do everything that Coolidge did. This strategy succeeded until coffee was served. The president poured his coffee into the saucer. The guests did the same. Coolidge added sugar and cream. His guests did, too. Then Coolidge bent over and put his saucer on the floor for the cat.

What's the moral of the story? Pick one:

(a) Never have dinner with Calvin Coolidge. (Not a big problem since he's dead.)

(b) Before you eat, always check the plates for cat hairs.

(c) Order tea, not coffee.

(d) Be yourself.

The envelope, please. The answer is … (d)! Now, I'm not advocating that you do what comes naturally (please, spare us *that*), but I am saying that you shouldn't pretend to be someone (or something) that you're not. Use your company manners, but stay true to yourself. After all, that's why that beautiful man or woman by your side started dating you in the first place, over the objections of his or her family. You want his or her family to like you for what you are, not what you can become to suit others.

Did You Know?

In response to the question "What do most people do on a date?" 9-year-old Jane replied, "Dates are for having fun, and people should use them to get to know each other. Even boys have something to say if you listen long enough."

Learn the Lingo

Body language is a form of nonverbal communication. Body language includes such gestures and movements as nodding, crossing your arms and legs, tapping your foot, jiggling your leg, and looking someone in the eye.

Body Talk

We like to flap our jaws and rearrange a lot of air molecules, but sometimes the real message is hidden behind the words—in nonverbal communication. Reading someone's *body language*, a form of nonverbal communication, can often tell you how he or she is responding to you. This is a great technique to use with your date's family, who are unlikely to come straight out and declare, "Martha, I like this one, even though he's a heretic and will burn in hell" or "Lou, I think we have a stinker on our hands here."

Take the following quick quiz to see how much you know about body language. Match each gesture or movement with its meaning. Write the letter of the correct answer in the space provided. You'll use some letters more than once.

Meaning

    a. Agreement and interest.

    b. Defensiveness, distance, and resistance.

    c. Boredom.

    d. You've outstayed your welcome.

    e. Lack of understanding.

Body language

_____ **1.** Leaning forward and facing a person squarely

_____ **2.** Blank stares

_____ **3.** Tightly crossed legs

_____ **4.** Looking at a watch

_____ **5.** Nodding

_____ **6.** Tapping a foot

_____ **7.** Looking someone in the eye

_____ **8.** Arms crossed

_____ **9.** Drumming fingers on the table

____ **10.** Taking a swing at your head with a six-foot zucchini

Answers

1. a	6. c
2. e or c	7. a
3. b	8. b
4. d	9. c
5. a	10. d

So when you meet your sweetie's kinfolk for the first time, remember to …

    ➤ Use body language that makes you appear calm and cool—especially if you're not.

➤ Use your body language to convey a positive impression—especially if you despise these people.

➤ Read their body language to discover how they *really* feel about you.

Did You Know?

A woman's definition of an ideal date changes with time. For example:

Age	Definition
17	He offers to pay.
25	He pays.
35	He cooks breakfast the next morning.
48	He cooks breakfast the next morning for the kids.
66	He can chew breakfast.

Two Outs, Bottom of the Ninth

A friend shared this story about introducing her boyfriend to her parents for the first time:

> "I am a 25-year-old Hispanic-American professional woman, living in Seattle, Washington. I came from a very strict Catholic family—Catholic school all the way. I met Rick at my first job in the aerospace industry.
>
> When I first started dating Rick, I did not tell my parents immediately because he is Jewish. When I had broached the subject of dating a Jewish guy in high school, my mother emphatically said 'No.' Then she added, 'Your grandparents would turn over in their graves if they knew you were dating a man who wasn't Catholic.'
>
> Before I introduced Rick to my parents, I was very conscious of the impression that my father might make on Rick. You see, my father often uses derogatory words and curses. I asked my father, 'Please don't use any vulgar words when you meet Rick.' My dad's response was, 'Why not? That's how a real man talks. Besides, it's his responsibility to accept me. I'm not changing for anyone.' What

he didn't understand was that, even if he meant no disrespect, it wouldn't be acceptable to Rick to hear this from him in an initial meeting.

So, it took me nearly a year to introduce Rick to my parents. The meeting was a disaster since we were all on edge. My mother deliberately made a pork roast (even though I told her that Rick doesn't eat pork), and my father was on his worst behavior. Rick and I are still dating, but I still cringe when I think about that first meeting."

—Maria, age 31

What happens if your sweetheart and your family don't hit it off right out of the gate? Or if you don't hit it off with your honey's side? It might take you years to convince your beloved's parents that you're really not the devil incarnate—or that he isn't.

Below are some steps you can take to contain the damage and improve the situation.

Truth or Dare

Start by making sure you're fighting a battle worth fighting. I got the following story from an acquaintance:

Mina, an 18-year-old Hindu girl from California, met Ali, a 19-year old Muslim, at school. They started going out, and Mina told her brother. He replied, "It's your life and your choice to make. But if our parents find out, don't count me in." Mina was shocked to hear her brother's words.

"This was my own flesh and blood going against me," she said. When Mina and Ali walked together on campus, Hindus stared at them.

Mina broke off with Ali six months ago and decided to marry a Hindu. To girls her age, she suggests, "Think before you leap into an interreligious relationship. Don't do it if you can't be honest to those around you and to yourself."

Don't Go There

Never plan on people changing their minds down the road. "Everything will be okay when we get married and have children," young lovers often think. Sometimes children do reconcile families, but other times they don't. Never play the odds unless you're willing to accept possible losses.

All relationships come with challenges, even when religious differences aren't a factor. Nonetheless, religion adds another layer of problems. It can be a very thick layer.

Yes, you might be able to work out your differences, but do you want to? Before you begin a campaign to make your beloved out to be the best thing since sliced pita/challah/bread, make sure this is really what you want—or are you just being insecure, rebellious, or playing through old family scripts?

Your sweetheart may indeed be the one for you ... or not. And even if it is the real thing, is the relationship worth risking the possible loss of your family? Only you can decide that.

If the religious barrier is insurmountable to you, don't invest any more time in the relationship unless your sweetheart is willing to convert. I know this sounds cruel and heartless, but reality isn't always the way we'd like it to be. (Chapter 18, "Rites and Rights," covers the issue of conversion.)

Damage Control

If you've decided that the battle is worth fighting, get everyone talking. Communication is vital, first between you and your squeeze and then between you and your family. Ignoring the problem won't make it go away.

Family Matters

There's an extensive list of resources, including Web sites and books, in Appendix B.

Don't Go There

In the heat of an argument, everyone says things they don't mean; it's why arguments are unpleasant. Never make a threat you're not willing to back up with action. Be careful not to say things that can't be unsaid, such as: "Accept my fella or I'm outta here."

If your family won't communicate with you concerning the religious issue, you may wish to get someone to mediate. Be sure to get someone whom all parties respect. A religious leader may seem like the logical choice, but this can set off a firestorm of controversy: *Whose* religious leader do you get? Instead, consider a neutral third party such as a counselor or psychologist.

If your lover won't talk about interfaith issue or tries to placate you with platitudes, give 'em the heave ho. A friend shared this story:

> "One of the other challenges that we face, though we've brushed it under the rug so far, is religion. We both come from childhoods spent going to Sunday school in Christian churches. My experience has been mainly nondenominational, whereas his has been Baptist and Pentecostal. I have had difficulties with his grandfather's church environments because I do not feel comfortable there, but my boyfriend won't talk about it at all. He just says, 'Uh-huh' and 'Don't start on the religion issue again.' Because of this problem, I feel cut off from my heritage."

As you talk to your sweetheart's family, educate people about your religion and learn about theirs. You can use the information in Part 2 of this book as a basis. The more you know about their beliefs and the more they know about yours, the easier it will be to find common ground.

It is vital to talk about culture and religion—no matter what the discussion reveals. Many of us are ignorant about others' cultures, and this generates more fear than the understanding so needed in this area.

The Least You Need to Know

➤ When you're dating someone of another faith, your attitude and behavior can make or break the relationship.

➤ If you make a good impression on your sweetheart and his or her parents, the odds are strong that they will come to like you as a person.

➤ Dress for success, consider whether or not to wear religious symbols, avoid charged situations such as holidays, and consider meeting on neutral ground.

➤ Treat the siblings well and avoid controversial topics but always be yourself.

➤ Recognize the importance of nonverbal communication.

➤ Carefully consider whether the battle is worth fighting: If so, keep the lines of communication open and educate yourself.

Chapter 10

I'll Be There for You: Dealing with Friends, Colleagues, and Strangers

In This Chapter

➤ Fantasy vs. reality

➤ Ways to be an unsupportive friend

➤ How to be a true friend

➤ How to be a truly obnoxious stranger

➤ Using religious differences as a mask

Soon after they started dating, Sanjay and Chrissie went out to dinner with Chrissie's closest friends, Mark and Nicole, for the first time. The evening got off to a strained start when Chrissie, Mark, and Nicole ordered beers but Sanjay demurred. "Hindus don't drink alcohol," he explained quietly. Mark and Nicole were uncomfortable, so they ordered a few too many beers.

Later, when Sanjay ordered a vegetarian platter, Nicole said, "Sanjay, you need red meat to stay healthy."

"Nicole," Chrissie answered sharply, "You know that Sanjay is a vegetarian. It's part of his religion. He's done just fine this far without any meat at all."

"Would you stop butting into their lives, Nicole?" Mark said. "Besides, you could afford to cut down on the fatty meat yourself."

"Excuse me?" Nicole shrieked. "Since when did you become such an expert on everything?"

Things didn't get any better as the meal progressed.

Sometimes the people you're counting on to support you the most when you're involved in an interfaith relationship—your friends—drop the ball. Friends are there for each other on television, but real life doesn't always imitate reel life. Colleagues can have problems dealing with interfaith romance as well. And amazing as it may seem, some strangers think it's their business to make comments about your date and ask embarrassing personal questions.

In the following pages, I'll arm you with the strategies you need to help your friends and colleagues become allies, not antagonists, in your love life. Then I'll help you deal with strangers who take offense at the notion of interfaith dating. You know the type: the brazen buttinskis who put their noses where they don't belong—in your love life. By the end of this chapter, you'll feel confident dealing with the slings and arrows that get thrown your way from friends and foes alike.

Reality Bites

Fantasy: Bridget and Bernie arrive at a reunion party given by Bernie's buddies at Zeta Beta Tau, a traditionally Jewish fraternity. They're holding hands and glowing with happiness. People casually smile and nod, offering pretzels. No one bats an eye at the interfaith couple.

Reality: Bridget and Bernie arrive at a reunion party given by Bernie's buddies at Zeta Beta Tau, a traditionally Jewish fraternity. Bridget is fuming because she'd rather be at the church-sponsored dance with her old friends, but Bernie refuses to step foot in a church. Bernie is livid because Bridget is wearing a very large cross around her neck. When the couple walks in, all conversation stops dead. "Bernie's dating a Catholic?" people whisper. "His parents must be beside themselves."

Reality Check

The truth usually lies somewhere between these two extremes. As you've no doubt discovered, some of your friends and co-workers will accept your new flame, while others won't. "My *real* friends will accept anyone I love," you fume. Maybe they will ... and maybe they won't.

Here's where you start thinking about being stranded on a desert island with a tender lover, cut off from the pressures of everyday life. On the island, the mosquitoes don't care that you're an interfaith couple—only that you'd make a tasty little snack. In the real world, however, friends and co-workers often find interfaith relationships to be tasty little snacks, savory tidbits to chew on when all other gossip runs dry. But for better or for worse, we need friends and must deal with co-workers and strangers, so we have to learn to cope with their pettiness as we celebrate their generosity.

Shaken, not Stirred

With luck, your friends will take more kindly to your interfaith lover than the preceding scenario suggests. Nonetheless, most people face some problems with their friends when they start dating someone of a different faith. These problems include ...

➤ **Fear.** Strangers to the tribe often cause anxiety since we fear that which is unfamiliar to us.

➤ **Sorrow.** Your friends may mourn the demise of the "old" you as they fear the emergence of a "new" you under the influence of a lover who follows a different belief system.

➤ **Confusion.** Your friends might wonder why you're dating outside of your religion and culture.

➤ **Anger.** People can become irate when the status quo is shaken. And you're the one shakin' it, lover.

Family Matters

Co-workers, I'm assuming that you're friends. Therefore, feel free to follow the directions for "Being an Unsupportive Friend."

➤ **Envy.** Yes, even your best friends can envy you. In this case, they might be jealous that you're breaking out of the old ways, especially if they are unable to do so.

Twelve Steps to Being an Unsupportive Friend

Listen up, friends and colleagues. The following are my 12 easy steps for being unsupportive of your friend's interfaith relationship. (Note: You can use these steps at any point in your friend's relationship. They are guaranteed to make a challenging situation into a bad one.)

1. **Make disparaging remarks about the date's faith.** Criticize your friend's latest choice, always bringing up problems that religious differences can cause. Comments such as "Your parents must be furious" and "How can you celebrate the holidays now?" go a long way toward showing a lack of support and proving that your friend has made a horrible choice—not of potential mate but of a friend. (Note: This technique works even better if you keep hammering your point home.)

2. **Tell tasteless, insulting religious jokes.** It often seems like we have an endless supply of tasteless, insulting religious jokes. However, if you run short of material, you can just take any old ethnic joke and insert the correct religious reference. Always specifically target the date's religion; it's much more effective than

insulting all religious people in general. Jokes such as this are a great way to perpetuate baseless religious stereotypes, too.

Act of Faith

Devout Hindus wear a *tilak* on their forehead between their eyes. Women wear a round red dot; men wear an elongated dot. The point is known by various names such as *bindi*, *Ajna chakra*, *spiritual eye*, and *Third Eye*. In ancient times, this spot was believed to be the major nerve in the human body. Traditional Hindu women apply the bindi with a cosmetic, but bindi are now available in a wide variety of self-adhesive forms. These include plastic gems, thread loops, and even Day-Glo products. These ornate bindi are gaining favor with non-Hindu women who argue that the bindi is the most visually striking and fascinating form of all body decoration.

3. **Bring the religious issue into the office.** This one's important for colleagues as well as friends: Even though someone's love life is no one else's business, make sure that everyone in the office knows what's going on with your friend's love life. This is especially effective in small, closed offices in which one or more people are known to be prejudiced, but if you work hard enough at it, you can fan the flames in a large, apparently tolerant office as well.

4. **Ask embarrassing personal questions about the person's beliefs.** Asking about sexual habits and preferences is always good for putting someone on the spot, but questions about food, clothing, body decoration, worship, and family matters can also be intrusive. Make sure to ask these questions in a loud, clear voice to get the maximum amount of embarrassment out of them.

5. **Predict a dire future, filled with unhappiness.** So what if you can't really predict the future; hey, who can? Don't let that stop you from saying things like "Children of mixed marriages never adjust, you know."

6. **Don't waste any time; try to disrupt the relationship long before the walk down the aisle by being nasty and unsupportive.** When your friend introduces his or her date, throw a temper tantrum about how you are losing your best buddy to an infidel! A heretic! Try this wail: "My best friend! My oldest, dearest friend. This is the thanks I get for all my years of loyal friendship?" Don't forget to mention how you waited in line for 10 whole days for Grateful Dead tickets.

7. **Compete with your friend's lover for his or her attention.** Call at least three times a day, always at inconvenient times. Of course, this technique works much better if the couple is living together. Then you can call at 6 A.M., 6 P.M., and midnight. At first they might think you're just another misguided telemarketer, but if you always ask to talk directly to your friend, they'll get the point.

8. **Try a little sabotage.** For example, compare your friend's current date to past ones you liked better, as in "Ah, Amber, now that was a beautiful/brilliant/bodacious babe. And she was the right religion, too." Comments such as "Why would you date a [insert name of religion]?" are a good way to undermine any love relationship. You can set up a series of blind dates with attractive replacements, too.

9. **No matter how small a slight, never let it go by.** Never forgive and forget. Holding a grudge can force your friend to make a choice: It's either you or the new love.

10. **Add to the mess.** If the relationship gets a little rocky, fan the flames. Be sure to say "I told you so" early and often. Bring up various real or imagined slights you received at the hand of your friend's sweetheart, too.

11. **Give an ultimatum.** If the fools persist and actually continue dating, refuse to go out with them anymore.

12. **If all else fails, break off the friendship.** Why not cut off your nose to spite your face? You'd be surprised how many people do when it comes to their friends dating someone they don't approve of.

Don't Go There

Beware: It can be especially difficult to date someone of a different faith when you're working in a family business or a religion-based business.

Twelve Steps to Being a Helpful Friend

You're smart and cool, so you got my point. Below are the ways you can actually *help* your friends deal with interfaith relationships.

1. **Never make disparaging remarks about the date's faith.** Better yet, make the religion issue a nonissue. It's no one else's business anyway.

2. **Nix the religious jokes.** They're *never* funny.

3. **Keep your friend's personal life out of the office.** (And while you're at it, keep your own beliefs and love life to yourself, too.)

4. **Never ask personal questions about anyone's beliefs.** However, get as much information as you can about the person's religion in general. Remember that

Family Matters

A negative prediction can often become a self-fulfilling prophecy. If you tell someone that a relationship will fail, you just might help cause its downfall. You don't want to be making your friend unhappy, chick pea.

knowledge is power in all realms of the human experience, but most especially when it comes to interfaith dating.

5. **Leave predictions about the future to cheap carny acts and other self-proclaimed mystics.** Never presume to know how a relationship will turn out.

6. **Support your friend.** If you can't support him or her, keep your mouth closed.

7. **Never compete with your friend's lover for his or her attention.** There's more than enough to go around. And if there isn't enough time for everyone, be a grownup and wait your turn.

8. **Don't undermine your friend's love life, no matter how noble you think your motives might be.** Hands off.

9. **Forgive and forget.** We all have enough baggage without picking up some extra.

10. **"Don't make no mess, won't be no mess," a wise woman once told me.** If your friend's love life gets a little rocky, stand back. If your friend asks you for advice, stand further back. You're not an expert, and any advice you offer can come back and bite you in the backside.

11. **Don't say things you're likely to regret later.** When in doubt, don't say anything—even if you have to bite your tongue.

12. **Never cut off contact over religious differences.** There are enough troubles in the world without adding to them. Do your very best to keep the lines of communication open, no matter how different your religious beliefs.

Turnabout Is Fair Play

Since I'm an equal-opportunity advice-giver, I also offer the following ways for lovers to destroy any hope of getting along with their old friends. (Hey, two can play this game. Why leave all the fun to the supporting players?)

1. **New love, new life.** Never include your old friends in any plans you make with your new girlfriend or boyfriend, even if you're doing the same stuff you used to do all the time. Imagine that they've suddenly sworn off bowling and biking. Ditto on clubs, restaurants, and video games.

2. **Kindergarten baby, stick your head in gravy.** If your friends persist in trying to maintain contact, feel free to throw a temper tantrum. Other great techniques include slamming down the phone, refusing to answer e-mails, and snubbing your friends in the hallway. If you ignore them, maybe they'll pack up their tents and sneak away.

3. **Assume your friends are prejudiced.** What happens if your friends really don't like your new lover? Automatically decide that your friends won't accept your sweetie because of his or her religion—even if all evidence points to the contrary.

4. **Look for an offense where none exists.** Get hypersensitive. This can create a permanent rift, even between previously close friends.

5. **Criticize your friends' religion to your lover at any and all opportunities.** Push their buttons with words like "misguided," "confused," and "lost." Try to hit all the sensitive points.

See a common thread here? Each of these tongue-in-cheek "suggestions" …

➤ Is dishonest and unfair.

➤ Tears down your friends.

➤ Shows a lack of consideration.

➤ Backs you into a corner.

➤ Demonstrates unrealistic expectations.

➤ Does not respect boundaries.

It's natural to have problems with your friends and co-workers when you get serious about someone—especially someone who follows a different belief system. After all, change, even positive change, is threatening by its very nature. Try the following strategies for keeping everything on an even keel:

➤ Stay cool.

➤ Be mature.

➤ See the situation from your friends' eyes.

➤ Keep the lines of communication open.

➤ Remember that sometimes the best action is no action. You may have to back off and let things simmer down.

You can only change yourself, rarely others. You might lose a few friends if you become seriously involved with someone of a different religion, and sometimes that just can't be helped. No one has to put up with prejudice and cruelty, especially from their "friends."

Strange Encounter

I never cease to be amazed at the rudeness of strangers. Just when I think I've seen it all, I see a little more. A few years ago, for example, I had some foot surgery to correct problems caused by years of wearing high-heeled shoes. Although I was in a cast hobbling on crutches for six weeks, I continued my usual routine. Every single place I went, total strangers decided it was their God-given right to ask me what had happened. "What's wrong with your foot?" they asked. When I politely said, "It's actually none of your business," nearly all of them got insulted. "Well," they huffed, "if you feel that way about it." I did.

So many things are none of our business, and other people's romances rank right up there on the "butt out" chart. You can make the world a better place by minding your own business, but what can you do with strangers who persist in minding your business by making judgments about your beliefs based on your appearance or your date?

You can …

1. Ignore them. Even the most boneheaded bonehead eventually gets the message.
2. Smile, nod, and ignore them. Use this method if you're feeling especially charitable. I rarely am.
3. Say, "It's none of your business." Then walk away.

Under no circumstances should you engage strangers in a debate about their moronic comments and your beliefs. Today, even the most benign-looking citizen might be a pistol-packing granny, and no one wants to get involved in a case of religion rage.

Dream Lover

I believe that most of us have a mental blueprint for the type of person we're attracted to. Examine your past relationships to see if you agree with me. Better yet, look at a handful of old married couples. Amazing how much alike they look, isn't it?

But what do you do if you fall in love with someone outside your specifications? Just as you can view a glass as "half full," you can view the positive aspects of your differences. Start by realizing that "different" isn't always bad. It can open up many new experiences and joys to your life.

Shooting Yourself in the Foot

A surprising number of the interfaith couples I've interviewed are their own worst enemies. They often sabotage their relationship without even realizing it. For example, a man who fears commitment might use religion as an excuse to explain why he won't propose. "I'd marry her if only she wasn't [insert religion here]," I've heard. When the woman offers to convert, the man flees in a panic.

Likewise, a woman who is driving her man away because she drinks or smokes too much might use religious differences as the reason for the breakup. This time the dialogue goes: "He doesn't like me because I'm [insert religion here]." No, honey, he doesn't like you because you smoke like a chimney and drink like a fish.

Hidden in Plain Sight

Religious differences are often used to cloak these issues as well:

➤ Unsavory friends

➤ Drug and alcohol abuse

➤ Personality problems

➤ Differing goals (such as children vs. child-free)

➤ Differing lifestyles (such as city vs. country)

➤ Spending habits

➤ Physical issues (body type, sexual preferences, and so on)

This isn't to say that religion can't break up a romance; it can and often does. It *is* to say that you should be sure to identify the real cause of trouble in Romance City before you blame it on religion.

The Least You Need to Know

➤ Your friends and co-workers may feel threatened, sad, and confused by your choice of mate.

➤ Support your friends in interfaith relationships by making religion a nonissue and respecting their privacy.

➤ Don't say things you're likely to regret later and try not to cut off contact.

➤ If you're the lover, keep your friends in your life, assume the best of them, and keep religion out of the mix. Try to see the situation from your friends' point of view.

➤ Ignore strangers who think it's their right to make comments about your choice of dates. It's not.

➤ Don't use religion as the excuse for a breakup when it's not.

Chapter 11

Making It Work

In This Chapter

➤ What makes an interfaith relationship thrive?

➤ The importance of acknowledging differences based on spiritual needs

➤ Tips for succeeding in an interfaith relationship

➤ Why couples counseling may be right for you

Driving home from work one day, a man stopped to watch a local Little League base-ball game that was being played in a park. As he sat down behind the bench on the first base line, he asked one of the boys what the score was.

"We're behind 14 to nothing," the boy answered with a smile.

"Really," the man said. "I have to say you don't look very discouraged."

"Discouraged?" the boy asked with a puzzled look on his face. "Why should we be dis-couraged? We haven't been up to bat yet."

Hope springs eternal, the poets claim ... and well it should. Otherwise, why would we exercise, redecorate, or flirt? It pays to be hopeful, whether it's your first at bat in a Little League game or your interfaith romance.

In this chapter, I'll teach you how to hit a home run in the game of interfaith love. First we'll discuss the importance of recognizing the religious differences that exist in interfaith relationships. Then I'll help you learn how to deal with these differences creatively and effectively. Finally, we'll discuss why you may want to get some couples counseling before you get engaged to or marry someone of a different faith.

Allies, Not Adversaries

I found the following story in my mailbag. How does it compare with your experiences with interfaith dating?

"Tim and I met at school about two years ago. I was a transfer student and ended up in his math class. I'm a tall blonde from a well-to-do family; Tim is short with dark, curly hair. His family lives from paycheck to paycheck. There are other differences as well.

Tim's family is very religious. His grandfather is a preacher at their church, his father wants to be a preacher, and they attend every single church meeting and function. My family is the complete opposite when it comes to church. We used to be more involved in the church, but as the years passed, we slowly stopped going to church. None of us has been to church in years.

I think Tim fell in love with me at first sight; well, that's what he says. As we started to get serious and think about a future together, we began talking about issues that we had tried to hide or forget about. Religion was the one thing that made it harder to decide whether to stay together or split.

I am Church of Jesus Christ of Latter Day Saints, and Tim is Church of Christ. Whenever we would try to talk about the issue, we always ended up fighting or one of us would just leave. I thought that our relationship was ending, and I began thinking that maybe we shouldn't keep trying to fix the religion issue, that what was meant to be was meant to be.

But I loved Tim and wanted him to be the man I grew old with. I knew he felt the same way.

So we began to study each other's religion, and we discovered that we do believe in the same principles. Then I started attending his church meetings, and he came to a few of mine. Our love exploded. We began to understand each other better, and we both had a willingness to learn about each other's differences.

I think that us trying to fix the religion issue also fixed other problems in the works. Now our relationship is stronger than ever, and we're planning to get married!

I attend his church, but I am not a member of it. I still have the same beliefs that I did four years ago, but I am willing to compromise and make a little sacrifice for my husband and my family.

There's no denying that opposites *do* attract because difference is exciting. How else to explain that little thrill we get when we know we're going over the line by dating someone that Papa and Mama just won't like?"

—Janice, age 29

Love is a wondrous thing, and sometimes, no matter how good our intentions, we do fall in love with someone who hails from a different (read *unsuitable*) background. Often, that unsuitability is based on religious differences. The decision to break it off or go ahead is based on many factors, of course.

If you *do* decide to go ahead with an interfaith relationship, your romance will have the best chance of succeeding if you and your mate deal with differences effectively rather than try to ignore them. "Denominational differences don't cause breakups," said Michael Lawlor, director of Creighton's Center for Marriage and Family. "It depends on what the couple does together religiously and how they deal with differences." The following sections suggest some ways that you can help strengthen your interfaith relationship.

Family Matters

How do you define a "healthy" romance"? Here's my definition: Partners care for and about each other and help each other achieve their fullest potential.

Through the Looking Glass

Start by recognizing that there *are* differences—always. And those differences can be more complex and wide reaching than you think.

For example, many Jews feel they're relegated to the fringe of American society. This feeling can persist even if the person was born in America to two parents who were born in America. Take the case of Deborah. Here's what she says:

Did You Know?

According to a small child of my acquaintance, you can tell when two people are in love: "If they go out to eat and order one of those desserts that are on fire. They like to order those desserts because it's like their hearts are—on fire."

> "I was raised in a heavily Christian community and always felt like an outsider. It was continually smashed in my face that I wasn't part of the main culture. In elementary school, teachers asked me, their only Jewish student, to go from class to class every December to explain Hanukkah. My mother made potato pancakes, and we were like a traveling sideshow act, the freaks showing off a little foreign culture. I couldn't understand why they didn't ask some Catholic kids to do this dog-and-pony show. After all, wouldn't that be more educational and less exclusionary? The teachers may have thought they were doing me a favor, but this stupid yearly ritual made me feel even more of an outsider."

—Deborah, age 33

Deborah's boyfriend, Ed, a Catholic, can't understand why this was such a big deal to Deborah. He's also bothered that all of Deborah's friends are Jewish. "I feel like the outsider when we get together with Deb's friends," he complains. "I like all Deb's friends, but it's like they belong to a secret club and I don't know the password."

"And I can't understand why she seems to form this instant bond with anyone who's Jewish—from the grocery delivery boy to the office secretary. Once Deb discovers they're Jewish, it's like a family reunion."

Act of Faith

People on the fringes of their different faiths tend to be attracted to each other more often than people with strong religious ties who follow different faiths. If the Christian partner is devout but the Jewish partner isn't, chances are the romance won't endure. This is especially true if the Christian partner tries to pull the Jewish partner into Christianity. The Jewish partner tends to panic and flee to Judaism. So when a Christian asks out a Jew, by the time they're talking about marriage, there's a good chance that the Jewish partner has started nurturing a strong commitment to Judaism. Pfft!—even long-term relationships collapse under those circumstances.

"I have friends from all different faiths," Ed continues. "Heck, I don't even know what religions half of them follow, and I don't much care. But this is such a big thing to Deb. Even if we end up married and I convert, I'm not sure I want my whole life to revolve around all the same people."

Ed's confusion is understandable and his dilemma a common one. People usually feel most comfortable with people who share their background and values. It's crucial to realize that religion is more than a set of beliefs; it's also an ethnic and cultural heritage. While being with Deborah has made Ed more attuned to the anxieties of Jewish people in a predominately Christian culture, he's still baffled by the outsider's view of American culture that many Jews feel.

Look Before You Leap

Next, closely evaluate your relationship to decide if you want to move to the next step: marriage. You've no doubt already got your lists of "good husband" and "good wife" qualities all set—we prepare that when we're still teenagers! But interfaith issues add a new layer of complexity to the relationship. Here's what Anne-Marie, a Catholic who has been married to a Hindu for more than a decade, discovered *after* the wedding:

> "Neither of our families was over the moon when we started going out and certainly not when we married. I was introduced to his family as his girlfriend and gradually got used to their ways. I was a Catholic and converted to Hinduism. Although I am now Hindu, I am white. People stare at me. It's almost like being in a zoo."

Try the suggestions in the following sections as you evaluate your relationship and decide if you want to kick it up a notch.

Time Is On Your Side

No matter how strong your passion, don't rush into anything. If it's real, it will last. If it's not, you'll find someone who complements you even more fully. Or, as my mother used to say, there's a lid for every pot.

In that first flush of passion, it's tempting to throw caution to the winds and get hitched pronto. Don't. If you do decide that your sweetie is "The One True One," opt for a long engagement—at least a year. You can use this time to work out some of your interfaith issues. Go for the big issues:

➤ What religious identity do you have?

➤ How do you both feel about your respective religions?

➤ Will one partner convert?

➤ If not, how will you meld religious observations?

➤ What objections from family and friends do you anticipate? How will you deal with these?

➤ If you plan to have children, in what religion (if any) will they be raised?

Don't Go There

Couples who rush into marriage often avoid talking about the key issues in their relationship, especially religion. They use the wedding plans as a diversion. Don't let this happen to you.

Identity Crisis

As Popeye liked to say, "I yam what I yam," and you are what you are. This is a very good thing. Be secure in your own identity. As you learned in Chapter 3, "Present Your ID, Please," it's important to probe your character and goals before you enter into a commitment with anyone.

It's tempting to remake yourself in someone's image, but in the long run, neither you nor your honey will be happy with the "new you" because it won't really be *you*. I know too many unhappy people (mainly women) who remade themselves to fit someone else's measure. The measure changed, and they were cast adrift.

If your religion is important to you, say so up front. Don't try to ignore it, minimize it, or deny it. Your beliefs are an integral part of who you are.

Learn the Lingo

A **rabbi** is a Jewish religious leader. The word "rabbi" means teacher.

A **kibbutz** is a cooperative farm in Israel.

Family Matters

Partners have the most difficulty reconciling degree of faith because spirituality can't be explained.

Along with this, be sure to acknowledge your depth of belief or your partner's. I found the following letter in my mailbag:

> "The summer after we graduated from high school, my high-school steady went to Israel to work on a kibbutz. There, he became an Orthodox Jew and is now deeply religious. I am Jewish but not religious. My boyfriend has since returned to America, finished two years of college, and is considering becoming a rabbi. We resumed our romance, and he talks about us getting married.
>
> I can't imagine following all the rituals involved in Orthodox Judaism, especially keeping a religious home. No one seems to understand my problem: 'You're both Jewish,' my friends say. 'So what's the big deal?'"

Depth of faith *is* a big deal indeed. Unfortunately, people often assume that the biggest problems in interfaith relationships arise from difference in formal religious labels, as in Catholic-Hindu or Jewish-Muslim romances. However, this is not the case. Religious trouble in interfaith romances just as often springs from differences in each partner's depth of religious feeling.

In many couples, one partner is intensely spiritual and the other is not. In the case I previously described, the couple shared the same level of belief early in their relationship, but then the situation shifted. Even though they are both Jewish, they have very different levels of belief. It's clear that this couple is in trouble.

Here's the scoop: You can compromise on a lot in a relationship but not on depth of faith. That's because it is a need, a matter of training, or a temperament.

Pressure Plays

Don't force your beliefs on your partner.

Getting your partner to convert seems like a nice way of solving the issue of religious difference. After all, if you both wear the same label, the issue disappears ... except it doesn't. The previous point about level of spirituality illustrates this.

A surprising number of otherwise intelligent people have tried to convert me to their faith or to a greater devotion to my own. Some of these misguided do-gooders have used tedious lectures, while others have tried written tracts (figuring that a writer always responds better to writing).

Let me give you the lowdown: A person who wants to change his or her beliefs will; someone who doesn't want to change won't. (More on this in Part 4, "Celebrating Our Differences: Interfaith Marriages.")

And while we're here, always respect your partner's background. To respect someone's beliefs, you have to understand them first. Then, if you can't respect his or her beliefs, you'll know this isn't the person for you.

The Parent Trap

Visiting with your honey's folks will help you understand his or her roots and will give you a peek into life in the future. Keep in mind that we tend to become more and more like our parents as we get older. Try to spend a few days at their home or on vacation with them. Being confined in a camper or cruise ship with them can be revealing.

A close friend of mine, a Jewish woman from Long Island, was engaged to a Christian Fundamentalist from Kansas. One week into a cruise with him and his family, she realized that she'd either jump ship or push him and his family overboard if they were forced to spend one more minute together. Although she had visited his parents before, until then, she hadn't realized how similar her honey was to his parents—and how different she was. No doubt they felt the same way about her. Fortunately, everyone realized that this relationship just wouldn't make it to shore, so to speak.

Don't Go There

Many devout Jewish families view their children's participation in any Christian ritual, or even entering a church, with anguish and horror.

Did You Know?

My husband jokes that, if I become like my mother, he's going to kill me and bury me in the back yard next to our long-dead dog. Interestingly, my brother-in-law says the same thing about my sister. We think the men are joking, but we're not so sure.

The Couple That Plays Together, Stays Together

The best thing about being in love is that it's fun. You get a best friend who just happens to be as much fun horizontal as he or she is vertical.

When you come up for air, share common interests and concerns. Obviously, first try to participate in each other's religious life. The more you know about your honey's beliefs, the more able you'll be to decide if you're compatible. If your beliefs mesh, it will be easier to work out the relationship in the long run.

Family Matters

According to my husband, the number one requirement for a solid relationship is "the couple has to like each other." I think he has a point.

All good relationships are built not only on love, passion, mutual respect, and kindness, but also on shared interests. Here are some areas to consider exploring together:

➤ Sports (watching and playing)

➤ Travel

➤ Culture (movies, theater, literature, music)

➤ Card games

➤ Socializing

➤ Gardening

Every couple needs a rich and fulfilling social life. After all, we all get by with a little help from our friends. If you surround yourself with similar interfaith couples, you'll have a support network to help you deal with the problems you'll likely face as the years go by. In addition to getting help from your friends, you can give some, too. Your experiences can help your friends resolve the issues they face in their relationships.

Danger, Will Robinson

Never ignore outside pressure. I know a staggering number of people who play ostrich. You know the type: They bury their heads in the metaphorical sand and pretend nothing's wrong when a whole lot is very wrong. As you date, acknowledge the pressures you face and see how you deal with these issues individually and together. Do they make you or break you?

Along this line, consider the warnings you get about intermarriage. Specifically, weigh what your friends and family think about your relationship. Ask yourself these questions:

➤ Who has warned me about intermarriage? What motives might they have?

➤ Which warnings aren't realistic? Why?

➤ Which warnings are realistic? Why?

➤ How will my honey and I deal with these warnings?

Who Ya Gonna Call?

Before Emily Shimamora Cohen got married, December was a time for Christmas music, pork lo mein, and joyous gift exchanges. Since marrying Marc Cohen, however, the first-generation Chinese-American has pledged to keep pork out of the house, observe Hanukkah, and raise the couple's daughter, Beth, as a Jew.

Don't Go There

Some relationships are founded on stress, such as people who survive a plane crash together or deal with the death of a mutual friend together. When the stress disappears, these couples either manufacture more problems to occupy their time or fall apart. Stress is not a healthy basis for a long-term relationship.

The transformation didn't happen overnight, nor does it ever for people who marry into another culture or religion. In fact, the ordeal can be overwhelming, according to couples who seek guidance from rabbis, ministers, and counselors before getting hitched.

Emily and Marc were a couple who decided to enter couples counseling before becoming engaged. Emily and Marc found that the group discussions helped them to identify their differences. In counseling such as theirs, a rabbi and an interfaith counselor moderate the discussion groups to help couples reconcile their issues before getting married and to help the already married couples cope better.

Did You Know?

About 80 percent of the Jews in San Francisco marry outside the faith, according to Fred Rosenbaum, director of Lehrhaus Judaica, a Jewish-studies adult school in Berkeley. Demographer Gary Tobin of San Francisco confirms that figure, which represents one of the highest intermarriage rates in America.

You and your honey may want to try some sessions with an interfaith counselor before you go any further in the relationship. A counselor specially trained in interfaith issues can help you and your partner work through some issues that may be difficult (if not impossible) to resolve on your own. Speak with other interfaith couples to get recommendations or contact local churches and temples in your area for referrals.

The Least You Need to Know

➤ Interfaith romances are most likely to succeed if partners deal with differences effectively.

➤ Start by recognizing that these differences exist and may affect areas of your life you haven't thought about.

➤ If you decide to get married, opt for a long engagement. Get to know yourself and carefully weigh your partner's spiritual needs as well as your own.

➤ Never force your beliefs on your partner, get to know his or her folks well, and share common interests and concerns.

➤ Build a network of similar couples, consider warnings, and deal with outside pressure.

➤ Consider couples counseling before you make the leap into matrimony.

Part 4

Celebrating Our Differences: Interfaith Weddings

Why do weddings matter? After all, aren't they just a prelude to the important event, the marriage? Wedding ceremonies ...

➤ *can usher us into a sacred time and space.*

➤ *can formally establish and anchor the meaning we desire for a marriage.*

➤ *have the power to shape and bring together the very direction of a marriage. That's because a wedding ceremony can set the tone for a home and a life.*

Fortunately, gone are the days when you couldn't have any say-so in your wedding. In this section of the book, you'll find out how to make your wedding meaningful for everyone in attendance, no matter what their religious beliefs. Most of all, find out how to make your wedding ceremony satisfy you and your honey.

Chapter 12

Tempest in a Tabernacle: The Wedding

In This Chapter

➤ How weddings spark unresolved issues

➤ Why the engagement ritual matters

➤ Money, power, and control

➤ Misunderstandings that arise from different backgrounds

➤ A happy ending

With their lovely gowns, lavish food, and lively dancing, weddings are understandably billed as joyous occasions. People are supposed to look forward to weddings with pleasure. Yet most people think it's inevitable that, at some point, the happy couple, their families, and their friends will feel a sinking feeling in the pit of their stomachs when the word "wedding" is mentioned—especially if the bride and groom follow different faiths. Fortunately, it doesn't have to be that way.

In this chapter, you'll learn why weddings are such emotional—and important—events in general, but especially when an interfaith couple is involved. I'll first explain how expectations and unresolved feelings about weddings can cause difficulties for everyone involved. Then we'll see how wedding problems can often be traced back to the engagement. Next we'll discuss the relationship of money, power, and control. You'll see how different religious and cultural backgrounds can cause major-league misunderstandings.

Interfaith marriages suffer the strains of all unions and then some. But there can be a happy ending, as the story that concludes this chapter proves.

Wedding Bell Blues

My mailbag is stuffed to the brim with stories of interfaith weddings gone awry. Below is a typical one. See how it compares to your expectations and experiences:

Melissa Catalano, a successful real estate broker, was justly proud of her skill as a negotiator. She knew how to find a way for everyone to come out ahead—or to think they had. "I'm an expert at creating 'win/win' situations," she told me. That was *before* she and her fiancé Ken Goldberger started to plan their wedding. Then she became an expert at clenching her fists, gnashing her teeth, and pulling her hair out.

Learn the Lingo

A **chuppah** (or **huppa**) is a Jewish wedding canopy. It symbolizes the home.

Did You Know?

The legal age for marriage with parental consent ranges from 12 for women and 14 for men in some states to 16 for women and 18 for men in other states. The required age for marriage without parental consent varies from 16 to 21 for women to 18 to 21 for men.

"My family automatically assumed we would get married in our parish church. My priest would officiate. Of course, there would be a mass. Ken's side automatically assumed that we'd get married in his temple, standing under a *chuppah*. His rabbi would officiate. Of course, there would be a full service, and he'd smash the glass at the end.

As we planned the wedding, Ken and I quarreled more and more. We had just assumed that all the pieces would fall into place, but they didn't. Within a week, I was ready to elope and honeymoon at the North Pole—anywhere far, far away."

Ideally, by the time you're ready to get married, you and your honey have decided to follow one religion, have a blended ceremony, or forego religion completely and get married by a justice of the peace. But if making these decisions were *that* easy, hell would be frozen over, and we'd all be ducking to avoid the flying pigs.

When you and your beloved disagree over the wedding plans, guess what's going to happen? It's not a pretty sight. Why all the fuss and feathers? Like Melissa, you probably feel drawn to your heritage but want to accommodate your honey and his family. Like Ken, you love your bride and want to be nice to her family, but you don't want to feel disloyal to your religion.

When you're planning an interfaith wedding, the decisions come faster than bills after Christmas/Chanukah. Ham or brisket? Church or temple? Rabbi, priest, minister, judge, or Uncle Duke of the Church of the Large Donation? Let's see why these decisions are so important and are likely to cause difficulties between the couple and among family members as well.

When You Wish Upon a Star

In America, a wedding is seen as a time when children become adults. For one shining moment, an ordinary woman becomes a princess. Like babies, all brides are beautiful, the center of attention, a miracle. The groom is seen as a prince, a knight in shining armor whisking his beloved off to a magical land of eternal happiness.

A wedding is such an emotional moment because it is a life-changing event. As a transition in the lives of all those involved, a wedding always stirs up strong emotions. Here are some emotions that people may feel when they're getting married or helping their children plan a wedding:

➤ Excitement	➤ Envy
➤ Anticipation	➤ Worry
➤ Fear	➤ Panic

Family Matters

When their children marry, parents often feel a sense of loss ("My baby! My baby is leaving home!") along with joy ("Now we can finally clean up that pigpen of a room").

Past Tense

At the same time, unresolved feelings often bubble to the surface. Perhaps your honey had a horrendous previous wedding and got off on the wrong foot with his or her ex as a result. Hurt feelings aren't the sole realm of your honey, however: A sibling or in-law might have just as much trouble dealing with your nuptials because of what happened at *his or her own.* Perhaps a relative was forced to compromise on religious issues and felt like he or she lost the "battle"; maybe one set of parents got their way with another child and feel they have the right to bully you and your honey as well.

Consider this: There are only two ways to gain membership in a family—to be born (or adopted)

Hold On!

Don't Go There

Be forewarned: A previously married spouse or a parent whose past wedding experiences have been unsatisfying is likely to view your wedding as a chance to rectify old wounds. You're likely to be the one caught in the crossfire as he or she presses to get what *he or she* wants at the wedding, not necessarily what you (and your honey) want.

into it and to marry into it. Even if you moved away from home a long time ago, your marriage signals a huge psychological change in the family structure. What happens at the wedding ripples through the family for the rest of everyone's life.

My Way or the Highway

The following experience came from an acquaintance on the coast:

> "Two years [after we started dating], Larry and I married. Planning the wedding to accommodate his Judaic roots and my Christian family soon proved improbable, so we were wed by a justice of the peace at a small, family gathering. Religion doesn't seem to matter much when you date—but it matters to me now. Neither Larry nor I were regular worshippers in a traditional way, though each of us retained our religious upbringing in a spiritual way. I attended Larry's family's holiday functions, and he attended my family's dinners. Still, I have always wished I had a religious wedding ceremony."

Did You Know?

During the 1980s and 1990s, an increasing number of women kept their maiden names when they married. Increasingly, however, more and more newlywed women are taking their husband's last names. Sociologists are scurrying to explain why.

A wedding is ostensibly for the bride and groom, but your honey, his or her family, and even siblings often make self-serving suggestions and even unreasonable demands. The stew of everyone's expectations, wishes, and demands can make for a real Mylanta moment. It's a sucker bet that something is going to go wrong and someone is going to pitch a fit.

Here's some of the weight that a wedding carries:

➤ Family expectations
➤ New commitments
➤ Responsibility
➤ Change in status
➤ Change in identity

I clearly remember the feeling I had soon after I was married when someone first referred to me as "Mrs. Rozakis"—I looked behind myself to see where my mother-in-law was standing. You see, it had not yet dawned on me that *I* was now a Mrs. Rozakis; I still thought of myself under my maiden name. It took me a surprisingly long time to identify myself as "Mrs. Rozakis." I knew the day had finally come when I looked for myself in my high school yearbook but my picture wasn't there. "How can this be?" I thought. "I was on the yearbook staff!" Of course, I was looking under Rozakis, not my maiden name.

Add the issue of an interfaith wedding ceremony, and the water can get very choppy indeed. Since weddings are fraught with emotional weight, they often cause people to act in ways that you wouldn't expect.

Ring Ding

Some parents get upset long before the wedding. The pressure may start with the engagement ring (or lack thereof). Here's my friend Shoshana's story:

> "When I got engaged to Ahmed, I couldn't get the kind of ring I wanted—I had to wear his grandmother's ring. Now, I didn't want to make trouble with Ahmed's family, but I wasn't even allowed to change the setting. The ring was really out-of-date and looked terrible on my hand. But family tradition demanded that it be kept in pristine condition so I could pass it down to *my* son or daughter. That way, I guess, the ring could make them as miserable as it had made me."

Note that this story doesn't even have a religious component: It's just an everyday story of family expectations in the face of an engagement.

Other friends have told me stories of having their honey's family pick out their engagement ring ("Of course you'll use my jeweler, sweetie") or even counsel them not to get an engagement ring at all. ("Sonny boy is still paying off his college loans. Don't you want him to get out of debt before you start demanding fancy jewelry?")

A few couples refuse to be bullied, but the majority of people give in to the pressure to keep the peace. Often, they're young and unused to dealing with these pressures. Later, they often regret their decision. "My mother-in-law wanted me to get the same shape and size ring as all the other daughters-in-law so there wouldn't be any competition," said one woman. "I gave in because I didn't want to be seen as a troublemaker. I didn't like the ring when I got it. I still don't like it, years later. In retrospect, I should have stood my ground."

Did You Know?

It was the accepted practice in Babylon 4,000 years ago that, for a month after the wedding, the bride's father would supply his son-in-law with all the mead he could drink. Mead is a honey beer, and because the calendar was lunar based, this period was called the "honey month"—or what we know today as the "honeymoon."

Hindsight is 20/20; it's always easy to look back and know what we *should* have done. As someone who gave in a lot more than she should have while planning her wedding and has regretted it ever since, here's my advice: Stand your ground from the very beginning. There's no call to be snippy, but the sooner you make your wishes known, the easier it will be to set appropriate limits and boundaries as you plan the rest of the wedding festivities.

Whose Wedding Is It, Anyway?

Money, as you are doubtless already aware, represents forces and values far beyond a mere summing-up of one's liquid material worth or simple purchasing power. Money, especially in our ostensibly classless, proudly democratic, and ferociously free-market society, symbolizes pride. It represents freedom. It serves as an obsession, a measure of self-worth, and a Holy Grail all rolled into one. (Plus, if you have lots and lots of it, restaurant owners are nicer to you, and you usually get your way—especially when it comes to planning a wedding. It's the cynic's Golden Rule, folks: The one with the gold rules.)

Weddings are more sensitive than a teenager with acne because they're not only a public declaration of a couple's love, they're an open show of the bride's social status. Even if the bride and groom are paying the tab themselves, the scope of the wedding reflects on everyone in the family. Trust me: You don't want to be in the firing range when participants play "Can you top this?" with the finances.

Since different religions have different wedding customs, money becomes a crucial issue. Traditional Hindus, for example, often have elaborate wedding ceremonies that involve relatives from all over the world and can last for days. People from other faiths who might be used to a punch-and-cookies affair on the church lawn may find a Hindu wedding tough on the purse.

Money Business

Because planning the wedding is linked to financial issues, those who foot the bill often have the ultimate say in what type of wedding it will be—or they feel that they do. Some families will amiably negotiate the amount of money they have to spend and try to decide fairly who will pay for what. Others, in contrast, use money as a weapon to get their way. "I'm paying for it, and I'm going to get what I want!" one father told his daughter.

In the good old days when father knew best and things were left to the Beaver, the family of the bride arranged the wedding and paid for it. Even the language of weddings—"giving the bride away"—placed the responsibility squarely on *her* family's wallet. The groom was responsible for the liquor, transportation, and photography.

Fortunately for all involved (especially for those of you who have 10 unmarried daughters or one child in college), this tradition is being shattered. Today, more and more couples split the expenses according to who can afford what. As a result, resentment can arise when the bride's parents get stuck footing the whole bill when they were expecting the groom's parents to fork over their fair share.

Hey, Big Spender

Think that's all that can go wrong when money issues come up? Think again. Here are some other problems that can arise over the wedding expense:

1. **Keeping up with the Joneses.** It's common to find one side overspending on a wedding to impress their friends and neighbors. We went to a wedding where the groom's side provided suede yarmulkes trimmed in gold and printed with the bride and groom's name and wedding date. These hats were *expensive.* (The usual yarmulkes are made of inexpensive satin.)

2. **Headliners.** One side may find a more impressive officiant than the other to outshine the opposition. Does a Catholic bishop trump a Protestant minister?

3. **Suddenly devout.** One side might suddenly become super-religious to overshadow the other side's faith. It's amazing when people who haven't set foot in a house of worship since the Flood suddenly demand a full-dress wedding with all the trimmings. While they may indeed be moved by a late religious awakening, such a show is often done to outdo the other side.

4. **Oops!** The bride and groom can be left in a hole by well-meaning but profligate parents—or fiscally irresponsible ones.

Culture Clash

A friend shared this horror story:

Arina, born in Afghanistan, was excited about her brother's upcoming wedding to Mina, a young woman from India. Arina didn't have time to talk to her brother and Mina about the wedding. In keeping with her own Afghani tradition, Arina wore a white dress, a symbol of luck and happiness for the wedding couple.

Don't Go There

Don't wear black or white to a traditional Chinese wedding. Both colors are associated with death.

That morning, Arina showed up at Mina's house to help her prepare for the wedding. When Mina saw Arina, she started to tremble and her faced turned ashen. Mina's other relatives acted equally upset when they saw Arina. Some turned away; others were openly hostile. "What have I done wrong?" Arina wondered. Before the wedding, Mina's aunt took Arina aside and explained that wearing white to an Indian wedding is a very bad omen. It is thought to bring back luck, even death, to the couple. Only a bitter enemy would wear white to a wedding.

Arina thought she was honoring the wedding couple by wearing white; the bride and her family took her outfit as a sign of the worst possible ill wishes.

Cultural differences can wreck havoc at weddings. Sometimes even the best intentions are misinterpreted due to differences in region, background, and heritage. Here's another example:

Did You Know?

In pre-Revolutionary China, arranged marriages were the norm. It was common for a bride and groom to meet for the first time on their wedding day.

Family Matters

Recognize that you are marrying not just your honey but his or her entire family as well.

The Hawthorne family sent out invitations for the forthcoming wedding of their daughter Carol to Guatemalan-born Ernesto Colon. Since the Colon family lived in California and the wedding would be held in Florida, the Hawthornes enclosed maps to the catering hall and information about hotels in the area. They listed the names, rates, and amenities at three different hotels. They also suggested that guests make their reservations as soon as possible since hotel space was limited.

The Colon family was so outraged when they received their invitations that they refused to go to the wedding.

The Hawthornes believed they were being considerate by including hotel information. To the Colons, however, the family of the bride should have welcomed the groom's family into their home, no matter how crowded they might be. The Colons interpreted the information about hotel reservations as rejection. After all, the Colons had traveled across the country to attend their son's wedding; weren't they at least entitled to simple hospitality?

Once they discovered the reason for the misunderstanding, the Hawthornes felt embarrassed. They didn't change their plans, however, because having strangers as houseguests was not part of *their* cultural heritage. In an effort to maintain a semblance of family relations, the Colons finally decided to attend the wedding and stay in a motel, but their feelings were not soothed. Relations between the Hawthornes and Colons are still not good.

Sometimes Dreams *Do* Come True

My dear friends Rosemarie and Andy, one of the most loving couples I know (and one of the most intelligent), have managed to blend two faiths seamlessly. Here is their story:

"When Andy and I were planning our wedding, we faced the challenge of deciding where to get married. Andy is Jewish, and I am Catholic. I had always dreamed of getting married in church. As a child, I attended mass each week with my family, and I would also accompany my Mom to church when she sang for weddings, which was just about every weekend. I was a little girl at the time, peering over the balcony of the choir loft, watching bride after bride walk down the aisle with their long white gowns gliding perfectly behind them. This was a magical image to witness week after week. I would often imagine the day when it would be me. That memory was a part of my childhood and of me.

The only problem was that Andy was Jewish and was not at all comfortable being in a church, let alone getting married in one. So after long discussions, we compromised and had our ceremony at the C.W. Post Interfaith Chapel. We had a beautiful ceremony shared by a priest and a rabbi. Our families were very happy and we were thrilled because we were married."

But over the years, Rosemarie thought more and more about her wedding. "I always felt like something was missing, as if a piece of my life was not complete," she said. "I was no longer the little girl gazing down from the choir loft, but I still felt that a spiritual link was missing for me personally." Rather than letting her discontent fester, Rosemarie decided to do something about it:

Family Matters

Tracey, Rosemarie and Andy's wonderful daughter, offered this hint about raising children in an interfaith marriage: "I was raised as both a Catholic and a Jew. This was a wonderful heritage because it gave me a complete sense of my entire ancestry and who I am."

"After 10 years of marriage, we had grown and matured, and Andy had a better understanding of what my faith meant to me. We had shared so much in those 10 years, and still not getting married in church was something I wish we could have experienced. On our tenth wedding anniversary, Andy gave me a gift from his heart. He agreed to renew our vows in a Catholic church.

Andy was completely comfortable doing this for me. He knew that my intent was not to change his beliefs or impose my own faith on him. He was doing this for me as a person, as an individual who believed in their faith. This generous act was what our marriage has been about. We are two different people with two different faiths. Andy couldn't comfortably do this for me at age 22, and I respected that. At 32 he could, and it meant the world to me. We had a small, simple ceremony with our children and family gathered around us.

Our renewal was a renewal in us. It was establishing that our love meant giving when you don't totally understand the other person's perspective, but you care enough to try to understand. It meant giving up something that meant a lot to me at the time but finding the ability to be selfless because I loved him. Patience, understanding, communication, respect, and compromise are key in any relationship. An interfaith marriage requires these qualities all the more."

Act of Faith

Any palm readers out there? If so, the "marriage line" is the line under the little finger that begins outside of the palm and extends inward to the palm. The marriage line not only indicates marriage but all forms of romantic relations including relations with lovers, mistresses, and friends. Commonly, it is said that one marriage line indicates one marriage, and two lines indicate two marriages. If there are several marriage lines but none with any clarity, it suggests a late marriage.

As Rosemarie and Andy's story demonstrates, you may not be able to solve all the issues surrounding your wedding initially, but if you get off to a strong and loving start, you can have a successful marriage. As a bonus, you might even get the wedding you want later!

Bridge Across Troubled Waters

You're no idiot. You know that starting out as a couple is more difficult than mastering underwater fire prevention. As the wedding approaches, you're still feeling each other out and trying to be on your best behavior. You're simultaneously thrilled to discover all that your partner is … and crushed to discover all that he or she is not.

So while you're traveling the emotional interstate with your honey, why not build some bridges with your prospective in-laws at the same time? Read on to find out how to craft the wedding you and your honey want, while forging bonds with your future family.

The Least You Need to Know

➤ Recognize that everyone brings his or her own emotional baggage to the wedding preparations and ceremony. This colors our actions and reactions.

➤ Remember that religious differences are often accompanied by cultural differences as well.

➤ Stand fast on big issues; give in on the little ones.

➤ You can get the interfaith wedding you want, and many people do.

➤ In the long run, it's the marriage that matters, not the wedding ceremony.

Chapter 13

A Jewish Wedding Ceremony

In This Chapter

➤ Ceremony choices

➤ One couple's experiences

➤ Jewish wedding traditions

➤ Finding a rabbi to officiate

➤ The actual ceremony

➤ An interfaith couple's Jewish wedding

"When I met my husband, he made it clear that he wanted to raise the kids Jewish," said Nicole, who grew up a Jehovah's Witness.

"We had been dating two weeks," Larry recalled. "She said fine. It was a lot easier throwing yourself into a relationship knowing we didn't have the religious hurdle."

This chapter opens with a survey of the choices that interfaith couples have when it comes to wedding ceremonies. Next, you'll read about the option that one interfaith couple made—a Jewish ceremony—to see if it's the right way to go for you and your honey. The rest of the chapter explains the elements of a Jewish wedding ceremony from start to finish. By the time you finish this chapter, you'll be equipped to decide whether you and your sweetheart want to be married in the Jewish tradition.

Did You Know?

The Ethical Cultural movement, a religious fellowship, was founded in 1876 by Felix Adler. In Adler's words, the movement stresses the "supreme importance of the ethical factor in all relations in life—personal, social, national, and international—without dependence on uniform theological or metaphysical beliefs."

Family Matters

Fundamentalist Christians often feel that they must convert people they care about to their faith. The conversion reassures them that these people aren't "lost" and separated from God.

Yours, Mine, or Ours?

When you marry someone of a different faith, you have the following choices when it comes to the wedding ceremony:

1. **Follow your faith.** For example, let's say you're a Reform Jewish man marrying a Hindu woman. If she agrees, you would get married in a Reform Jewish synagogue, following all the Jewish customs.

2. **Follow your partner's faith.** In this instance, assume you're a Presbyterian man marrying a Muslim woman. You would get married in the Muslim mosque, following Muslim rituals.

3. **Combine both faiths.** Depending on the faiths, this may not always be possible. For example, Orthodox Judaism and Fundamental Christianity do not allow intermarriage. Clearly, this is an issue that requires careful thought and a great deal of communication between partners. If the faiths can be combined, you would have two religious leaders officiating and follow the customs of both religions.

4. **Select an entirely new faith.** Some interfaith couples decide to adopt a new faith as a compromise. Unitarianism and Ethical Culture are often chosen because they are accepting of intermarriage.

5. **Eliminate the religious aspect by having a civil ceremony.** In addition to a justice of the peace, couples can get married by any judge. Federal judges have especially nice chambers.

The Best of Both Worlds

Here's how one interfaith couple, Maria and Stan, solved the wedding issue. See if their solution fits your needs.

"When I met my future husband, I had only dated Catholics. In part, this was because my mother was Catholic and my father was Lutheran. We followed my mother's faith, so I had experienced the rupture that resulted from my dad's 'odd man out' religious status in our family. I was all set to attend college, establish a career, and marry a Catholic. All my plans fell apart when I met Stan. By the end of the evening, Stan and I knew we were meant for each other.

The crunch came with the religious difference: I was raised Catholic; he was Jewish. My friends and family said that he should convert; if not, he should at least be religiously passive so we would have a Catholic household and Catholic children. His parents were adamantly opposed to this choice.

After conversations that stretched long into the night, we decided to adopt both traditions. 'The kids will be confused,' some friends argued. 'They'll be alienated, and they won't know who they are,' many of our relatives objected, drawing on theory rather than any experience they'd actually had. We started with a Jewish wedding because it was very important to Stan and his family.

It wasn't easy because the bigotry was on both sides. Stan's graduate career was almost derailed when an acting chairman questioned that someone married to a Gentile could be serious about Judaic studies; when Stan later became a professor, his college lost potential donors because he was married to a Catholic. From the Christian end, the bigotry was institutional, including homilies against the hypocritical Pharisees and 'the yoke of the Law.'

For us, the problem differences were more cultural than religious. Jews and Gentiles often have different expectations about food: what it means and how much of it there should be at a celebration. We worked out these problems by identifying them and then keeping in mind that they are merely differences in cultural pattern, not matters of right and wrong. Then we worked out compromises.

Don't Go There

From the time of Ruth the Moabite, who chose to cling to her Jewish mother-in-law ("Whither thou goest ... thy people shall be my people"), interfaith marriage has been an especially thorny battle for Jewish people. To some Jews, the melting pot has become a meltdown because intermarriage is accomplishing what centuries of oppression could not—the extermination of the Jewish people.

And the children? They're all adults now and are not alienated, confused, or any of those other terrible things we were warned about. Our older son once said he thought it was because we were each so sure of who we were ourselves, they never felt there was a problem. Our younger son admits he did sometimes have thoughts like, 'Boy, Dad will be sorry for grounding me when I become a Christian,' but in fact feels his spiritual life has been enriched and enlarged by not being limited by a set of precut assumptions."

—Maria, age 47

Mazel Tov!

As the preceding experience shows, Maria and Stan decided to compromise and follow both religions. To settle the wedding issue, they opted for a Jewish ceremony. This may or may not be the right choice for you and your sweetie. If it is, what should you do first? Start by learning as much as you can about the ceremony. To make your research easier, let me introduce you to the basics of the Jewish wedding ceremony.

The Basics

Before you can get those invitations printed, you need to cover the key elements of any wedding—when, where, how much, and the biggie: What shall I wear? And here they are …

1. **Time.** In traditional Jewish practice, weddings don't take place on the Sabbath (Friday night through Saturday day) or on major Jewish holidays. If you plan to get married on Friday night or Saturday afternoon, you'll have a harder time finding a rabbi and run the risk of offending more observant Jewish guests.

2. **Place.** Although a Jewish wedding is most commonly held in a temple, hotel, catering hall, restaurant, or home, it can be held anywhere at all—consider this if you're the outdoorsy type. Opposite to a Christian wedding, the bride's family and friends usually sit on the right side, and the groom's family and friends usually sit on the left. As you plan, remember that some synagogues restrict photographs and videos because of the distractions they cause. Officials may not allow you to lob handfuls of rice at the couple after the ceremony either.

3. **Fees.** The best things in life may be free, but synagogues still have to pay for heat, lighting, and repairs. Find out the fee structure for the synagogue rental before you book the wedding so you can figure it into your budget.

Did You Know?

Orthodox Jews recommend that the wedding be held outdoors so that the offspring of the marriage might be as numerous as the stars. I'd worry about rain.

4. **Clothes.** The bride can wear anything she wishes, but nearly all brides in formal Jewish weddings wear the traditional American white wedding gown. The groom wears a dark suit or tuxedo. Divorced or widowed women are free to wear elaborate white gowns if they wish and many do. Others wear fancy suits, tea-length gowns in pastel colors, and so forth.

Guests dress appropriately, and men are expected to wear a *yarmulke* (skullcap) during the service. Not to worry, men: The bride and groom provide yarmulkes if you've left yours in your other suit. Jews are equally relaxed about a yarmulke falling off. If yours takes a dive, there's no harm done—just put it back on. (Men with hair often secure their yarmulkes with bobby pins or clips.)

Orthodox Jews dress very modestly, even at weddings. Clothes must reach to the neck and extend below the knees. Clothes can't be tight or revealing. Long sleeves that cover the elbows are also required.

Learn the Lingo

A **ketubah** is a Jewish marriage contract.

The Ceremony

Before the actual wedding ceremony, the husband gives the wife a *ketubah,* a marriage contract. In interfaith marriages, some rabbis give the couple a ketubah; others do not. Be sure to ask for a ketubah if you want one. They are often lettered with elaborate calligraphy and make a beautiful addition to your new home.

A Jewish wedding can vary greatly. In addition to differences among the Orthodox, Conservative, and Reform branches, each rabbi and synagogue has its own interpretation of tradition.

In general, the ceremony itself lasts 20–30 minutes and consists of the following elements:

1. The groom is led to the chuppa, usually escorted by both of his parents. (A relative can stand in for absent or deceased parents.)

2. The bride is brought to the chuppa, usually escorted by both of her parents. (A relative can stand in for absent or deceased parents.)

3. Both sets of parents (or stand-ins) remain standing with the bride and groom as part of the ceremony. They do not take a seat with the congregation, as is common in Christian weddings.

4. The rabbi gives the invocation.

5. Blessings are recited over wine, and the bride and groom drink from the cup.

6. The rabbi gives a brief sermon, usually an explanation of the importance of marriage in Judaism. Rabbis who know the family can offer personal reflections on the bride and groom and their suitability for each other.

7. If the bride and groom wish, they may insert some special readings or prayers into the ceremony.

8. The bride and groom exchange vows and rings. In Reform ceremonies, the plain gold wedding band is placed on the bride's left ring finger. (In Orthodox and Conservative weddings, the ring is traditionally placed on the bride's right index finger.) In Reform ceremonies, there may be a double-ring ceremony if the groom wants to wear a ring as well. (Make him wear a ring, ladies; those rings mean "Hands-off—this one's taken!") The bride and groom can write their own vows if they wish or can supplement the traditional ones.

9. Blessings are recited over wine, and the bride and groom drink from the cup. (Yes, I know you've already done this. You get to do it again, so get a good-quality wine. None of that cheap stuff.)

10. The rabbi pronounces the couple married.

11. The rabbi offers the closing benediction.

12. At the end of the ceremony, the groom smashes a glass (or a small piece of glass) with his right foot to symbolize the destruction of the Temple.

Act of Faith

According to some sources, the groom breaks a glass as a reminder that, even during the most joyous Jewish occasions, we must mourn the destruction of the Holy Temple, as it says in Psalms: "... if I do not raise you [Zion] above the height of my joyous occasions ...." Jews believe that God's kingdom will not be complete until the Holy Temple is rebuilt.

According to other sources, however, the breaking of the glass is a good luck custom that originated in the Middle Ages when a loud noise was supposed to drive away evil spirits. No matter what its precise meaning, the glass is always well wrapped, so don't worry about Aunt Edna becoming a human pincushion.

The Rabbi

Because marriage under Jewish law is essentially a private contractual agreement between a man and a woman, it doesn't technically require the presence of a rabbi or any other religious official. This is not the case in Christian marriages. It is common, however, for rabbis to officiate, partly because the presence of a religious or civil official is required under United States civil law and partly in imitation of the Christian practice.

If you and your honey decide you want a Jewish wedding (or an interfaith ceremony involving a rabbi), start by finding one who will officiate. This isn't as easy as you might think because, according to Jewish law, a Jewish wedding contract is valid only when entered into between two Jews. A Jew and a non-Jew can have a valid civil wedding but not a valid Jewish wedding, according to some Jews.

Further, Judaism teaches that men and women must marry and have a family to achieve complete humanity as given to them by God. Since the home in Judaism is the equivalent of the altar or communion chalice in Christianity, many rabbis feel they cannot consecrate a home that may not be Jewish. As a result, few Conservative rabbis and no Orthodox rabbis will perform an interfaith ceremony.

Start by looking for a Reform or Reconstructionist rabbi. Even some of these rabbis, however, will not perform interfaith ceremonies.

Also recognize that rabbis are free to impose their own requirements in exchange for performing the ceremony. For example, they may require you to undergo premarital counseling or promise to raise the children as Jews.

How can you find a rabbi? Try these sources:

➤ Recommendations from interfaith couples who have had Jewish wedding ceremonies

➤ Recommendations from Christian clergy, who often know of rabbis who will officiate

➤ The Reform and Reconstructionist synagogues in your area

➤ Jewish youth groups in the local universities

➤ Jewish Web sites on the Internet

➤ The Rabbinic Center for Research and Counseling, 125 East Dudley Avenue, Westfield, NJ 07090

Learn the Lingo

A **cantor** is a trained musician who leads the worship services at a larger synagogue. Cantors are also teachers of religion.

If you can't find a rabbi, a *cantor* can also officiate at an interfaith ceremony. In the Reform tradition, rabbis and cantors can be male or female.

Now that you know what's done in a traditional Jewish wedding, you can decide which elements to include and which ones to change. For example, you may not

147

wish to have both sets of parents stand with you; often in interfaith marriages, the parents take seats with the rest of the guests.

Don't Go There

Some European-born Jews now living in America call their parents-in-law by the Yiddish words "shviger" (mother-in-law) and "shver" (father-in-law). Other Jews, however, consider these terms insulting. My advice? Never assume; always ask.

L'Chayim!

L'Chayim (li-KHAY-eem) is the Yiddish/Hebrew toast to life. It's used the way you would use "Cheers!" in English. Let's offer L'Chayim to this happy couple:

"I was raised Methodist and educated in Catholic parish schools. I'm going to have a Jewish wedding because my fiancé is Jewish, and after researching Jewish weddings, I fell in love with the beautiful ceremony, which so powerfully mixes the purely joyful with the solemn. I'm especially looking forward to the part where David steps on the glass and everyone yells 'Mazel Tov!'

Am I converting? No. In fact, I'm going to wear my grandmother's cross to the wedding to represent my 'something old.' I'll also wear the bracelet David's mother gave me when we got engaged. Her husband gave it to her on their 25th anniversary. She told him then that when David 'found his girl' she would pass it on. After presenting me with the bracelet, she also gave us a hundred dollars and a box of Jewish pastry. She calls me 'mummula' and other Yiddish endearments and fusses over me extravagantly. I feel confident that David and I will have a happy and fulfilling life together because of rather than despite our religious differences."

—Krystal, age 28

The Least You Need to Know

➤ Carefully decide whether you want to be married in your own faith, your partner's faith, a combination of the two, another faith, or a civil ceremony.

➤ Traditionally, Jewish weddings are not held on the Sabbath (Friday night through Saturday day).

➤ The wedding can be held anywhere, and guests dress appropriately.

➤ A rabbi usually officiates at a Jewish wedding, although a cantor can also. It can be very difficult to find a rabbi willing to marry an interfaith couple.

Chapter 14

Christian Wedding Ceremonies

In This Chapter

➤ The Catholic wedding ceremony

➤ The Greek Orthodox wedding ceremony

➤ A Protestant wedding service

➤ An interfaith couple

"A life without religion is a life without principles, and a life without principles is like a ship without a rudder."

—Mahatma Gandhi, *Autobiography* (1924)

This chapter explains the basics of a Catholic wedding ceremony, a Greek Orthodox wedding ceremony, and a Protestant wedding ceremony so that you and your fiancé (or fiancée) can decide whether you wish to consecrate your vows in one of these traditions.

By the time you finish this chapter, you'll have the facts you need to make an informed, intelligent life decision about whether a Christian wedding is right for you and your honey.

The Catholic Wedding

An acquaintance passed on this story about her friend Rita. How closely does it mirror your experiences with mixed matches?

"We have differences, yes we do. I am Catholic; he's Christian Pentecostal. He doesn't like the figures inside the Catholic churches, and I don't like that he has to pray for everything. We have learned to deal with it by respecting each other because we're a couple. He doesn't like my religion, I know, but when I explained how much it meant to me to get married in the Catholic Church, he agreed, happy to make me happy on our special day. Once we were married in the church, I felt that our hearts were truly joined."

As Rita understands, a Catholic wedding is a union of not only bodies, hearts, and minds, but also souls. The Catholic Church stresses careful premarital planning to help make sure that Catholic unions will endure. Let's look at that planning now.

Learn the Lingo

A **diocese** is a church district under the jurisdiction of a bishop.

Don't Go There

Avoid priests who claim they don't need to file any paperwork to perform an interfaith ceremony. Your wedding may not be valid in the Church if the proper documents haven't been filed.

Before the Big Day

As of yet, there's no uniform set of rules for Catholic marriage preparation that applies to all of America. The Catholic bishops will decide the matter. In the meantime, I suggest that you visit your family priest or a local parish priest to find out the requirements in each particular diocese.

Below are some general guidelines that hold true in all *dioceses*:

1. **Paper trail.** To get married in the Catholic Church, you're required to complete specific documents well in advance of the big day. The Catholic partner in an interfaith couple must supply two documents:

   ➤ **A baptismal certificate.** If your Mommy didn't paste your baptismal certificate into your baby book or squirrel it away in the family safe-deposit box, call or write to the church where you were baptized, and they will send you a copy. Just be sure to leave yourself plenty of time to receive it in case there's a mix-up or short staffing in the records office.

   ➤ **A letter of freedom.** This letter testifies that, according to the church's records, you're free to marry because you're not currently married in the eyes of the church. Get this letter from the parish where you now live, not the one where you grew up.

Some dioceses require additional documentation, such as affidavits from family members swearing that you are free to marry in the Church. The non-Catholic partner may also have to provide documentation that he or she is free to marry in accordance with Catholic standards.

2. **Pre-Cana Counseling.** Although the name varies, *pre-Cana* is the most common term for the Catholic premarital programs that help couples prepare for their new life together. Pre-Cana programs are usually required for all couples who wish to get married in the church, whether both partners are Catholic or just one. Couples are usually counseled in groups led by happily married Catholic couples who are specially trained for this responsibility. However, some priests conduct pre-Cana themselves.

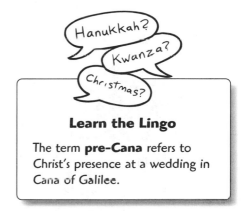

Learn the Lingo

The term **pre-Cana** refers to Christ's presence at a wedding in Cana of Galilee.

Before 1965, the non-Catholic partner had to promise to raise all children that resulted from the marriage as Catholics, but this promise is no longer required.

3. **Dispensation.** In the case of an interfaith marriage, the priest has to file a *dispensation* to receive special permission to officiate at the ceremony. If the non-Catholic half of the couple wants to have a dual ceremony (such as Catholic-Jewish or Catholic-Hindu), the priest must request a dispensation to participate. Once the dispensation is approved, the marriage is considered valid in the eyes of the Church, even if the priest is not actually present at the ceremony.

Discouraged yet? Don't be! Although this preparation sounds very complicated, it's actually easier to get married in the Catholic Church than in the Jewish synagogue. That's because the Catholic Church doesn't have such strong objection to intermarriage.

The Basics

Okay, all the documents are filed, and you've been counseled in the Church. You're not quite ready to zip up your dress, ladies, or fasten your necktie, gentlemen. First, attend to these matters:

1. **Place.** Since there's no uniform rule about interfaith weddings in the Catholic Church, some dioceses allow such unions on their premises, while others may not. For example, the New York archdiocese (where I live) allows an interfaith

couple to be married in any sacred space such as a chapel, church, or synagogue as well as a secular space such as a catering hall or hotel. However, outdoor weddings are not permitted. But outdoor weddings may be allowed in Maine or Michigan, so consult with your dioceses.

Family Matters

Instead of throwing rice or puffed rice or any other cereal projectiles, why not supply guests with little bottles of soapy water and have them blow bubbles? It's lovely, and it prevents litigious guests from suing you because they slipped on rice kernels.

2. **Time.** Always book the church well in advance, especially if you're planning to get married in a church during peak season, May and June. It's not that hard to find a catering hall, a room in a firehouse, or even someone's backyard for a reception. But if you want a church wedding, only a church will do, and they can be in short supply in your area.

   Sunday mornings are busy times in the Church, so it's hard to book weddings then. As with the Jewish tradition, weddings aren't scheduled during major holidays such as Christmas and Easter, again because parishioners have first dibs.

3. **Clothes.** As with Reform Jewish weddings, the bride can wear anything she wishes, but nearly all Catholic brides today opt for the traditional American white wedding gown. The groom wears a dark suit or tuxedo. Divorced or widowed women are free to wear elaborate white gowns if they wish, and many do. Others wear fancy suits, tea-length gowns in pastel colors, and so forth.

   Nearly every female guest I've seen at formal evening weddings recently—whether Catholic, Jewish, or interfaith—has worn black, which I think makes the entire affair look like a funeral. To make a stand, I've taken to wearing sky-blue, red, or purple. Give me some help here; take a stand for colorful weddings!

4. **Restrictions.** Some churches restrict photographs and videos. Many churches don't allow rice to be thrown; they don't want your Uncle Fenster taking a header down the stone steps.

5. **Fees.** As with any wedding location, expect to pay to rent the church. Be sure to find out the fee structure before you book the wedding so you can figure it into your budget.

The Ceremony

In the Roman Catholic tradition, there are two types of marriage ceremonies:

➤ A wedding ceremony without a Mass

➤ A wedding ceremony incorporated into the Mass

A wedding ceremony without a Mass lasts about 20 minutes, including readings and hymns, and is very similar to the Protestant wedding ceremony. A wedding ceremony with a Mass usually lasts about an hour.

Some dioceses don't permit a Mass to be said at an interfaith marriage with two clergy of different faiths running the show. However, if you want a Mass, consult with your diocese to find out its individual policy in the matter.

Below is the general outline for a wedding ceremony with a Mass:

1. As Catholics enter the church, they bless themselves by dipping the fingertips of their right hand into a font containing holy water. Then they make the sign of the cross. Non-Catholics walk right in without making the sign of the cross.

2. Guests choose their own seats or are guided to their seats by the ushers. Opposite to a Jewish wedding, the bride's family and friends usually sit on the left side, and the groom's family and friends usually sit on the right.

3. Some Catholics may make the sign of the cross while genuflecting (bending the knee as a sign of reverence) when they reach the pew. Some may go directly to their seats and sit down, while others may kneel and pray before sitting; either is acceptable. While non-Catholics are welcome to genuflect, they are not required to observe these signs of respect and awareness of the body of Christ present in the church.

4. The groom walks down the aisle.

5. The bride walks down the aisle, usually accompanied by her father or a stand-in.

6. The priest begins the Mass with prayers. Throughout the Mass, take your cues from those around you. The priest will also give instructions. There will be readings and prayers. At times, you will be required to stand. Sometimes, there may be kneeling, but non-Catholic guests can just sit quietly while others kneel.

Did You Know?

Catholics make the sign of the cross by touching their forehead, heart, left shoulder, and then right shoulder.

Family Matters

Increasingly, couples are providing personalized instruction booklets to help guests follow the wedding rituals. Consider creating booklets for your wedding as well. Not only do they make guests feel more comfortable, they also make lovely souvenirs.

7. When the congregation is invited to recite the Lord's Prayer, Protestants should be aware that Roman Catholics omit the final few lines: "For Thine is the kingdom, the power and the glory, forever and ever."

8. During the wedding ceremony, vows and rings are exchanged.

9. There will be the "sign of peace." The priest might say, "Let us offer each other a sign of peace," an indication for everyone to turn to their neighbors, shake their hands, and say, "Peace be with you" or some other friendly greeting. Sometimes relatives or very close friends will hug, and a mother may kiss her child at this point.

10. Communion is served. The commemoration of Christ's Last Supper, Communion is the ceremony in which bread and wine are consecrated and taken as the body and blood of Christ. To take Communion, people walk down the center aisle to take the bread (often a wafer) and come back up the sides to their seats.

11. The register is signed.

12. The priest introduces the newly married couple. At this point, people may applaud, depending on local custom.

Now that you've learned about a traditional Catholic wedding, you can decide whether this ceremony suits you and your beloved. Remember that you may wish to incorporate a Catholic ceremony with the traditions of another faith, having two religious leaders officiate.

Don't Go There

Communion in the Roman Catholic Church is reserved for baptized Catholics only.

Act of Faith

A survey of recently married couples revealed the following choices for background music during the church ceremony: "Love Theme from *The Godfather*;" Bach, "Largo from *Concerto #5*;" Handel, "Air from *Water Music*;" Beethoven, "Adagio *Cantabile*;" Bach, "Air on the G String;" "Sunrise, Sunset" from *Fiddler on the Roof*; Sousa, "Liberty Bell March" (you might know it as the *Monty Python* theme); Bach, "Jesu, Joy of Man's Desiring;" and Mouret, "The Rondeau" (the *Masterpiece Theatre* theme).

A Greek Orthodox Wedding

Yassou! Before a Greek wedding, the bride and groom receive Holy Communion. The sacrament of marriage begins with a betrothal ceremony in which the priest blesses rings and places them on the right hand (not the left) of both the bride and the groom. The rings signify the bond in the name of the Father, Son, and Holy Spirit rather than a human agent.

During the marriage ceremony, the couple is crowned. The best man assists in this part of the ceremony. The couple then drinks from a wine cup called "the common cup of joys and sorrows." They also circle a ceremonial table three times to honor the Holy Trinity.

Weddings in the Greek Orthodox Church and the Ukrainian Orthodox Church are essentially the same, with slight variations.

A Protestant Wedding

The Protestant Church came out of the Roman Catholic Church in the Protestant Reformation of the early 1500s. Therefore, all the traditions of the Catholic Church are part of the Protestant Church. Among others, Protestant denominations include Anglican, Baptist, Presbyterian, and United churches.

Generally speaking, Protestants don't forbid interfaith weddings (although Pentecostals, Fundamentalist Christians, and Mormons frown on them more than others). Neither do they regard them as a betrayal of an individual's Christian heritage. As a result, interfaith weddings in which one partner is Christian are often celebrated in Protestant churches.

Most mainline Protestant ministers are willing to share the celebration with a rabbi or other religious leader. There are requirements, of course, but Protestants give interfaith couples a lot of wiggle room when it comes to sharing the spotlight at the altar.

Did You Know?

Traditionally, the attendants at a Greek wedding wear a charm in the form of a small eye that protects the wedding guests from bad luck.

Don't Go There

Beware of stepping on toes. If you're having two religious leaders officiate, the one who leads the planning process is usually the clergy person of the institution where the wedding is being held.

Follow the Rules

Depending on the specific minister, parish, and Protestant denomination, the following conditions must often be met before the couple can be married:

1. Often, one partner must be a member of the specific Protestant denomination.

2. Sometimes, one partner must be a member of the particular parish in which the couple wishes to be married.

155

3. Nearly all Protestant pastors require a period of counseling and evaluation before they agree to marry a couple. If you plan to have two religious leaders officiate, such as a rabbi and a pastor, they will often work together to avoid duplication in counseling.

Tailored to Fit

Below is the typical Protestant wedding liturgy. It can easily be adapted to suit an interfaith wedding and accommodate two officiating clergy, a Protestant and a non-Protestant.

1. The guests file into the church while music plays in the background. The music is often live, but it may be taped as well. (I'm especially partial to harps, flutes, and female singers at interfaith Protestant-based weddings, but to each to his own.)

   Guests are likely to be greeted by ushers who will escort them to their seats in the church. The seats on the left side of the church facing the altar are reserved for the bride's family and friends; the seats on the right side are for the groom's family and friends. If one side is expected to outnumber the other, it is customary to mix the seating.

2. The bride's and groom's parents enter and are seated in the front. The bride's mother is the last person to be escorted to her seat.

3. The wedding procession enters. The groom, best man, and ushers stand to the right of the altar. The bridesmaids, maid/matron of honor, flower girl, and ring bearer walk up the aisle, followed by the bride. She may be escorted by her father or another male relative, but this is optional.

4. The wedding liturgy begins, opening with a brief statement about the religious nature of marriage. This is followed by an invocation (prayer). The pastor and other clergy (if there is more than one officiating) will tell the guests when to stand and when to sit.

5. Next comes the declarations of consent, when each partner agrees to marry the other. (If the bride is escorted by her father, she now joins the groom.)

6. This is followed by readings from scripture and other sources. Then may come a brief homily or other responses.

7. The bride and groom repeat their marriage vows. (This is where I start crying.)

8. Rings are exchanged. The ceremony can be single ring or double ring.

9. The declaration of marriage is next.

10. Prayers or intercessions, often including the Lord's Prayer, follow.

11. The blessings of the marriage are next, followed in some liturgies by the Eucharist. About 15 years ago, Protestant churches moved away from serving Communion at weddings, but the practice is now being brought back by some.

In an interfaith ceremony shared by two different clergy, such as a minister and a rabbi, the ceremony will be divided between the two. If you want this type of ceremony, look for clergy who are willing to work with you and each other to make the ceremony fair and meaningful. This way, neither side will feel slighted, and everyone will feel the emotional significance of the rite of passage.

Some Protestant clergy will even include aspects of other traditions even if they are the only officiant. While it's rare to find a Protestant pastor who can sing like a cantor, the right pastor will work with you as a couple to make your wedding suit you both.

Act of Faith

Here is the Lord's Prayer (Psalm 23) from the King James Bible:

"The Lord is my shepherd; I shall not want.

He maketh me to lie down in green pastures: he leadeth me beside the still waters.

He restoreth my soul: he leadeth me in the paths of righteousness for his name's sake.

Yea, though I walk through the valley of the shadow of death, I will fear no evil: for thou art with me; thy rod and thy staff they comfort me.

Thou preparest a table before me in the presence of mine enemies; thou annointest my head with oil; my cup runneth over.

Surely goodness and mercy shall follow me all the days of my life; and I will dwell in the house of the Lord forever."

The Prophet

Although the Protestant wedding ceremony follows a general plan, there's flexibility for individual needs. You and your honey may wish to insert brief poems, songs, or material you have written yourself.

For example, many interfaith couples are fond of passages taken from *The Prophet* by Kahlil Gibran. Here's a famous excerpt that may work for you and your honey. It appeals to many interfaith couples because it allows for individual differences as much as togetherness:

"Then Almitra spoke again and said, And what of Marriage, master?

And he answered saying: You were born together, and together you shall be for evermore. You shall be together when the white wings of death scatter your days. Aye, you shall be together even in the silent memory of God.

But let there be spaces in your togetherness.

And let the winds of the heavens dance between you.

Love one another, but make not a bond of love:

Let it rather be a moving sea between the shores of your souls.

Fill each other's cup but drink not from one cup.

Give one another of your bread but eat not from the same loaf.

Sing and dance together and be joyous, but let each one of you be alone,

Even as the strings of a lute are alone though they quiver with the same music.

Give your hearts, but not into each other's keeping.

For only the hand of Life can contain your hearts.

And stand together yet not too near together:

For the pillars of the temple stand apart,

And the oak tree and the cypress grow not in each other's shadow."

God Bless You!

Here's how one interfaith couple resolved their wedding conflicts. See how their struggles compare to your own.

"The biggest conflict we had while dating was my religious faith. Although I had been raised a devout Catholic, I was an agnostic when we met. Angela grew up Lutheran and could trace her roots back to Germany. She has every inch of her life in the Lutheran church. So her condition for marriage was plain: 'We will get married in the Lutheran church.' Every other difference was smoothed out in time, but the one that was as firm as diamonds was, 'We will get married in the Lutheran church.'

I began going to church with her about two years into the relationship. But God and I were like distant relatives who hadn't been on speaking terms for years. It was too humbling and difficult a prospect to take for a very proud man such as me. Another year and a half went by, and we got engaged.

But God and I were still not speaking, and Angela's demand remained on the table. I realized I would have to take a step toward God and find out for myself if I indeed was as sure of my shaky belief as Angela was of her faith in Christ. But a decision like your faith is an emotional one, not a logical one.

I made the leap, and we were married in the Lutheran church. It was the right decision for me."

—Robert, age 31

The Least You Need to Know

➤ If you get married in the Catholic Church, you will need certain papers and premarital counseling. Interfaith marriages require special dispensation from priests.

➤ A Roman Catholic wedding may be celebrated with or without a Mass. Regardless, the ceremony follows a set ritual.

➤ A Greek Orthodox wedding includes a betrothal ceremony, crowns, and other rituals.

➤ A Protestant wedding liturgy can usually be adapted to suit an interfaith wedding and to accommodate two officiating clergy, a Protestant and a non-Protestant.

Going to the ~~Church/Temple/~~ ~~Chapel~~ Building and We're Gonna Get Married

In This Chapter

➤ Chinese wedding ceremonies

➤ Hindu marriage rituals

➤ Japanese nuptials

➤ Mormon marriages

➤ Muslim weddings

➤ Unitarian wedding ceremonies

➤ Ecumenical unions

A lot of people complain about life in a mobile society, but at least one group—religion historians—says it isn't all bad.

"Fifty years ago, whatever religion your parents were, you were," says Martin Marty, author of *Modern American Religion* (University of Chicago Press, 1996). "Today, with emigration, intermarriage, and geographic mobility, you're much freer to shop."

To help make your "shopping" easier, this chapter explores Chinese, Hindu, Japanese, Mormon, Muslim, and Unitarian wedding customs. Together, you and your honey can decide which traditions best reflect your unique religious feelings. The chapter concludes with a section on ecumenical unions and writing your own vows to help you make your special day even more personal.

Chinese Wedding Ceremonies

Today, most Chinese weddings in North America incorporate Western influences, with brides wearing white wedding gowns. However, some brides do wear the traditional *chiansam*. If there is a church ceremony, it's likely to be Protestant or Catholic (see Chapter 14, "Christian Wedding Ceremonies"). Traditional Chinese elements might be blended into the celebration. The tea ceremony is the most popular tradition.

Learn the Lingo

The **chiansam** is an Asian woman's form-fitting outfit with high slits up the sides of skirt.

Did You Know?

Red is the traditional good-luck color for Chinese people.

If included in the wedding, the tea ceremony is most likely to take place after the church service. The ritual follows these general guidelines:

➤ The bride and groom show their respect to their elders.

➤ Tea may be served to just the groom's parents or to both sets of parents.

➤ The bride and groom kneel together and thank heaven and earth.

➤ The bride kowtows (bows) to the groom's parents (and often her own).

➤ The groom greets the bride's parents without kowtowing.

➤ The bride then serves tea to the groom's parents. In return, the groom's parents give the bride an expensive gift, often jewelry, as a symbol of acceptance into the family.

➤ The bride next bows to the groom's siblings, starting with the eldest brother and his wife.

➤ The bride pours tea for them, and they present her with gifts such as jewelry or money in a red envelope.

Chinese-American weddings may also include the 12-course Chinese banquet, which is a very good reason to consider having a Chinese-style wedding if your honey is so inclined. (And please invite me!)

Hindu Wedding Ceremonies

Hindu wedding ceremonies vary greatly depending on geographical location, family customs, and personal taste. Even within India, there are differences in the clothes, ornaments, rituals, food, and the length of the wedding celebration, which in some cases can last for several days.

Interfaith Hindu weddings that incorporate both religions often have two different ceremonies telescoped into a one-day celebration. Since there are many variations in Hindu weddings, the bride and groom select the traditional elements that hold the most meaning for them.

There are many rituals that take place before and after the actual wedding ceremony. Here are some of the most important rituals to consider adapting to your own interfaith Hindu wedding ceremony:

➤ At the wedding ceremony, there could be a sacrificial pit where a holy fire is lit. A priest will officiate.

➤ At some point during the ceremony, the couple may circle the holy fire, chanting and throwing in offerings such as rice. Most often, the fire is circled seven times.

➤ The bride and groom may exchange garlands of fresh flowers, placing them around each other's neck.

➤ The father of the bride offers her hand in marriage to the deities and then to the groom, with the groom assuring him that he will take care of her.

➤ An important part of the ceremony is "tying the knot," when the groom ties a gold necklace around the bride's neck.

➤ During the *saptapadi* portion of the ceremony, the bride and groom take seven steps together toward a long and happy marriage; with each step, the couple prays for different blessings including wealth, happiness, strength, and devotion.

Did You Know?

In traditional Hindu weddings, an auspicious date and time for the marriage ceremony would be chosen based on astrological charts.

Don't Go There

Americans pride themselves on their informality, but people from most other places in the world do not see this as a virtue. Instead, informality often equals disrespect. Younger people should be especially careful to address older people by their titles or as custom dictates, especially during an emotionally charged event such as a wedding.

➤ At some point during the ceremony, the bride may stand on a stone (representing firmness and stability) to signify loyalty and faithfulness in the marriage.

Japanese Wedding Ceremonies

As with Chinese weddings, in North America, most Japanese weddings follow Western traditions. The bride wears a formal white wedding dress; the groom wears a dark suit or a tuxedo. The religious services are usually Protestant-based and are often held in churches, catering halls, restaurants, and hotels.

Traditionally, Japanese give money rather than objects as wedding gifts. The money is placed in a special envelope decorated with a gold cord tied with a special knot. The size of the gift depends on the guest's relationship to the couple: The closer the relationship, the larger the gift. Traditionally, guests receive a gift as well as give one.

Mormon Wedding Ceremonies

The following letter was passed on by a friend. Is the couple's experience similar to your own?

> "Julie was the only member of her family who joined the Mormon Church. Our decision to get married in a Mormon temple created an awkward situation for everyone involved. Mormon temples can only be entered by church members in good standing since they are considered sacred. Therefore, Julie's family would not be able to see the ceremony.
>
> There were definitely some very understandable grumblings from members of Julie's family. After all, Julie is the only daughter in her family. Still, her parents tried to be supportive, and they made the trek from Wisconsin to Salt Lake City, Utah.
>
> My family and I cared about how Julie's parents would feel. My mother was especially determined to make the event as pleasant as possible for Julie's family, despite the odds. The ceremony went as well as could have been expected, but I was worried after. I wondered what Julie's parents were thinking and if they were going to harbor any resentment against us for deciding to get married in the Mormon temple.
>
> Despite the awkwardness of that day, the relationship between my in-laws and me has grown. I remember shaking in my boots when I asked Julie's father for her hand in marriage, and I don't shake half as much now as I did then when I talk to him. I figure that this is mainly due to attempts on either side to make it work.
>
> Julie's parents have tried hard to accept me and my different religious views. From my perspective, things have turned out positively for two reasons. First, we have tried to establish bonds through common interests. Second, and probably more important, Julie's parents have been understanding and tolerant."
>
> —Scott, age 31

There are two different Mormon wedding ceremonies: the *temple ceremony* and the *chapel ceremony.*

Mormon Temple Ceremony

Performed by a temple official, the temple ceremony is "reserved for active members of the Mormon Church who adhere to certain standards," says Bishop Glenn Pruden of the Mormon Church in Hamilton, Ontario.

Mormons are not allowed to discuss the temple ceremony with non-Church members, so if you are considering this type of wedding ceremony, check with your local Mormon temple to get the particulars.

Mormon Chapel Ceremony

The chapel service, however, is open. Anyone, not just Mormons, can attend. It is very similar to a Protestant wedding service but is shorter and simpler, often lasting only 15 minutes. The bride would most likely wear a formal white wedding gown, and the groom a suit or tuxedo. The ceremony follows these general guidelines:

➤ The guests enter the chapel and are seated.

➤ The wedding party walks down the aisle to the strains of solemn organ music.

➤ The service, led by the bishop of the *ward*, opens with a prayer. This is followed by music and the bishop's speech about the holiness of marriage.

➤ The bride and groom exchange vows and rings and sign the register.

➤ The wedding party exits and greets their guests at the door.

Learn the Lingo

The Mormon **ward** is the congregants, similar to a Protestant, Jewish, or Catholic congregation.

Muslim Wedding Ceremonies

Since followers of Islam come from all different cultures, the wedding ceremony varies from place to place. Here's the basic ground rule: Muslim women must marry Muslim men; Muslim men can marry non-Muslim women, but their children must be raised Muslim.

Before the wedding ...

➤ The offer of marriage comes from the female, relayed to her sweetheart by her father or another male relative.

➤ The couple must agree to marry of their own free will.

➤ If he accepts the marriage offer, the groom gives his bride-to-be a substantial gift, called a *mahr.* The gift can be a home, property, or school tuition, for example.

During the wedding …

➤ Any Muslim who understands the wedding traditions can perform the ceremony, although many mosques have marriage officers who fulfill this function.

➤ The actual ceremony is very short and simple, lasting about five minutes.

➤ Men and women are separated at a Muslim wedding—including the bride and groom.

➤ As a result, the bride is not present at the actual ceremony but is in a different area with the other women. She has a male representative standing in for her.

As you learned in previous chapters, traditional followers of Islam are usually not receptive to intermarriage. Be sure you understand the Muslim traditions completely before you decide on intermarriage.

Unitarian Wedding Ceremonies

What about lovers of different religious backgrounds who find it difficult to accommodate the needs of all the traditions? Instead of foregoing a church ceremony altogether or accepting all the customs and formal rituals of one partner's religion, you may want to consider looking into the Unitarian Church.

Did You Know?

In the United States, Thomas Jefferson, Benjamin Franklin, and John Adams were all Unitarians. Members reject the Trinity concept in favor of monotheism, in which God is considered one entity, hence the name "Unitarian."

Unitarian Universalists believe in an individual ethical value system rather than ritualistic formalities and dogma. Since personal choice in spiritual matters and ceremonies is central to the religion, Unitarian ministers are free to adapt the form and content of ceremonies to incorporate words and music that are important to the couple getting married.

Unitarian ministers regularly conduct marriage ceremonies in which one or both of the parties are from mixed-faith backgrounds.

The minister and the couple work together to design an individualized wedding ceremony that also incorporates any legal requirement to register the marriage. The wedding can be tailored to reflect the philosophical views of the couple. To this end, the wedding ceremony can include meaningful quotations, poems, or personal pledges, for instance. Where the law allows, the wedding service can take place anywhere.

Ecumenical Wedding Ceremonies

But what happens if you want to accommodate both faiths at the wedding ceremony? An increasing number of interfaith couples are choosing to have an *ecumenical* wedding ceremony with a representative from the bride's religion and one from the groom's religion co-officiating.

In most cases, these weddings are very inspirational because they demonstrate the mutual respect both families have for each other and their backgrounds.

With some solid planning, real consideration, and a dollop of luck, you may be able to satisfy everyone and have it your way as well, as the following anecdote shows.

In an ecumenical wedding of a Jewish groom and Lutheran bride, the groom's grandfather asked if the minister could include the Jewish "breaking of the glass" tradition. In addition, the groom wanted something special added to make sure his bride's family wouldn't feel left out. The minister agreed, and the following passage was inserted just before the groom broke the glass:

> "It is said that life as we know it unfolds in a perfect way, yet it is not perfect. What does this mean? One meaning is that there is a perfection to life, even when what we call the imperfect occurs. In the Jewish tradition, this is recognized and symbolized with the breaking of the glass. So now, with the breaking of this glass, we pray that [bride's name] and [groom's name] will always see the beauty of their life together, including the broken glass in their life. Amen."

Learn the Lingo

Ecumenical means "general, universal." Ecumenical wedding ceremonies incorporate traditions from different religions and cultures.

Don't Go There

Many priests and ministers are willing to co-officiate, but Mormons, Muslims, and Orthodox and Conservative Jews are far less likely to cooperate.

Chief Considerations

If you and your sweetheart decide to have an ecumenical wedding ceremony, here are some hints for making it a success:

Family Matters

As you design your ecumenical wedding, try this "homework" from Jewish tradition: Write a marriage contract and find seven readings that express your ideals and hopes for the marriage. You may wish to include the agreement and readings in your ceremony.

1. **Carefully consider the location.** You know the three rules of real estate: location, location, location. The same rules hold for interfaith wedding ceremonies. Some rabbis won't participate in a wedding that takes place in a church, for example. There may also be family tension over the location of the ceremony.

2. **Carefully consider the religious symbols to be used.** Negotiating over which religious symbols and customs to include in your service is a good way to obtain a deeper understanding of each other's values, as well as design a mutually satisfying wedding.

3. **Carefully consider the language.** Specific references to the partner's deity may offend. Jewish families may be upset by references to Christ or the Trinity, for instance.

4. **Carefully consider the people who will officiate.** Be sure you know and trust the religious leaders you have chosen to officiate. You want religious leaders who will do what *you* want, not what *they* want.

5. **Carefully consider communication.** Make your wishes known to the religious leaders who will officiate. One couple I know left everything up to the rabbi and minister. The actual ceremony was beautiful—but not at all what the couple wanted. And whose fault was that? (Hint: Not the rabbi's and minister's ...)

6. **Carefully consider the date.** Remember that Jews don't get married on the Sabbath (Friday night through Saturday day), and Christians don't usually schedule weddings on major holidays. Check the calendar carefully and book your wedding well ahead.

Over the Edge

While we're on the theme of consideration, consider staying within the bounds of convention. If your wedding is too close to the fringe, the odds are good that you'll offend some family and guests, as the following story shows:

"Stephan and I were starry-eyed idealists. To us it was spirituality, not religion, that was of ultimate importance in life. There was one God, we believed, and many ways to worship that sacred mystery. To that end, we felt free to select from any and all traditions in creating our wedding ritual. Together, we fashioned a wedding ceremony that would embody our eclectic approach. In the end, our marriage moved many people with its brave and pioneering spirit, but it also offended others with its nonconformity. The people we offended never forgave the slight."

—Joanne, age 48

The story of a marriage only begins at the wedding and hopefully travels far beyond it. But a couple's intentions set so much in motion on their wedding day! The elements and mood you choose for your ritual—such as inclusiveness, prayer, or honor for one another's family and traditions—are important because they will continue to reverberate throughout your married life.

A wedding is a hinge in time when it's possible to make—or break—a lifelong family relationship. A successful interfaith wedding is the beginning of a remarkable journey in which partners learn how to negotiate the peculiar challenges of the interfaith terrain. Whether or not you are a religious person, interfaith marriage presents an ongoing challenge in remaining true to your individual self and roots while simultaneously learning to build the bridges of tolerance and understanding.

The Least You Need to Know

➤ Today, most Chinese and Japanese weddings in North America incorporate Western influences, with Protestant or Catholic services.

➤ Hindu and Muslim wedding ceremonies vary greatly depending on geographical location, family customs, and personal taste.

➤ There are two different Mormon wedding ceremonies: the temple ceremony (for active church members) and the chapel ceremony (similar to a Protestant wedding service).

➤ Unitarian churches have long been a haven for interfaith weddings.

➤ Many interfaith couples have an ecumenical wedding ceremony with a representative from the bride's religion and one from the groom's religion co-officiating.

➤ With interfaith marriages, carefully consider the location, religious symbols, language, officiants, communication, and date.

Design Your Own Wedding Vows

The groom's tux can be a little tight in the shoulders, the bride's gown can sag a bit at the hem, but the wedding vows have to fit perfectly. It can be especially difficult to get the right fit when it comes to interfaith wedding vows, however. The Christian vows may seem too, well, *Christian,* and the Jewish vows just too *Jewish.* And we haven't even considered other religions.

The solution? Design your own vows. Tailor your sentiments and speech to express the unique love you and your sweetie share and your feelings about your individual and shared religious faith.

In Chapter 15, "Going to the ~~Church/Temple/Chapel~~ Building and We're Gonna Get Married," you learned about creating an ecumenical wedding ceremony. In this chapter, I'll provide you with hints, templates, and model vows to make it easier to create the heart of your wedding, whether it's a religious ceremony, an ecumenical affair, or a civil service. You'll be able to include just the right amount of religion, emotion, and heritage to make your wedding ceremony the day of your dreams.

Religion-Free Zone

If you and your sweetheart have decided to steer clear of all religious references in your wedding ceremony, you'll probably want to start by exploring a civil ceremony. Here are two examples of vows that might be exchanged in a civil ceremony:

Did You Know?

Should your vows be short or long? Use the models here as guidelines. Figure on speaking no more than three minutes. It's a wedding, not a political rally.

"[Name], I take you to be my lawfully wedded [husband/wife]. Before these witnesses I vow to love you and care for you as long as we both shall live.

I take you, with all your faults and your strengths, as I offer myself to you with my faults and my strengths. I will help you when you need help, and will turn to you when I need help. I choose you as the person with whom I will spend my life."

In the following sections, you'll see how several couples expanded this basic nonreligious vow to make it their own. Notice how each of the vows expresses deep love and commitment—yet is unmistakably personal and unique.

Light of My Life

The following vow expresses a deep and abiding love. Perhaps its sentiments suit your feelings as well.

Don't Go There

Even if you're Billy Crystal, Steve Martin, or Jay Leno, your wedding isn't the time for humor. Your wedding is a solemn, important day, especially with the added strain of interfaith conflicts. Be serious during the ceremony; save the humor for the best man's toast.

"As you have been by my side through my darkest hours, so I will be a light in your life. I will listen to your concerns and not judge. I will join you in laughter and support you in tears. As you have cared for me in times of illness, so I will keep you sheltered when storms arise. I will comfort and console you. I will be the rock that you stand on, the staff that you lean on, and the wings that allow you to fly. As you have inspired me to follow my dreams, so I will help you achieve your goals. I will encourage you in your endeavors and nourish your spirit as you walk through life. As you have loved me, so I will love you. Above all else, I will allow you to be you."

Wings and Roots

Although the following vow is brief, it nonetheless carries some heartfelt emotion and memorable lines. Each person can say these lines, or they can repeat them together with prompting from the officiant.

> "We will forever value each another, share our most private thoughts, and love each other. We will live each day as if our last, vowing never to go to bed angry. If sorrow enters our life, we pledge to one another that together we will see things through. As we grow old, we will look into each other's eyes and know that with each breath we take, our love will grow. These are the words I feel and speak from my heart."

My Love Grows Daily

I like the following statement because of its simple, straightforward declaration of love and devotion.

> "I love you.
>
> I pledge to grow in my love for you.
>
> I pledge to nurture our love for it is loving you that nurtures my soul.
>
> I pledge to share our love together as one.
>
> I love you because you are the only one for me.
>
> To know you is to know love—and through you, know true love.
>
> I love you because you complete me.
>
> I cannot know union without you—for it is by joining you that I learn about love's union and where it comes from.
>
> I see your love for me in your eyes. It shows me what true love is.
>
> I promise to support your growth in all ways.
>
> I promise to honor you by being open to all the expressions of your inner self.
>
> Above all, I promise to be true to you and true to myself so that we may grow in our love that joins us as one.
>
> Let us fly together in harmony our whole lives long. May gentle winds carry us all the way to heaven."

Did You Know?

Should you read your vows or memorize them? Memorizing them is unquestionably more effective, but be sure to have a copy on hand if you freeze at the last minute.

Religious, but Personal

Your vows can speak to your individual faiths as well as your shared beliefs. Consider including a religious element in your vows if you or your honey is devout. This is especially important in a civil wedding ceremony, so neither partner feels cheated out of the wedding vows long dreamed.

You may also want to include a reference to religion in the vows if any parents or other important relatives are religious. The reference doesn't have to be anything overt; a subtle allusion will often be enough to forestall trouble down the road. Why? It indicates a willingness to maintain traditions.

Of course, you would never throw in a reference to the Supreme Deity to shut up meddlesome Aunt Edna or placate rich Uncle Herman. Such a tactic is likely to backfire—big time. Instead, work with your honey to decide what role religion will play in your lives together and then tailor your wedding vows to reflect your shared beliefs.

Below are some ways that different interfaith couples resolved the issue to their satisfaction. See which vows come closest to expressing your religious feelings.

My One True Love

The following vow was written by a bride for her groom. You can easily adapt it by presenting the same sentiments from the groom's point of view. Notice the subtle references to faith.

> "I accept you to be my husband, secure in knowledge that you will be my friend, my faithful partner in life, and my one true love. On our wedding day, I give to you in the presence of all those in attendance my promise to stay by your side as your wife in sickness and in health, in joy and in sorrow, as our faith and love carries us through good times and bad.
>
> I promise to love you, comfort you in times of distress, laugh with you and cry with you, grow with you in mind, worship with you, always be open and honest with you, and cherish you for as long as we both shall live."

Walk with God

The following vow links a deep and abiding religious faith to marriage.

> "I take you, [beloved's name] to be my wife [or husband]. I will speak the truth to you in love. I will encourage you and strengthen you in your walk with God. I will not let the sun go down on my anger; instead, I will be gracious, tenderhearted, and forgiving even as God has forgiven me. I will be peaceful, content and joyful in every situation we encounter knowing that God is at work."

Act of Faith

Where do you get a marriage license? The rules vary from state to state. In New York, for example, the couple must apply in person for a marriage license to any town or city clerk in the state. The application for a license must be signed by both the bride and groom in the presence of the town or city clerk. Although the marriage license is issued immediately, the marriage ceremony may not take place within 24 hours from the time that the license was issued. In New York, the marriage license is valid for 60 days and costs $30 in New York City, $25 outside the city.

Heaven Sent

The vow printed below has a reference to God at the very beginning:

> "I prayed to God for a companion who could understand me and accept me as I am and for a special friend who would share laughter and tears—and God sent you.

> [Beloved's name], I promise to love you with all my heart, mind, strength, and faith. I promise to be faithful, now and forever. I also promise to respect your faith even as I follow my own.

> I will be there when your strength fails you, and may my strength always be there for you. Side by side, step by step, may our great journey together begin, here now from this day forward.

> I gladly accept the obligations that go along with this pledge. With continued love, friendship, trust and communication, I, [name], take joy today in committing my life to yours."

God's Blessing

The following vow places God at the center:

> "I [groom's or bride's name] do take thee [groom's or bride's name] to be my lawfully wedded wife, to honor, respect and to hold thy needs before mine own, to keep you as my one true love as God has ordained, for all of my life. This day I affirm before God and all witnesses, my undying loyalty and pledge to forsake

all others for you. To uphold in sickness and health to be your best friend, sharing in our happiness and sorrow, to always have compassion and love without reservation or reward. Though life may be rich or poor, to you alone will I hold. To you this day before God I pledge this vow to you."

Speaker for the House

Not only can you individualize what you and your beloved say to each other, but you can also tailor what your officant and other speakers say during the ceremony. Follow these steps to design an interfaith ceremony:

1. Check with the minister, priest, rabbi, or justice of the peace to see if he or she has any pre-made ceremonies that suit your needs.

2. If so, be sure to read the speech carefully to make sure that it captures the exact degree of faith that you and your beloved follow.

3. If not, see if the officiant is willing to have you script the ceremony. If not, find someone who will work with you.

4. Make your wishes *very* clear so all participants understand where you and your honey stand on the religious issue and agree to abide by your desires.

5. To make sure that every part of your wedding ceremony fits together smoothly, be sure to read the vows and speeches well ahead of the blessed day. See that everyone is expressing the same sentiments in the same tone. Reading through everyone's speeches can also help prevent embarrassing gaffes.

Act of Faith

The following religious pledge is suitable for a couple renewing their vows: "I call upon those here present to witness that I renew the gift of myself to you, which I first made, when God bound us together on our wedding day. I renew my loving promise to you. I promise to be true to you in good times and in bad, in sickness and in health. I will love you and honor you, all the days of my life. I am sorry for any want of love, any selfishness, any times I have sinned against our marriage. I promise for the time to come to give myself in love, to both you and our children, trusting in God, who lives in our home."

The Spirit of the Native Americans

Here's a beautiful Native American blessing that you may wish to make part of your wedding ceremony. It's infused with spirituality but doesn't contain any overtly religious references. Your maid of honor, best man, or religious officiant can read it to you and your guests:

> "Now you will feel no rain, for each of you will be shelter for the other.
>
> Now you will feel no cold, for each of you will be warmth to the other.
>
> Now there will be no loneliness, for each of you will be companion to the other.
>
> Now you are two persons, but there is only one life before you.
>
> May beauty surround you both in the journey ahead and through all the years,
>
> May happiness be your companion and your days together be good and long upon the earth."

The speaker may wish to build on the vow with advice such as this:

> "Treat yourselves and each other with respect, and remind yourselves often of what brought you together. Give the highest priority to the tenderness, gentleness, and kindness that your connection deserves. When frustration, difficulty, and fear assail your relationship—as they threaten all relationships at one time or another—remember to focus on what is right between you, not only the part that seems wrong. In this way, you can ride out the storms when clouds hide the face of the sun in your lives. Remember that even if you lose sight of the sun for a moment, it is still there. If each of you takes responsibility for the quality of your life together, it will be marked by abundance and delight."

Did You Know?

The most popular months for Jewish weddings are April, June, October, and December. Keep this in mind as you plan your wedding.

Don't Go There

What should you do if your honey won't write his/her vows? First figure out why the reluctance: Does your honey have unresolved feelings about personal vows and prefers a traditional religious service? Does your honey hate to write? Does your honey manage time badly? Worst of all, has your honey decided that marriage with you isn't in the cards? Resolve the issue before you go any further.

Rock of Ages

The speech below has a religious component, but it's general rather than faith-specific. Perhaps it will be right for your interfaith ceremony.

"Above you are the stars, below you are the stones, as time doth pass, remember ...

Like a stone should your love be firm; like a star should your love be constant.

Let the powers of the mind and of the intellect guide you in your marriage, let the strength of your wills bind you together, let the power of love and desire make you happy, and the strength of your dedication make you inseparable.

Be close, but not too close. Possess one another, yet be understanding.

Have patience with one another, for storms will come, but they will pass quickly. Be free in giving affection and warmth.

Have no fear, for God is with you always."

The Couple's Prayer

Consider whether "The Couple's Prayer" melds your religious traditions and beliefs. Remember, you can adapt this speech, as well as any of the texts presented in this chapter, to your faith and specific family situation.

"Lord, they stand before you happy and hopeful, yet also somewhat frightened. We believe that You brought them together and that You are with them now. We also know that the road ahead will have both good times and hard times. We ask now that You bless them and be with them in the following days.

Help them to live up to the vows they made to each other today. Keep their love fresh, alive, and growing. Remind them always to approach each other with gentleness and patience. Teach them how to communicate and trust more completely. Never let them take one another for granted.

Guide them as we strive to hear You speaking to them through their religious traditions. Make them faithful to Yourself, as well as to each other. May their life together be a sign to others that people can live together in peace in spite of differences.

Make their home a place of peace and growth where people are always welcome. Help them reach out to others to share the love and blessings they themselves have experienced.

If You bless them with children, make them good and loving parents. Help them always to remember that they are first of all Your children. Guide them as they try to raise their children to be full and complete human beings aware of Your love, and help them to step aside when it is time to let go.

Thank you for their family and friends, both those present and those unable to be with us today. Their love and friendship have led them to be what they are today. May their celebration strengthen their awareness of Your love and their commitment to love others. Amen."

Smooth Sailing on the Sea of Married Life

The following ceremony strikes a good compromise in many ways. See if it expresses your sentiments. If so, you may wish to share it with your justice of the peace or other officant and adapt it to your individual needs.

Officiant: This marriage is an event in the lifetime of a love. Neither I, nor all society, can join these two lovers today. Only they can do what they have chosen. They are joining themselves, each to the other. As they find union with one another, they proclaim that union today and pledge its future. By our participation in this celebration, we do but recognize and honor their intention to dwell together as husband and wife.

Groom: I promise you [bride's name], that I will be your loving and loyal husband from now on. I will share with you all of life's joy and sorrow, pleasure and pain, until death parts us.

Bride: I promise you [groom's name], that I will be your loving and loyal wife from now on. I will share with you all of life's joy and sorrow, pleasure and pain, until death parts us.

Officiant: Each of you has rings for each other. Would you exchange them?

As they are exchanging rings, the Officant says:

As a ceaseless reminder of this hour, and of the promise you have made to each other, these rings speak of the oneness you now experience as husband and wife.

Now you will feel no rain, for each of you will be shelter to the other.

Now you will feel no cold, for each of you will be warmth to the other.

Now you will feel no loneliness, for each of you will be a companion to the other.

Now you are two bodies, but there is only one life before you.

Go now to your dwelling place, to enter the days of your life together.

And may your days be good, and long upon the earth.

Because they have so affirmed, in love and knowledge of the other, so also do I declare that [groom's name] and [bride's name] are now husband and wife.

Act of Faith

According to law, there's no specific marriage ceremony required except that the parties must state in the presence of an authorized member of the clergy or public official and at least one other witness that they take each other as husband and wife. Even though the form of the ceremony isn't proscribed by law, the officant is. To be valid, a marriage ceremony must be performed by someone sanctioned by law. Mayors, city clerks, justices, judges, and ordained members of the clergy can all perform weddings. Be careful of ship's captains; in New York state, for example, they're not allowed to perform weddings.

Readings

In addition to your vows and the officiant's speech, many weddings include readings. Select the passages that express your feelings for each other, marriage, and your faith. Here are some popular religious readings.

Religious Passages

You may wish to combine some of the shorter passages into one reading or invite several different people to read short passages each.

➤ Braham-Sutra. *When the one man loves the one woman and the one woman loves the one man, the very angels desert heaven and sit in that hour and sing for joy.*

➤ Corinthians 13:4–7. *Love is patient; love is kind and envies no one. Love is never boastful, nor conceited, nor rude; never selfish, not quick to take offense. Love keeps no score of wrongs; does not gloat over other men's sins, but delights in the truth. There is nothing love can not face; there is no limit to its faith, its hope, and its endurance.*

➤ Genesis 1:28. *And God blessed them, and God said unto them, Be fruitful, and multiply, and replenish the earth, and subdue it.*

➤ Genesis 2:18–24. *And the Lord God said, It is not good that the man should be alone; I will make him a helpmate for him. And out of the group, the Lord God formed every beast in the field, and every fowl of the air; and brought them unto Adam to see what he would call them: and whatsoever Adam called every living creature, that was the name thereof. And Adam gave names to all the cattle, and to the fowl of the air, and to every beast of the field; but for Adam there was not found a helpmate for him. And the Lord caused a deep sleep to fall upon Adam, and he slept: and he took one of his ribs, and closed up the flesh instead thereof; and the rib, which the Lord God has taken from the man, made he a woman, and brought her unto the man. And Adam said, This is now bone of my bones, and the flesh of my flesh; she shall be called Woman, because she was taken out of Man. Therefore shall a man leave his father and his mother, and shall cleave unto his wife: and they shall be one flesh.*

➤ I Ching. *When two people are as one in their inmost hearts, they shatter even the strength of iron or of bronze.*

➤ John 15:9–12. *As the Father hath loved me, so have I loved you: continue ye in my love. If ye keep my commandments, and abide in His love; even as I have kept my Father's commandments, and abide in his love. These things have I spoken unto you, that my joy might remain in you, and that your joy might be full. This is my commandment: That ye love one another as I have loved you.*

➤ Mark 10:6–9. *From the beginning of creation God made them male and female. For this cause shall a man leave his father and mother, and cleave to his wife; and they shall be one flesh: so then they are no more twain, but one flesh. What therefore God hath joined together, let no man put asunder.*

➤ Psalm 128:1–4. *Blessed is every one that feareth the Lord; that walketh in his ways. For thou shalt eat the labor of thine hands; happy shalt thou be, and it shall be well with thee. Thy wife shall be as a fruitful vine by the sides of thine house, thy children like olive plants round about thy table. Behold, that thus shall the man be blessed that feareth the Lord.*

➤ Talmud (Ketubot 8). *Blessed art thou, O Lord, King of the Universe, who created mirth and joy, bridegroom and bride, gladness, jubilation, dancing, and delight, love and brotherhood, peace and fellowship. Quickly, O Lord our God, may the sound of mirth and joy be*

Don't Go There

Writing wedding vows isn't something we do hidden in the bathroom, like flossing or plucking stray hairs. Instead, sit down with your sweetie and hammer your vows out together—as a couple. You should still floss and pluck alone, however.

heard in the streets of Judah and Jerusalem, the voice of bridegroom and bride, jubilant voices of bridegrooms from their canopies and youths from the feasts of song. Blessed art thou, O Lord, who makes the bridegroom rejoice with the bride.

Literary Passages

And some words of wisdom from two of our greatest writers.

William Shakespeare

"Love is not love
Which alters when it alteration finds,
Or bends with the remover to remove.
O, no! It is an ever-fixed mark,
That looks on tempests and is never shaken.
It is the star to every wandering bark,
whose worth's unknown, although his height be taken."

George Eliot

"What greater thing is there for two human souls than to feel that they are joined for life, to strengthen each other in all labor, to rest on each other in sorrow, to minister to each other in all pain, to be with each other in silent unspeakable memories at the moment of the last parting?"

Did You Know?

Does the thought of delivering your vows make you quake in terror? If so, relax. Then check out my *Complete Idiot's Guide to Public Speaking.* Everything you need to know about writing and delivering great speeches—for all occasions—is here.

The Art of Marriage

Perhaps you've heard the following reading, "The Art of Marriage." It's very popular for its homey and accessible message.

"The little things are the big things.

It is never being too old to hold hands.

It is remembering to say "I love you" at least once a day.

It is never going to sleep angry.

It is at no time taking the other for granted; the courtship should not end with the honeymoon; it should continue through all the years.

It is having a mutual sense of values and common objectives.

It is standing together facing the world.

It is forming a circle of love that gathers the whole family.

It is doing things for each other, not in the attitude of duty or sacrifice, but in the spirit of joy.

It is speaking words of appreciation and demonstrating gratitude in thoughtful ways.

It is not expecting the husband to wear a halo or the wife to have wings of an angel.

It is not looking for perfection in each other.

It is cultivating flexibility, patience, understanding, and a sense of humor.

It is having the capacity to forgive and forget.

It is giving each other an atmosphere in which each can grow.

It is finding room for the things of the spirit.

It is a common search for the good and the beautiful.

It is establishing a relationship in which the independence is equal, dependence is mutual, and the obligation is reciprocal.

It is not only marrying the right partner, it is *being* the right partner."

Write This Way

Now comes the moment of truth: actually sitting down and writing your vows. Buck up: it's really not that hard. Start by saying what's in your heart of hearts.

You can make your vows extra special by including specific references to your partner's fine qualities. Here are some qualities to consider:

➤ reliability

➤ values

➤ conduct

➤ kindness

➤ decency

➤ dedication

➤ honesty

➤ ethics

➤ sense of humor

➤ consideration

➤ determination

➤ caring

Don't Go There

In your wedding vows, be specific about your lover, but never embarrassing. Save the personal details, inside jokes, and naughty bits for the breakfast table and bedroom.

You may also wish to use old-fashioned language to give your vows a more formal flavor. The following chart shows some possibilities.

Standard Diction	Old-Fashioned Diction
you	thee, thou
your	thine
shall	shalt
have	hath
are	art
you	ye
fear	fearest (etc.)

The following pair of vows are beautiful for the depth of their emotion and sincerity. See how this bride and groom individualized their vows, and decide if this approach works for you.

Don't Go There

NEVER write your honey's vows for him/her. First, you can't presume to know what your honey feels in his or her heart. Second, what's next? You do all the household chores and work full time? I don't think so!

Wife's vow:

[Groom's name], since we have been together, you have provided me with strength, security, confidence, honesty, love, and guidance. Where there has been cold, you have brought warmth; where my life was dark, you have brought light. In my darkest trouble, in my coldest silence, I looked for you and you were there. You are truly my knight in shining armor. You may not realize it, but you have helped me and saved me in so many ways and I love you for that. I am honored that you will have me as your wife and I am proud to have you as my husband.

I believe that we were meant to be together from the start. I will always love you with all my heart.

Groom's vow:

[Bride's name], you are a star from the heavens to love, honor, and cherish, for all the days of my life. You are my pearl of choice, my strength at my side.

My love for you will never fade.

You are my love, my life, my wife.

May God bless our marriage in peace and happiness for all time.

But perhaps the following passage, when it comes to interfaith marriages, says it all:

> The secret of love and marriage is similar to that of religion itself. It is the emergence of the larger self. It is the finding of one's life by losing it. Such is the privilege of husband and wife—to be each himself, herself, and yet another; to face the world strong, with the courage of two.

> To make this relationship work, therefore, takes more than love.

> It takes trust, to know in your hearts that you want only the best for each other.

> It takes dedication, to stay open to one another, to learn and grow, even when it is difficult to do so.

> And it takes faith, to go forward together without knowing what the future holds for you both.

> While love is our natural state of being, these other qualities are not as easy to come by. They are not a destination, but a journey.

> The true art of married life is this spiritual journey. It is a mutual enrichment, a give-and-take between two personalities which diminishes neither, but enhances both.

The Least You Need to Know

➤ Interfaith couples should consider writing their own vows to make sure they clearly express their individual and shared religious faith.

➤ The vows can be nonreligious pledges or religious promises.

➤ Consider selecting religious or secular readings to add to your wedding ceremony.

➤ Use the sample wedding ceremonies and vows as you create your own.

➤ You *can* have the interfaith wedding ceremony you want—but only you and your sweetheart can make it happen.

Chapter 17

All in the Family—But Whose? The Issue of Conversion

> ### In This Chapter
>
> ➤ Events that spark religious conversion
>
> ➤ What conversion means to different faiths
>
> ➤ Converting to Christianity
>
> ➤ Converting to Judaism
>
> ➤ Weighing a possible religious conversion

Robert Benchley, the American humorist and critic, took a course in international law while he was a student at Harvard University. On the final exam, Benchley was asked to discuss the arbitration of an international fishing dispute between the United States and Great Britain. He was supposed to pay special attention to hatcheries, protocol, and dragnet and trawl procedures.

Benchley, who was not prepared for the exam, began his essay by announcing that he knew absolutely nothing about the point of view of the United States with respect to any international fishing controversy; he also confessed that he did not know where Great Britain stood on the issue. "Therefore," Benchley asserted in the introduction to his essay, "I shall discuss the question from the point of view of the fish."

Like Benchley, people who consider religious conversion have learned to look at an issue from another point of view. In this chapter, you'll explore all facets of the conversion issue to decide whether you want to convert to your honey's religion. This is a very difficult and emotional issue for most people since it involves their heritage and culture as well as their spiritual beliefs.

"Whither Thou Goest, I Will Go"

The following letter came from my online mailbag. How close is this couple's experience to your own?

"I had been raised as a Protestant; Sanjay was Hindu. When we had to decide where to get married, the religious difference started to come to the surface. Sanjay felt that his parents wouldn't come to the wedding if it was in a church. Since I knew my parents would come to my wedding no matter where it was, I felt that I should agree to marry in Sanjay's temple. I spoke with my beloved pastor to see if he would perform a joint ceremony, and he flat-out refused. I was deeply shaken by this.

Sanjay and I had also started to have discussions about our future children—would we raise them as Christians or Hindus? At one point, Sanjay suggested that any girls could be raised Christian and any boys raised as Hindus. After mulling that over for quite a while, I found it more and more disturbing. It just didn't sound like a family to me with two factions going their separate ways.

After much soul-searching and a great deal of reading about Hinduism, I decided to convert. Through the years, there have been differences, of course. But with love, you learn to compromise. I found that, although I practiced Hinduism, it was impossible for me to give up Christmas. So each year we had a tree and decorations.

Sanjay and I recently renewed our wedding vows while on a cruise and rededicated ourselves to each other. And the words that always return to me are 'Whither thou goest, I will go.'"

—Carole, age 48

Did You Know?

Converts tend to be better informed and more committed than many who were born into the faith.

More Americans than ever are exploring and experiencing religious conversion. No one knows exactly how many people a year are involved, but most of the major world religions are gaining numbers in America, according to David Barrett of Global Evangelical Movement Research, which supplies demographic statistics to the *Encyclopedia Britannica*.

The United States remains a predominantly Christian country with 200 million people, or 85 percent of the population, claiming Christianity. Still, there were fewer than 1 million Muslims here 20 years ago, and today there are four times as many. There were 200,000 Buddhists then, almost a million now.

These spiritual journeys tend to occur sometime between the age of 18 and 35. Many times they begin with a jolt, such as …

➤ A life-threatening illness.

➤ The death of a loved one.

➤ The loss of a job.

➤ A failed relationship.

➤ A sense that there must be more to life.

➤ A serious interfaith love affair.

Religious inquiry takes a lot of work because …

➤ Long-held beliefs are challenged.

➤ Family and friends are not always supportive.

➤ Changes in old habits and attitudes may be in order.

I've Looked at Life from Both Sides Now

A colleague passed along this story:

> "Emily and I initially met in Massachusetts between my two tours of duty as a missionary for the Church of Jesus Christ of Latter Day Saints (Mormons). She was not a Mormon when we met.
>
> We became friends. Emily, then a Presbyterian, asked me about my beliefs in God. This was the beginning of a long and slow discussion of beliefs that culminated in her receiving Mormon missionaries into her own home in Minnesota. Soon after, she was baptized into the Mormon Church."

When you get engaged to a person of a different faith, someone is likely to ask you if you're interested in converting. Actually, make that *a lot* of somebodies. You're especially likely to get asked about conversion if your honey is very religious and his or her faith doesn't take kindly to people outside the fold. But even if this isn't the case, you can count on being asked the question at least once.

Walk This Way

A man who converted described the experience this way:

> "It's hard to compare religious conversion to anything else. Marriage didn't change me, but this really did. It must be what birth is like. You start fresh, a whole new life."

Before you can decide whether conversion is an option for you or your sweetie, you have to know what "conversion" means. Different religions regard conversion very differently. To Catholics, for example, conversion means accepting a new religion. To Jews, however, conversion means accepting a culture as well as a religion.

Converting to Christianity

I found the following conversion story in my e-mail:

> "My family wasn't much into religion. We celebrated the Jewish holidays, and I attended Hebrew school for a while, but then I dropped out.
>
> After college I dated Michael, a Catholic, who is now my husband. He went to church every Sunday, and I asked if I could tag along. I'd ask him questions, and he'd explain the meaning of things. I began to wonder if there was something in Catholicism for me.
>
> I started taking religious instruction. My family didn't know anything about it, and my first hurdle was telling my father. I was very nervous, but he surprised me. He said, 'I think it's wonderful that you've found faith.'
>
> I thought my grandparents would disown me, but they were great, too. And my mom was fine with it. The one who got upset was my maid of honor at my wedding, who is Jewish. On the night before my wedding, she said I was deserting her and Judaism. I told her I'll always know I'm from the Jewish faith, but I wanted to be part of a religion I feel strongly about.
>
> Entering the Catholic Church was a monumental change. It changed my inner life, my attitude about myself and other people. It teaches that we have to forgive, and sometimes now it feels like my faith is working overtime."
>
> —Debbie, age 34

Family Matters

According to Jewish law, a Jew married to a non-Jew is still considered Jewish. All children of Jewish mothers are considered Jewish as well. The children of a Gentile woman married to a Jew are considered Gentile unless they convert.

Learn the Lingo

Baptism is immersion or sprinkling with water, part of a person's conversion to Christianity.

The central ritual of Christian conversion is *baptism*, immersion or sprinkling with water. This external ritual symbolizes the person's internal acceptance of

Jesus Christ as his or her Redeemer. Christians believe that God, in his grace, chooses to enter your heart through the Holy Spirit to give you this faith. Although nuances vary among denominations, Christians believe that baptism cleanses individuals of sin and gives them a new life, one that will not be ended by death but will continue into eternity.

A non-Christian doesn't have to convert to Christianity in order to participate in much of the life of a Catholic or Protestant church where the spouse is a worshipper. This is not true of all Christian faiths, however. Fundamentalists, for example, place special emphasis on bringing the nonmember into the fold.

Don't Go There

Even today, most Jews view baptism as betrayal. Nearly all would say that it is impossible to be Jewish and Christian at the same time.

Converting to Judaism

A friend shared her experience with religious conversion:

> "I decided to convert from Catholicism to Judaism. My Hebrew name became Ruth, daughter of Israel, and I was reminded of the Biblical movie, *The Story of Ruth,* which I had watched on TV as a young girl. The story seemed so romantic to me.
>
> We were married in a Jewish catering hall complete with its own chapel. It is traditional that a mother who is marrying off her last child is crowned with flowers at the wedding—and since I was an only child, my mother was crowned!
>
> We were blessed with two wonderful sons, Jonathan and Justin, who grew up with Christmas and Hanukkah gifts, Easter baskets and Passover seders. I joked to people that we celebrated every holiday on the calendar! Both boys celebrated their bar mitzvahs and are now 18 and 21. Our differences only added to our delight in each other and brought a richness to our lives."

—Louise, age 52

Converting to Judaism means entering into a covenant between God and the Jewish people. According to the Jewish Bible, God made a convenant with Abraham, father of the Jews, promising to make Abraham's descendants into a great nation. As a sign of this convenant, Abraham *circumcised* himself and all the men and boys in his home.

Learn the Lingo

Circumcision is cutting off the foreskin of the penis.

The following table shows the conversion process to Judaism for men and women.

Converting to Judaism

Gender	Ritual
men	*milah* (circumcision)
	kabbalat mitzvot (acceptance of the commandments)
	tevilah (immersion in the mikvah, a pool of water)
women	*kabbalat mitzvot* (acceptance of the commandments)
	tevilah (immersion in the mikvah, a pool of water)

However, the various branches of Judaism differ greatly in what is meant by a commitment to live a Jewish life and even differ in the conversion process itself. If you think that converting to Judaism is for you, start by finding a rabbi willing to guide you through the process.

Now that you know what's entailed in conversion to Christianity and Judaism, it's time to think about whether or not conversion is an option for you.

Look Before You Leap

Some converts are enthusiastic that they decided to adopt their spouse's religion, believing that it greatly strengthened their marriage. The following respondent falls into this camp:

> "I was born in Peru and raised a Catholic. Nine years ago, I stopped going to church. I always believed in God, but nothing held my attention at services.
>
> We came to this country seven years ago. Not long after, the Mormon elders, the leaders of the Mormon Church, came to my mother's house and invited her to their church. It was something different, and she went. Not long after, she and my sister became Mormons. Last February, my husband and I were baptized Mormons.
>
> My marriage changed a lot after that. My husband and I are more understanding of each other now. And he changed. We're much happier together. I think that's what God wants."

But not all converts feel the same way about their decision, as in Sharda's case:

> "I am a Hindu woman who fell in love with Hasan, a Muslim. Hasan insisted that I convert to Islam at the time of our marriage and that the children be brought up as Muslims. I gave in, but a few years later, Hasan took a second wife, which is allowed under Islamic law. I must accept his second wife because,

if I divorce Hasan, he will get custody of the children. I have lost my religion and my culture and even the intrinsic bond of man and wife."

Should the possibility of an interfaith marriage lead you to think about converting to your partner's religion, consider what will be gained by such a drastic move. Is marriage alone sufficient to motivate a religious conversion?

Trouble in Paradise

I heard the following story from a distant friend:

Krishnan was a very devout Hindu. So the priests at the temple were surprised when he told them he was marrying a Catholic girl. He explained that she wasn't very religious so there would be no conflicts.

In the first years of his marriage, he kept up his religious practices. But gradually he stopped coming to the temple because his wife wanted him home on the weekends. When the children were born, he intended to bring them up as Hindus, but his wife objected, so he gave up this idea to keep his wife happy. To keep peace in the family, Krishnan then converted to Catholicism. To this day he feels sad, guilty, and resentful about his conversion.

> **Family Matters**
>
> Religious differences become most potentially explosive during the wedding and again when children are born.

Here are the three main problems that can arise when one partner converts to make another partner happy or to resolve tension in the relationship:

1. **Resentment.** The partner who converted often resents having had to make the sacrifice.

2. **Loss of identity.** Children may come to see the converted parent as disenfranchised and therefore identify with his or her original religion.

3. **Excessive zeal.** The convert may actually become too religious, making the partner uncomfortable with his or her increased level of belief and observance.

One Size Doesn't Fit All

A marriage counselor I know has seen many interfaith marriages crash on the rock of religion. He assesses, "When the husband and wife don't follow the same religion, the greatest victims are the children. These children who are not able to have any spiritual guidance will have nothing to pass on to their own children. It will lead to more and more unhappy situations."

Don't Go There

In any intermarriages, the non–Muslim spouse must convert to Islam. Keep this in mind if you fall in love with a Muslim.

If we accept what this marriage counselor believes (and I'm not sure that I do), then religious conversion can perhaps "solve" some of the challenges of an interfaith marriage, but only if the convert enters into the tradition wholeheartedly and without reservation. I'll argue that conversion is only a viable option if you are somehow dissatisfied with your own religion or lack thereof. Today, we celebrate individualism, which means that religious conversion is rarely the best option for most people.

Further, conversion doesn't always bring harmony. Most people who marry someone of a different faith find that their life is enriched not by a common religion but rather by love, commitment, respect, caring, and compromise. In many cases, respect for differences in your spouse's belief system is a better way to bridge the differences that interfaith marriages bring than conversion.

The Least You Need to Know

➤ To Catholics, conversion means accepting a new religion.

➤ To Jews, conversion means accepting a culture as well as a religion.

➤ The central ritual of Christian conversion is baptism, immersion or sprinkling with water.

➤ Converting to Judaism varies among the different branches of Judaism, but it usually takes about a year and involves several rituals.

➤ Conversion is a serious life-changing process. If you are converting to please a spouse, consider such a move very carefully.

Chapter 18

Rites and Rights

In This Chapter

➤ Danger signs

➤ The three C's: communicate, compromise, and collect (information)

➤ Pulling together to create a successful interfaith wedding ceremony

➤ What marriage means

➤ Ways to make an interfaith marriage a success

So you're engaged to be married. Congratulations! But your future spouse has a different religious background? Don't despair. Your wedding planning doesn't have to result in conflict between you and your honey or between the families.

This chapter contains some important tips for making both your wedding and your marriage a success. Some of these hints come from friends, acquaintances, and colleagues; the others are from my experience in a long-term, successful interfaith marriage.

First I'll provide some words of wisdom about the wedding, including hot potatoes to watch for—and drop! Then come strategies for encouraging everyone to cooperate to create a successful interfaith wedding ceremony.

I'll help you resolve the crucial issue of what marriage is (and isn't) before the big day to save you a lot of hardship down the road. Next, I'll teach you how to work with your spouse to set and enforce priorities that will help you build a strong, enduring marriage. Finally, we'll discuss the possibility of taking a page from Betty Crocker and using family meals to build unity and cohesion.

One Potato, Two Potatoes

How can you tell if you and your spouse are running into the wedding bell blues as you plan your nuptials? Here are some hot potatoes to be on the lookout for ... and drop!

1. **Making what other people think and feel more important than what you think and feel.** Danger bells should ring if you're letting parents, consultants, clergy, vendors, friends, your favorite wedding Web site, and even your honey make your decisions for you.

2. **Being afraid to take care of yourself and your honey because it might hurt other people.** If you're always walking on eggshells, it's time to reevaluate the wedding-planning process.

Don't Go There

Warning lights should flash when the bride is very young (as in under legal age) and the groom is pushy. But before you pull the plug on the nuptials, consider the consequences. Do you run the risk of losing your child if they marry anyway? Will you be unable to help your child later if the marriage sours?

3. **Being insensitive and inconsiderate of other people's feelings.** It's time to step back if you're not considering a way to make the wedding work for you and significant others. Being considerate of others shouldn't become so much to deal with that it makes you selfish in your planning.

4. **Treating yourself like a second-class citizen.** If you're running yourself into the ground with exhaustion, you're off track. Planning an interfaith wedding does suck away a lot of air, but there should always be enough left for you to breathe.

5. **Putting off spending sufficient and quality time with your honey.** If you find yourself saying, "We'll have time tomorrow" or "Who has the energy to talk right now?" you're in trouble. Focus on the big idea: There should *always* be enough time for you and your honey.

6. **Not taking control of what is going to be said at your ceremony.** If you're letting your clergy or someone else make decisions for you, you're not going to get the wedding you and your honey want. Take the time to study the ceremony script or to have someone assist you in writing and editing the script so that your wedding day means exactly what the two of you want it to mean. This is especially crucial with ecumenical weddings, in which two religious leaders officiate.

The Three C's

According to my friend Adam, age 10, you can make a marriage work by "telling your wife that she looks pretty even if she looks like a truck." You can't go wrong with Adam's advice, but you might need a little more to go on when it comes to planning the wedding. Let me add my two cents' worth to Adam's suggestion:

1. **Communicate.** Get your families together to discuss what traditions are most important to each family and to the two of you. If that's not possible, ask both sides to e-mail you or call you with what they feel is most important. Yes, it is your wedding, but other people in the family deserve to have a say—especially if they're footing the bill. You certainly don't have to include everything that everyone wants, but it is nice to ask people for their opinions before you make your decisions.

2. **Compromise.** If it works for you, include as many traditions as you can from each religion in the ceremony. For example, Lois's father is a devout Episcopalian, and she and her fiancé, Todd, asked him to read a Bible passage that meant a lot to him during the wedding service. Lois and Todd asked Todd's mother, a Unitarian, to read a poem that she loved. They had the other parents light a candle together. Everyone participated, and many traditions were included.

3. **Collect.** Read a lot about interfaith marriages and ceremonies. To make this easier for you, I list lots and lots of sources in Appendix B, "Resources on Interfaith Relationships." Remember, all weddings take serious planning, but interfaith weddings bring an extra layer of tension.

Play Nice, Kids

How else can you help bring two families together over wedding preparations while getting the wedding you want? Here are some ideas:

1. For the bride and groom ...
   - ➤ This is your wedding. If you have strong convictions on a specific issue, say so—or forever hold your peace.
   - ➤ Establish your identity as a couple by sticking together and making joint decisions.
   - ➤ If you *are* paying the entire cost of the wedding, you can theoretically have things exactly the way you wish. But be careful what you wish for ... you may get it. Instead of being a big baby, consider giving in on small issues to establish good relations with family from the get-go.
   - ➤ If you are *not* footing the bill, be prepared for some amount of compromise on significant issues.

197

➤ No matter who pays for the wedding, the wedding couple ought to discuss and decide on such important issues as the day, time, type of service (religious or secular), customs, location, guest list, music, and so on.

➤ Under no circumstances should you act as the negotiator between the two sets of parents. Even if you are the chief negotiator for the United Nations, it's not your job to arrange peace in our time. It is your job to get married.

2. For the parents and assorted in-laws …

➤ Remember that this is your child and child-in-law's marriage, not yours.

➤ Be there to help the bride and groom have the day *they* wish to have, not the day *you* think they should have.

➤ Even if you are paying for the entire wedding, be sure to consider the other set of parents involved.

➤ Respect other people's religion and culture, even if they are radically different from your own.

➤ Understand that you don't have to love this stranger who has stolen your child. All we're asking for here is a little respect. Ditto for the other set of parents and all their relatives.

3. For everyone …

➤ Try to have face-to-face meetings from the very start to allow both sets of parents to state their piece and make their demands.

➤ Nip problems in the bud. Don't let differences swell to disagreements and then become cause for World War III.

➤ Try not to prejudge, even if your prospective in-laws seem like they jumped into the gene pool while the lifeguard wasn't watching.

➤ See your parents-in-law as people, individuals with their own tastes and back stories. Don't just view them as "his parents" or "her parents."

➤ Different is not necessarily bad; it's just different. (Unless it involves hard-boiled eggs, Cool Whip, and a hula-hoop. Then it's very bad.) Try to make allowances for differences and reach compromises.

➤ Realize that everyone has an equal stake in making this marriage work. Even if you think that your son-in-law isn't the sharpest knife in the drawer. Even if you think your daughter-in-law is so dense that light bends around her. You want the kids to be happy.

➤ You can be brutally honest with yourself, but don't be so quick to spread that honesty around. Voice your concerns and then sit back. When in doubt, keep your mouth shut.

➤ Be aware that something is going to go wrong. Uncle Elmer will dance with a lampshade on his head (even if he has to bring it with him). Aunt Daisy will get potted and sing "Moonlight Bay" at the top of her lungs. There's no way around it.

➤ Realize that you're tense and frustrated with nerves on edge. You're likely to overreact at least once during the planning or party.

➤ Manners were invented to smooth the way over difficult social situations. If at all possible, follow the traditional wedding rules. These strict protocol edicts can help forestall explosions.

➤ Keep your sense of humor. If you and your beloved can laugh at some of the absurdity, you'll be able to defuse some of the tension.

➤ A little tolerance buys a lot of goodwill.

➤ Use common sense.

➤ Good luck!

Now, to make sure we're all on the same page, let's start with a definition of "marriage." Yes, I know that you know what marriage means, but do you and your honey share the same definition? You'd be surprised at the number of couples who don't see eye-to-eye on this crucial issue.

Marriage Is ...

We all agree with Charles Schulz that happiness is a warm puppy, but what is marriage? It's not as simple to define, and that's a good thing. After all, an issue as complex and crucial as marriage shouldn't be summed up in a simple phrase.

What does marriage mean to *you?* The following are some of the ways that a large group of couples of diverse backgrounds and ages completed this sentence during their engagement. While you're engaged, it's helpful to define marriage in writing because it helps you focus on the importance of the commitment you're about to make. Then compare your answers with your honey's to see where you agree ... and where you don't. Resolving the crucial issue of what marriage is (and isn't) before the big day can save a lot of hardship down the road.

"To me, marriage means ..."

➤ A communion of souls.

➤ Being partners for life.

➤ The end of a long search for what was missing in my life.

➤ Someone to show my emotions to.

➤ Minimizing the negative and focusing on the positive, yet not glossing over rough spots since problems can strengthen the relationship.

➤ Building a life together and working for common goals.

➤ Doing everything and anything I can for my spouse and always being by his side no matter what.

➤ Being responsible to each other, our family, and ourselves.

➤ Having time for ourselves.

➤ The commitment to spend the rest of my life with someone else.

➤ A time to share socks and sweatshirts officially.

➤ [That] there's a loved one at home for me to go to.

➤ A life-long commitment to love and respect another person.

➤ Sharing our lives, our good times and bad.

➤ [Being] there for her as a friend.

➤ A joined effort moving forward in life together.

➤ Someone to laugh with, cry with, and pray with.

➤ Lots and lots of love, support, and understanding.

➤ Becoming one with my sweetheart.

➤ Life full of happiness, love, and sharing.

➤ Being joined together forever with my soul mate.

➤ Waking up and seeing someone next to you who cares for you.

➤ Helping each other through everything we experience in life.

➤ Spending my life with the one person I truly love and trust.

➤ That I've chosen to spend the rest of my life with my best friend.

Now that you have a little more perspective on what marriage is, how can you help make yours work? You know that mixed matches often come prepackaged with additional problems. The strategies in the following sections can help you and your spouse deal with the unique situations that interfaith relationships bring.

Basic Training

No one ever said it would be easy to balance your needs with the needs of others—especially the needs of an entire new family with its own religious tradition. Hey, if it were *that* easy to link two (or more!) religions and create instant bliss, this book would be a whole lot shorter. But creating family harmony is possible—and it's very much worth the effort.

You realize it won't be easy to build bridges—and rebuild some that have been burned—but you also realize that it's a valuable way to spend your time. The return you get on your investment will last the rest of your married life. Below are some ideas to get you started dealing with the religious and cultural differences you're likely to encounter.

Work with Your Spouse

This is the key rule, numero uno, the whole enchilada. Dealing effectively with family, friends, and religious differences starts *first* with working conflicts through with your spouse. Remember that you're in this together.

Never put your spouse in a situation in which he or she has to choose between you and religion. If you do so, you're putting your spouse in a nearly impossible bind. Instead, try to understand the bond your spouse has with his or her faith and family. If possible, try to support that relationship.

Family Matters

You can also use these same suggestions to deal with marital conflicts that aren't rooted in religious differences.

Set Priorities

Fasting on Ramadan? Going to synagogue on Yom Kippur? Making sacrifices for Lent? With your spouse, decide what's important and what's not. This covers all of your life together, not just matters of faith.

For example, my husband and I have always let our kids eat anything they want anytime. Want ice cream 10 minutes before dinner? Fine by me … as long as you eat a reasonable dinner. But we're really, really picky about schoolwork. I don't think it's dawned on my kids yet that there is a grade below "A." Working as a team, set your family values. Then communicate your values to your family. *All* of your values to *all* of your family.

Hold On!

Don't Go There

A happy marriage *is not* like football; there are no successful end-runs in this game. *Never* cut your spouse out of the action when you deal with family and friends. And don't tolerate it if your spouse does.

Speaking of priorities, don't make promises you can't keep. Remember Hitler and Poland? Hitler promised the world that he'd stop gobbling up countries if he could only have Poland. So the Allies gave him Poland—and discovered that he had no intention of backing down. Placating people to keep the peace rarely solves the problem, especially if the issue is close to your heart.

Enforce the Priorities

Without being as inflexible as a teenager, stick to your decisions. For example, if you and your spouse don't want to erect a Christmas tree in your house, don't. If your

Family Matters

On touchy issues of faith, state your decision once and move on. The more you explain, the more defensive you'll seem. This weakens your position and leaves you vulnerable to attack.

Learn the Lingo

Triangulation occurs when a third party gets sucked into helping two people communicate with each other.

family and friends make a fuss, ignore it. Even if they drop off a honking big pile of presents.

Communicate Directly

Whenever possible, avoid communicating through a third party. Address the issue directly with the speaker. Let's say your brother-in-law made a disparaging remark about your beliefs. First tell your spouse what happened and how it made you feel. Then talk to your brother-in-law directly. Don't ask your spouse to talk to his brother about the issue.

Also, if something bothers you, address it as soon as possible. Don't let the situation stew. Sometimes it's a genuine problem; other times it might be a simple misunderstanding, as the following story shows:

Susan, a Jewish woman from Cincinnati, married into a family of Lutherans born in Germany. Whenever one of Susan's sisters-in-law went into the kitchen, she shut the door—often leaving Susan out. For years, Susan stewed over the situation, convincing herself that the women didn't want to be with her because she was Jewish. Finally, she got up the courage to ask her sister-in-law why she closed the kitchen door. "Why, to keep in the heat," she answered. "We always did that in Germany." Closing the kitchen door had nothing to do with Susan. A cultural misunderstanding had caused years of distress for Susan—which neither she nor her sisters-in-law ever realized.

Know Yourself

Shakespeare said it a zillion years ago, and the advice still holds today. Don't try to remake yourself into the person your spouse, family, or friends wants. For example, what if they're looking for little Susie Homemaker and you're a high-powered corporate attorney? You're under no obligation on your day off to hang the Christmas lights and bake 10 dozen butter cookies. Instead, hire a holiday decorator and see if your bakery delivers. Then get a manicure and a massage.

Get with the Program

Not every father-in-law lives to trek through the woods with an ax looking for the perfect Christmas tree; not every mother-in-law dreams of turning the pages of the

Advent calendar with her grandchildren. This is the new millennium, chickpea; Pops is more likely to be surfing the Net, and Granny's probably hang gliding. Put away the stereotypes and adjust your thinking to the reality of the situation. Don't expect what people can't deliver.

Learn to Cool Off

I tend to jump in where angels fear to tread. It's always headfirst, too. Fortunately, my husband is far more levelheaded, and he's learned to restrain me when at all possible. He says things like, "I think you want to hang up the phone now, spitfire" and "You really don't want to send that letter, dear." He's had success about half the time.

As I've learned the hard way, sometimes the best thing to do is nothing. Time heals many wounds—and wounds many heels.

While we're at it, play nice. Spare your spouse's family and friends the insults and character attacks. For example, Barry's father-in-law once called him a "knee-jerk liberal." "I had it on the tip of my tongue to call him a 'bloody fascist,'" Barry said. "Fortunately, I bit my tongue—even though he really *is* a fascist."

Of course, under no circumstances should you accept any religious or cultural slurs, whether they're aimed at you or any faith. Don't look for offense where none is intended, but never let any religious offense go without a response, even if you're told, "Oh, Uncle Adolph always says things like that" or "Those people use the same terms themselves, so what's the harm?"

Don't Go There

Don't confuse *responding* with *listening*. You're not obligated to do something just because your spouse, family, or friends want you to. However, you should always acknowledge their input.

Family Matters

Think of your spouse's family and friends as a potential resource to expand your support network. You can accomplish this by approaching them as you would any potential friend. Respect them, be interested in them, and listen to them.

Here are some appropriate responses when someone uses a religious slur:

➤ "That comment offended me."

➤ "I find your comment very insulting."

➤ "Please don't use terms like that."

And if you're feeling very charitable, you might say:

➤ "I'm sure you didn't mean to say that."

Don't Go There

When the going gets tough, the tough often stay neutral. Even if the situation has gone Bosnian, try to be civil if you can't be silent. Switzerland has the right idea—patient restraint. No one held a caucus and made you the family spokesperson.

Family Matters

You and your spouse are more powerful than you think. You're adults; you're a family unit. You can control visits, holiday celebrations, and access to grandchildren. Don't assume that you're powerless. People can't push you around if you don't let them.

Be Mature

Your spouse and parents have to love you; it's part of the deal. But no one else has to. Accept the fact that your spouse's family isn't your family and won't follow the same rules. Try to think "different"—not "better" or "worse." To make this work, give in on small points and negotiate the key issues.

Learn to see the situation from other people's point of view. Even if you don't agree, act like the big person you are. For example, I find pork abhorrent. No doubt this is because we never had pork when I was growing up. I never eat pork; I rarely cook it. Nonetheless, for years, my husband's mother made a pork roast when we came to her apartment for dinner. After wallowing in more pork than Congress produces, I came to see that she was trying to please her poor pork-deprived son. Big deal: I learned to have a salad before we ate at her house. My husband porked up in peace, and the only one to suffer was Babe, the poor porker.

Be Kind

Even if you have to grit your teeth, try to say something nice. And if you really can't say anything nice, shut up and smile.

Keep Your Sense of Humor

A very dear friend tells this story: "When I was pregnant with my first child, my father-in-law bought me a special gift: my very own funeral plot. 'Why a funeral plot?' I asked him. 'Well,' he replied, 'you might not make it through the birth, and I thought you should be prepared.'" I probably would have slugged the codger upside his head; my friend, in contrast, laughed and thanked him for his gift. (P.S. She and all her children are fine.)

Food Fight

Back in the old days (when cars were larger than TVs and only people of the female persuasion wore earrings), it was common for the groom's parents to hold a dinner to meet their future in-laws. When "the kids" announced their engagement, the groom's mother got on the (rotary) phone and called the bride's mother to set up a formal first encounter. Even if the in-laws had already met, this dinner was a done deal.

Today, we're more casual about life in general and weddings in particular. As a result, many couples set up their own first encounters. This is made easier by the fact that many couples live together before they tie the knot, so they have a place in which to cook and entertain. While it's certainly acceptable (and maybe even preferable) to meet everyone on neutral ground such as a restaurant, you know that nothing says lovin' like something from the oven.

There are also couples who don't meet their in-laws until they are married. As a result, the first meal encounter takes place after the nuptials. This often happens when one branch of the family couldn't make the wedding because they were busy saving the whales, splitting the atom, or serving time.

In either case, it takes enormous courage to stick your head in a lion's mouth, wear spandex after age 30, and cook that first meal for your in-laws or in-laws-to-be. Not to worry: Help is on the way.

1. First, stay away from lions. Leave that to *The Lion King*.

2. You never heard of a girdle?

3. Don't worry about cooking that first meal. It's a piece of cake!

Here's how to make sure the first meal doesn't turn into the Last Supper.

Four-Star Mom

Part of the problem with first-meal fright is your spouse's feeling about his or her family's cooking. Unless your in-laws have never applied heat to food, your beloved will adore the food that emerges from the family kitchen. So what if your mother-in-law burns corn flakes? So what if your father-in-law once made a martini with chicken soup? (My father actually did this, but that's another story.)

The flavors of home leave an indelible mark on a spouse's psyche. I make bread from scratch, brownies that win first prize in the county fair, and a killer pot roast. Nonetheless, my husband still has a soft spot in his skull for Chicken in a Bisket crackers and Snackin' Cakes, the foods of his youth. I could make this up?

And what if your spouse has a Supermom? She held down a job, cleaned the house, taught religious instruction, and made her own sauce (from the tomatoes and basil she grew in the lower 40). And your father-in-law? He's a grill master supreme. The

> **Hold On!**
>
> **Don't Go There**
>
> Catsup *is not* a vegetable—no matter what a former president claimed.

man flips burgers better than Ronald McDonald does. Your familiar cry, "The takeout is here, honey," isn't going to cut the mustard with these in-laws, kiddo. Neither will your usual dinner of Frosted Flakes tarted up with raisins (that's the fruit course).

Did You Know?

Make the meal at least once for you and your sweetie before the curtain goes up on the actual first meal with in-laws. You lessen your chances of culinary disaster if you're making a dish you've made before, especially if it's complicated.

Learn the Lingo

Kosher refers to a series of dietary laws followed by all Orthodox Jews and some Conservative and Reform Jews. The rules are complex, so check with a rabbi.

Hostess with the Mostess

So, to further good relations with your new family, I hereby offer a few tips for the perfect in-law meal. It won't leave your in-laws reaching for the antacid or thinking you're an idiot incapable of boiling water. Here are my guidelines:

1. **Attempt the impossible.** "Have you lost your brains, Rozakis?" you shout. "*I'm* going to make lobster Thermidore or prime rib with Yorkshire pudding? Why can't I stick with my usual 'Franks a Lot'?" No dice, you kitchen phobic. What you want is something really special, something that shows you care enough to cook the very best. With a new family, you have to chuck the ketchup and start dicing some herbs.

2. **Don't cheap out.** Use the very best ingredients. It's pretty hard to goof up $22-a-pound lobster. You'd be surprised how careful you get when the meal costs the same amount as the annual gross national product of a small Latin American country.

3. **Get big-name food.** This is not the time for scrod. Go for shrimp. Avoid chuck; you want T-bone, sirloin, or prime rib. Then refer to the food by name, as in "I know how much you like ostrich and buffalo kebobs."

4. **Consider religion.** Check to see what foods your new relatives do and don't eat. Mormons and Muslims don't drink alcohol, for example, and *Kosher* Jews don't mix milk and meat products.

5. Garnish. Parsley and plastic flags are always appropriate, but don't overlook the cunning little bamboo umbrellas that go in wussy drinks, turnips carved to resemble Barbra Streisand, and pipe-cleaner animals. These little accessories divert

attention from the scorched string beans. If all else fails and your food is totally inedible, your spouse's family will be so busy picking out the doodads that they'll never get around to actually eating.

6. **Blame it on the Bossa Nova.** If worst comes to worst, pretend you're a politician and point fingers. Chicken undercooked? Just can't trust that new oven. Soufflé collapsed? That's what happens during earthquakes. Figs not fresh? What trouble we're having with tariffs lately.

Family Matters

What if you really can't cook at all? In that case, make a dish from Guam, Sri Lanka, or Antarctica. No one will know if it tastes the way it should. After all, how many people eat porcupine on a regular basis? (Note: This won't work if your in-laws are from Guam, Sri Lanka, or Antarctica.)

In Case of Emergency ...

The best laid plans of mice and men (not to mention lovers) often go astray, so it's a good idea to have a back-up plan. Here it is ...

➤ **Serve more wine.** Good wine. (If they don't drink alcohol, try some designer water. So what if they think you're profligate?)

➤ **Turn on the football game.** People will think it's Thanksgiving and expect lousy food.

➤ **Serve more of everything.** At least no one will go hungry—if the food is edible.

➤ **Show the wedding videos.** Your in-laws will be too distracted by Aunt Mildred's striptease to remember that they came to your house to eat. (No video? Try the wedding picture proofs. In a pinch, a *Little Mermaid* coloring book might turn the trick.)

➤ **Announce that you've decided it's time to have baby.** This gives you at least nine months of good conversation.

As you cower under the kitchen counter, keep in mind that it's only a meal. Even if it's an unmitigated disaster from (watery) soup to (wormy) nuts, remember that it's still only a meal. You'll do better next time. Besides, in-laws rarely die from undercooked endive or burned fennel.

The Least You Need to Know

➤ As you plan your wedding, watch for danger signs including losing sight of your priorities, being inconsiderate, and giving control of your wedding to others.

➤ Communicate, compromise, and collect information.

➤ Everyone has to cooperate to create a successful interfaith wedding ceremony.

➤ Resolving the crucial issue of what marriage is (and isn't) before the big day can save a lot of hardship down the road.

➤ Work with your spouse to set and enforce priorities that will help you build a strong, enduring marriage.

➤ Be mature and kind.

➤ Consider using food to build bridges with your new family.

Part 5
And Baby Makes ...

How does the following story compare with your experiences?

When our first child arrived, so did the lump in my throat. We had agreed to raise our children in the Jewish religion. As a non-Jew, this seemed impossible and even hypocritical to both our families. I was reminded several times that children are usually brought up in their mother's religion. I am spiritually a Christian but it appeared more important for our children to be raised as Jews, as Judaism includes both a cultural and religious emphasis. Bob and I have always respected each other's religions, celebrating Jewish and Christian holidays.

As our married same-religion friends break up, it seems all the more clear that having respect for our differences has smoothed the marital road while enhancing and enriching the lives of our entire families.

—Lois, age 34

Here, we'll explore the options you have when it comes to raising children in an interfaith marriage. After all, I wouldn't want you to get sideswiped by the "December Dilemma"—Christmas or Hanukkah?—or other interfaith minefields.

Chapter 19

Sexpectations

In This Chapter

➤ Sex and interfaith couples

➤ Jewish views on sex

➤ Christian views on sex

➤ Muslim views on sex

➤ Dealing with religious differences about sex

There once was a farmer who was raising three daughters on his own. He was very concerned about their well-being and always did his best to watch out for them.

As they entered their late teens, the girls began to date. One night, all three of his girls went out on dates for the first time. The farmer greeted each suitor at the door holding his shotgun to make sure the young men knew who was boss.

The doorbell rang, and the first of the boys arrived. The farmer answered the door and the lad said,

> "Hi, my name's Joe,
> I'm here to see Flo.
> We're going to the show.
> Is she ready to go?"

The farmer looked him over and sent the two kids on their way.

The next lad arrived and said,

Learn the Lingo

Kosher refers to a series of dietary laws followed by all Orthodox Jews and some Conservative and Reform Jews. The rules are complex, so check with a rabbi.

"My name's Eddie.
I'm here to see Betty.
We're gonna get some spaghetti.
Do you know if she's ready?"

The farmer felt that this one was okay, too, so off the two kids went.

The final young man arrived, and the farmer opened the door. The boy began,

"Hi, my name's Chuck."

The farmer shot him.

Some issues are loaded ... but other issues are *explosive*. The issue of s-e-x is as explosive as they come, especially when applied to interfaith marriages. In this chapter, you'll discover how people react to their children's maturity and growing sexuality. Then we'll explore how several of the main religions regard sex. The differences in attitude can cause deep misunderstandings. Finally, I'll teach you strategies for dealing with these differences.

The Naughty Bits

Sex. Just say the word and people sit up a little straighter and start paying attention. Sex sells everything from soap to snack foods, cars to cappuccino. Let us not forget the obvious links to alcohol, cigarettes, and perfume—virtually every consumer good is sold through sex appeal. I'm sure that, right now, some overpaid suit on Madison Avenue is working on a way to sell dog food with sex.

Don't Go There

On average, people around the world first engage in intercourse at 17.6 years of age. Americans, in contrast, start earlier, at 16.2 years of age.

Movies and TV shows are rife with sexual innuendoes. There's even a laugh track to make sure we don't miss the juicy parts. The ratings system, designed to help adults screen their children's viewing habits, ironically makes it easier for kids to find the ribald shows—even if they don't get the jokes yet.

Increasingly, however, they *do* get the jokes ... and at a younger and younger age. You'd think this would make it easier for parents to accept their children's sexuality, but paradoxically, it can often have just the opposite effect. The nagging little issue that bothered us when the children were teens can become a screamingly big issue when they mature. These sensitive issues can be even more explosive in mixed matches.

Not with My Baby Girl You Don't!

Even though our society is permeated with sex, it can be difficult for parents to accept that their 30-year-old baby boy is "doing it" with his wife. It's no easier to contemplate their 30-year-old daughter having intimate relations with her hubby. Why do we find our adult children's sexuality so hard to accept? Primarily, our children's sexual actions ...

➤ Underscore our own mortality. If the kids are sexually active, then we must be old. *Really* old.

➤ Call our own values into question because our child can question his or her upbringing in the choice of a mate.

➤ Cause us worry. Will they be happy? Have they made the right choices?

As a result, many of us have a tough time making the transition from being parents of little kids to being parents of adults (not to mention grandparents). My friend Marci had the following story to share about her experiences on this front:

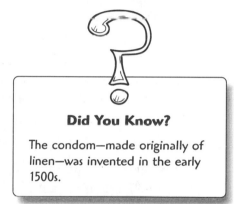

Did You Know?

The condom—made originally of linen—was invented in the early 1500s.

"I thought my parents and Ken's parents would be thrilled when Ken and I finally decided to have a child. We'd been married for three years when I became pregnant. When Ken and I announced our happy news, his parents seemed uneasy. An awkward silence settled over the room. It took several minutes before anyone congratulated us. Since Ken and I are both responsible, mature, and settled, I knew they weren't worried that we'd be bad parents. They just couldn't seem to believe that we would really be having a child. Ken's mother kept saying, 'My baby is going to be a father? My baby is going to be a father?'"

You spend years telling those hulking, surly teenage boys to keep their filthy hands off your pristine daughter. You caution her about getting "in trouble," "knocked up," or "in the family way." Suddenly, your daughter marries one of those lumbering, sullen boys, and you realize that he's really a shy, gentle young man. And now he's allowed to put his hands all over your daughter.

It works the other way, too. How many years did you spend furious at the bold hussies who called your innocent son at all hours of the day and night? They were shameless Jezebels. Suddenly, your son has plighted his troth, and the strumpet is revealed as a sweetie pie. And now she's *supposed* to touch him all over his body. No wonder everyone's in an uproar.

Makin' Whoopee

How did your parents explain "the birds and the bees" to you? Mine solved this problem the common way—by completely sidestepping the entire issue. I believe my mother said something along the lines of "Be careful" once during my teen years, but she could have been referring to my driving or my cooking. Both required great diligence on my part.

Don't Go There

The first known contraceptive was crocodile dung, used by Egyptians in 2000 B.C.E.

Despite today's sexual openness, our level of comfort about discussing sexual issues is most often based on our experiences as children. If your parents, relatives, and siblings were open about sexual matters, chances are you will be, too. If everyone in your family stayed buttoned up, however, odds are you're not about to babble to everyone about the great time you and your spouse had last night in bed with the whipped cream.

Not only do parents pass on factual information about the interaction of Tab A and Slot B, they also pass on their attitudes toward sex, their value system, and their sexual beliefs. Here are some issues about sex that your family conveyed to you, either consciously or unconsciously:

➤ What is good and what is bad about sex

➤ What is appropriate and what is inappropriate sexual behavior

➤ What is acceptable and what is not

➤ What is abnormal and what is downright weird

➤ How religion determines appropriate sexual practices

Perhaps this is one of the most difficult aspects of interfaith marriages, Ladies and Gentlemen, so think carefully before you say anything to your child or his or her sweetheart. Examine your own feelings about sex and its relationship to your faith.

Getting Jiggy with It

Q: What do you think your mom and dad have in common?

A: "Both don't want no more kids."

—Alana, age 8

All major religions hold marriage and the family in high esteem, affirming the spiritual and physical love of husband and wife as a joyful gift from God. Children are considered blessings to be cherished. Reduced to its basic terms, sex in the context of spirituality is thought of in one of two ways:

➤ Our religion says that sex is good; do it well.

➤ Our religion teaches that sex is important; do it right.

Act of Faith

Here are some useful Latin sexual phrases and their translations:

➤ Erectionus finalum. ("Anna Nicole Smith is here, Gramps.")

➤ Log floggit cum palma folliculus. ("If you don't stop it, you'll go blind.")

➤ Dumbassus! Hottie iste transvestitus! ("Fool! That gorgeous woman is a cross-dresser!")

Notice how careful I was to say "marriage and the family" in the same breath with "sex." That was quite deliberate, chick pea. Christianity, Judaism, and Islam all prohibit sex outside of marriage. However, there's a lot of leeway here with individual action. According to some polls, 85 percent of all married people said "I will" before they said "I do." And more than 50 percent lived together before they married. We can safely assume they weren't playing solitaire on those cold winter nights.

That said, let's look at the different attitudes each religion has toward sex. The following information represents the official religious teachings on the subject of sex. Recognize that individuals may feel differently, no matter how devout their faith. Therefore, never assume that your honey and his or her parents cleave unflaggingly to the party line.

Did You Know?

St. Paul, speaking from his Jewish background, even implied that it's impossible to have sex outside of marriage, as sexual intercourse constitutes de facto marriage.

Christian Views on Sex in Marriage

Both Catholics and Protestants view sexual intercourse in marriage as an affirmation of love and mutual support of both spouses. From that point on, however, we have a split.

Catholic Views of Intercourse

The Catholic Church teaches that the procreation of children is equally important a purpose as sexual pleasure. To follow this belief to its logical conclusion, Catholics believe that nothing should be allowed to interfere with the divinely ordered process of reproduction.

Learn the Lingo

The **rhythm method** of birth control involves abstaining from intercourse during the times of the female cycle when fertilization is most likely.

As a result, many medically accepted methods of birth control are not sanctioned by the Catholic Church, including barriers to conception (condoms, the sponge, IUDs, diaphragms) and the birth control pill. Only certain limited forms of birth control are allowed, most notably the rhythm method of contraception. However, according to recent polls, as many American Catholics use "artificial" birth control methods today as do Protestants.

The Catholic Church expressly forbids abortion. The Greek Orthodox Church and The Church of Jesus Christ of Latter Day Saints (Mormons) take the same stance. They also forbid artificial insemination, in vitro fertilization, and surrogate motherhood.

Protestant Views of Intercourse

Protestants agree with the Catholic view of sexual intercourse as a cornerstone of marital happiness, but they believe that sexual intercourse can be enjoyed without regard to reproduction. They see intercourse and sexual play as an affirmation of love and an end unto itself—without leading to the pitter-patter of little feet. As a result, Protestant couples are encouraged to use any medically approved form of birth control they wish, unless they want to conceive a child.

On the abortion issue, Baptists, Fundamentalists, and Mormons side with the Catholics on the issue of abortion. Other Protestants, however, agree with the compromise worked out by the Supreme Court and affirm that a woman has the right to determine whether or not she wishes to terminate a pregnancy.

Protestants accept assisted reproductive technology including artificial insemination, in vitro fertilization, and surrogate motherhood.

The following chart summarizes Catholic and Protestant views on human sexuality:

Belief	Catholic	Protestant
Intercourse affirms marital love	X	X
No artificial birth control	X	
Birth control allowed		X
Abortion forbidden	X	
Abortion allowed		X

Jewish Views on Sex in Marriage

According to observant Reform and Conservative Jews, marriage is not solely, or even primarily, for the purpose of procreation. Traditional sources recognize that companionship, love, and intimacy are the primary purposes of marriage, noting that woman was created in Genesis 2:18 because "it is not good for man to be alone" rather than because she was necessary for procreation.

A husband is responsible for providing his wife with food, clothing, and sexual relations (Exodus 21:10) as well as anything else specified in the ketubah (marriage contract). Marital sexual relations are the woman's right, not the man's. A man cannot force his wife to engage in sexual relations with him, nor is he permitted to abuse his wife in any way.

To the Jewish way of thinking, sexual relations within marriage are one of the greatest physical gifts that God has given humanity. Therefore, couples are encouraged to express their love physically. Under Orthodox Jewish law, a woman may even divorce her husband if he fails in his conjugal responsibilities.

Reform and Conservative Jews allow all forms of birth control and leave the abortion decision to the couple. Traditionally, Orthodox Jews did not allow certain forms of birth control, but recently, birth control pills were ruled permissible. Assisted reproductive technology and genetic engineering are accepted by Reform Jews and generally by Conservative and most Orthodox Jews as well.

Muslim Views on Sex in Marriage

Muslims believe that love should grow out of marriage, but it's not necessary at the outset. Rather, commitment, honor, mutual respect, and friendliness are the most important values a married couple can have as they begin their life together.

Islam emphasizes the continuation of the religion; therefore, Muslim couples are encouraged to have as many children as possible, and the number of children a couple has is linked with social status.

Family Matters

Followers of the Druze religion believe that a woman's self-fulfillment and marital satisfaction may be achieved chiefly by investing her energies in the family.

Can We Talk?

The following letter comes from a friend who wishes to remain anonymous for obvious reasons. He is a Reform Jew who views sex as a way to build love and intimacy in a marriage. His wife, in contrast, is a devout Catholic who views sex as a duty to be performed solely for the purpose of procreation. She has decided that sex is a chore to be performed with as little sensual pleasure as possible. Here's what the male half of this couple said:

"I called my father in complete bewilderment—the relationship that had seemed so wonderful was foundering and in such a humiliating way. He sympathized but pointed out that Ann Marie had grown up Catholic with a different religious and cultural attitude toward sex. I saw his point and felt a bit ashamed that I had argued as though we had worked all this out beforehand … we hadn't ever discussed the topic of sex and children. Ann Marie was a virgin when we got married, and we just figured that everything would work out all right. We saw eye to eye on everything else, so we'd clearly see eye to eye on sex as well. We didn't."

Did You Know?

As George Bernard Shaw said, "Marriage is popular because it combines the maximum of temptation with the maximum of opportunity."

Serious clashes occur when you marry someone who has a different attitude toward sex, especially if that attitude is based on religious differences.

If you and your spouse are equally conservative or liberal when it comes to matters of the flesh, regardless of your faith, things will likely be okay in the bedroom. If not, you'll want to work on solutions before you embark on a lifetime together. This is true even if you are both of the same faith but believe to different degrees.

For example, I know a man and woman who are both Jewish, well-educated, and highly sophisticated. The woman is Reform; the man is Orthodox. They are now divorced, in large part because of sexual differences based on religious beliefs. Here's what the wife told me:

"My ex-husband had an Orthodox Jewish upbringing, complete with a kosher home and a yeshiva [religious Jewish] education. To accommodate his beliefs, I kept a kosher home and became more observant—but it didn't help us in the bedroom. As a result of his beliefs, he insisted that neither he nor I completely undress during sex. He also insisted on making love in the dark: He would never make love during the day and wouldn't let me put on a light at night. He had been taught that a woman would be embarrassed at being seen during intercourse, so her dignity must be maintained by staying partially clothed and in the dark. This wasn't the only reason our marriage disintegrated, but it was definitely a major factor."

Patience Is a Virtue

Q: How would the world be different if people didn't get married?

A: "There sure would be a lot of kids to explain, wouldn't there?"

—Christopher, age 9

There's a wide gulf between intellectual, emotional, and spiritual understanding, so never assume that, just because you've talked about doing the deed a certain way, at a certain time, and for a certain purpose, you've got the problem licked. Other things may be licked but not the issues of sexual compatibility.

That's because sexual preferences determined by religion are rooted deep in the psyche. For example, traditional Judaism forbids sexual intercourse while a woman is menstruating and for a proscribed length of time afterward. Even a nonreligious Jewish man or woman may feel that sex during menstruation is repugnant; however, a Catholic man or woman bent on avoiding conception may feel just the opposite way.

Even if one or both of you agree to adjust your sexual practices to accommodate the other, it takes time to work through these changes.

Be Fruitful and Multiply

It is also essential that you and your beloved decide whether you want children and how many. Yes, I know you can't place an order as you would at a restaurant—"I'll take two boys and a girl, please, and make sure they're fresh"—but when a couple has sharp religious differences about reproduction, the decision to reproduce can make or break a marriage.

Remember that you can't change someone else; you can only change yourself. Women, never "surprise" your husband with a child he did not want; odds are he'll surprise you by believing you can't be trusted. And he will be right.

Loose Lips Sink Ships—and Marriages

You may decide to seek professional help for sexual incompatibility. Regardless, keep these issues to yourself—they're not for show-and-tell time around the water cooler or Thanksgiving turkey.

This might seem to be a sexual issue, but it's really a boundary issue. In this case, the dividing line is between privacy and secrecy. The words are not the same, any more than Ben and Jerry are the same or Michael Jackson and Diana Ross are the same.

Learn the Lingo

Privacy is discretion; **secrecy** is concealment. The first is open; the second is closed.

➤ *Privacy* is keeping things to yourself that you do not wish to share with others. Privacy involves personal issues such as sex.

➤ *Secrecy*, in contrast, is hiding something. Secrets are destructive because they can interfere with a healthy family relationship.

Privacy is keeping your business to yourself. *Secrecy* is Watergate. You want privacy; you don't want secrecy. Here's the bottom line: sexual incompatibility is nobody's business but your and your sweetie's and maybe a counselor's.

Did You Know?

For centuries, sexual relations in marriage also served a practical function; people needed the resulting offspring as a cheap source of labor.

Kissy Face

Sometimes cultural issues impact sexual behavior. The Japanese, for example, do not approve of body contact in public. Touching members of the opposite sex is especially repugnant. As a result, kissing in public is considered extremely offensive.

Even at Japanese weddings, these rules are not relaxed. Actually, they become more strongly observed. There is no hugging, no kissing, no touching on the part of the bride and groom and certainly not on the part of the wedding guests. Therefore, the Japanese have developed a complex system of bowing to express relationships.

Asians from countries other than Japan are equally disapproving when they see American men and women openly displaying affection in public. In their own countries, women are considered sexually licentious if they act this way.

The Least You Need to Know

➤ Few issues upset the family apple cart as much as sex.

➤ Your religious and cultural background often determines your attitudes toward sex.

➤ There can be serious clashes when you marry someone with different attitudes toward sex.

➤ The Catholic Church teaches that procreation is as important as sexual pleasure. Protestants and Jews do not.

➤ Islam emphasizes the continuation of the religion; therefore, married Muslims are encouraged to have many children.

➤ Religious differences can cause sexual problems.

➤ Have fun in bed but make sure you both agree on the definition of "fun." And close the curtains, please.

Chapter 20

Baby Talk

In This Chapter

➤ Choosing a religion for your interfaith child

➤ Presenting a united front

➤ Naming your child

➤ The issue of baptism

➤ The issue of circumcision

According to a child of my acquaintance, you just follow this rule for getting married: "The rule goes like this: If you kiss someone, then you should marry them and have kids with them. It's the right thing to do."

So you did the right thing and got hitched after you smooched. With the birth of your first child, any unresolved conflicts with your parents, families, and friends are likely to explode. Since half of America's grandparents see a grandchild almost every day, there's a lot of opportunity for family conflict.

In this chapter, we'll start at the very beginning with the issue of choosing a religious identity for your children and spreading the news to friends and family. Then I'll give you some suggestions for naming your child to avoid religious-based dissension. Finally, we'll move on to the highly charged rituals associated with a newborn, including baptism and circumcision (for boys).

Off on the Wrong Foot

Studies have repeatedly shown that whether you raise your child in one religion, two religions, or no religions has little or no impact on the child's mental health. However, the matter isn't as simple as that, as many interfaith couples have discovered. The marriage of Artie, a Reform Jew, and Geraldine, a religious Roman Catholic, illustrates this.

"Since our parents were so opposed to our marriage, we secretly eloped. We decided to keep our marriage a secret for another year, until [Geraldine] had finished college. I dropped out of college, got a job, and started saving money. We wanted our own place when we announced our marriage.

One evening, when Geraldine and I were making love in my bed, my parents came home and caught us in the act.

'How could you do this in our home?' my father screamed. My mother held his arm so he wouldn't hit me.

'It's not what it looks like,' I began.

'Oh, it's not?' Dad said sarcastically.

'Mom,' I explained, 'Geri and I are married. We've been married for five months.'

'When is the baby coming?' my father asked in a vicious tone.

'She's not pregnant,' I said defensively. 'We're in love.'

'Love,' my father bellowed. 'What do you know about love? You just want to get into her pants. And you, young lady, there are names for girls like you.' Geri fought back tears. 'Yes,' she said, 'Mrs. Taubman.' My father was taken aback and was silent for a few seconds. Then he began to laugh. My mother looked at him with astonishment. She began to speak. 'When my brother married a Methodist,' she began, 'my parents sat *shiva* for him. They tore their clothes and went into mourning for their dead son. Three weeks later, they changed their minds and invited him and his wife to dinner, hugging her and welcoming her to the family. But she never forgave them for first rejecting her. I am not going to make the same mistake.'

She held her arms open and beckoned to Geri. 'Welcome to the family, Geri,' she said. Geri went across the room and allowed herself to be hugged. Eventually, even my father called her 'my beautiful daughter-in-law.' What neither of them knew was that, by that night, it was already too late. Geri never forgave them.

Geri refused to convert, but when the kids were born, she agreed to raise them Jewish. She stopped going to church, but I knew she was just doing this to make me happy and keep peace in the family. She kept a Jewish home, but her heart wasn't in it."

This sad story illustrates a serious lesson: Both parents of a child must agree with the choice of religion for an interfaith couple to succeed. Further …

➤ The choice must be made freely by both partners.

➤ The choice should be made early on, preferably before any children are born.

➤ Parents must stand behind the religious choice and reinforce it—together.

Learn the Lingo

Shiva is the ritual mourning period in Judaism. See Chapter 24, "Christian, Jew, and Heaven Too?" for a complete description of Jewish mourning traditions.

United We Stand, Divided We Fall

Let's see what's happened to Artie and Geri a few years down the road:

Family Matters

All couples have to work as a team, not just couples of different faiths.

"On Saturdays, I took the kids to the synagogue for religious services, and we spent all the Jewish holidays at my parents' house. My parents adored the children and showered them with love and gifts. They were also very generous with Geri and me. They sent us on vacations and baby-sat the kids. They bought us furniture when we got our house, too. They had even chipped in for the down payment.

All this generosity annoyed Geri. She wanted to be independent. Although she kept her promise about raising the children Jewish, it was obvious that her heart was not in it. She accompanied us to the synagogue less and less often. She found excuses not to go to my parents' house for Hanukkah. She was hostile to everything related to Judaism. As we drifted further and further apart, it became clear that the marriage was in serious trouble."

As this story shows, an interfaith couple must work together, especially on the religious issue. It's vital that you and your honey work out your religious differences before junior makes his appearance. Trust me, here: After your little lambkins arrives, you'll be too busy changing diapers and trying to figure out why he's crying *again* to even think about his religion. A week later, you'll look up and realize you forgot to name the kid.

No matter what religious identity you and your spouse choose (even if you chose none), let your children and family know that you and your honey are happy with the decision you have made together. Present a united front, even if some lingering doubts remain. If you can't do this, you shouldn't be married to each other. I know that's harsh, but truth and reality are like that.

Don't Go There

Working through the religious issue is rarely quick or easy. As you create a policy and refine it over the years, remember to deal with each other with love, respect, and consideration.

Trouble in River City

What happens if you and your honey can't work out religious harmony before the babies arrive? What happens if you don't agree on this crucial issue? Unfortunately, your children will likely suffer the consequences.

How can you tell if you're headed down the wrong path? See which of the following descriptions fit your family situation. If any of them suit, you and your honey have some work to do.

1. **The Entropy Family.** My spouse and I argue over religion more and more. The constant battles are wearing us all down.

2. **The Backbiting Family.** My spouse and I criticize each other's religious values in front of the kids, our family, and our friends.

3. **The Church Mouse Family.** I feel like my spouse has taken over and I have no say at all in the family's spiritual beliefs.

4. **The Battle of the Titans Family.** My spouse and I compete for religious dominance in the family, like two superpowers battling over nuclear armaments.

5. **The All for Show Family.** My spouse and I give the kids conflicting signals, saying one thing about religion but doing another. We put on a good face for everyone, but things are a mess when it comes to real spirituality.

6. **The Puppet Family.** My spouse and I agree about religion, but my in-laws (or parents) keep butting in and calling the shots. Since we take money from them (or work for them, and so on), I feel powerless to complain.

7. **The Winner Takes None Family.** We split the kids down the middle—the girls follow one religion, the boys follow a different religion—which has just caused a huge family mess.

8. **The Lost in Space Family.** Well, we never got around to deciding on religion, so we're all drifting spiritually. I wish we had some spirituality in our lives.

9. **The Secrets and Lies Family.** My spouse has secretly kept his/her religion, even though we agreed to follow the same religion.

10. **The Cold War Family.** The religious issue has gotten so tense around here that my spouse and I talk through the children rather than to each other, as in "Ask your father if he wants a Christmas tree again this year" or "Ask your mother if she's going to do that nonsense with latkes again."

If one or more of these situations describes what you and your family are going through now, it's time to decide whether you care enough about yourself, your children, and your marriage to resolve the issue. I can guarantee that things won't get any better without some honest communication and compromise.

Let me get you started with some suggestions for building religious harmony.

We Can Work It Out

As an interfaith couple, your goal is to build love, tolerance, flexibility, and cooperation between you and your beloved before kids complicate the mix. If things have already gone south, there's still time to work on the religious issue. Why not …

➤ **Find common ground.** Especially if you and your spouse decide to raise your children in a dual-religion household, find common ground in both faiths. Stress the similarities in the belief systems, not the differences.

➤ **Be a family.** Show the kids that you're in this together. Work with your spouse, not against him or her.

➤ **Celebrate together.** Even if it's not your holiday, be present at the celebration so that you'll all function as a family, not as a bunch of people who happen to live together. Have the family join in your celebrations occasionally as well.

Family Matters

If you're moving to a new neighborhood, make it a priority to find out if there are any interfaith couples in the area. Having friends from similar backgrounds makes life easier for you and the kids.

➤ **Cultivate a wide variety of friends.** Socialize with other mixed-religion families so your children will understand that their situation is far from unique.

➤ **Spend time with the extended family.** Make it a point to socialize with your own families, too. Have your children spend time with their grandparents, if you're fortunate enough to have them. This helps children understand all sides of their religious heritage.

➤ **Respect differences.** Teach children to respect everyone's religion, not just their own.

What's in a Name?

A lot, when it comes from a different religious tradition. Here's a story torn from the pages of my own family album:

My husband is the oldest of three boys born to a Greek Orthodox father and a Roman Catholic mother who never resolved the religious differences in their marriage. When my husband was born, his paternal grandmother, Demetra, naturally assumed that her son and daughter-in-law would follow Greek Orthodox custom and name the baby after her departed husband, Aristedes. My husband's mother, in contrast, wanted to give her first child a common American name—Robert. She won.

Don't Go There

Traditional Jews consider it bad luck to make any preparations for the baby before its birth, such as setting up the nursery or having a baby shower. The furniture and so on is delivered to the house after the baby is delivered to the mother.

However, Grandmother Demetra's English wasn't that strong, and when she heard the totally unfamiliar name "Robert," she started shrieking, "Rabbit! Rabbit! What kind of a name is Rabbit?" The family compromised by naming my husband Robert Aristedes Rozakis. My mother-in-law uses the American translation, Robert Harris Rozakis. They baptized him both Greek and Catholic.

Here are my suggestions for naming your baby:

1. **Start with personal preference.** Select a name you like because of its sound or connotation. We picked Charles and Samantha: Charles because of its association with kings and Samantha because it sounds pretty.

2. **Consider religion-neutral names.** If family relations are already strained, consider selecting names that are religion-neutral. For example, many observant Jews would be upset if their grandson were named Christian or Jesus. Since my husband and I have two very different religious backgrounds, we also selected the names Charles and Samantha because they are religion-neutral.

3. **Know your religious customs and your spouse's religious customs when it comes to names.** Traditional Jews, for instance, don't select a name before the baby's birth or tell anyone the name before the official naming ceremony. On the grounds that English names are merely approximations of true Hebrew names, American Jews often use a name that has the same initial as the dead relative being honored: Our son's middle name, Lawrence, is after his maternal grandfather, Ludwig, who died five months before Charles' birth.

4. **Make sure the name goes with your last name and other kids already born.** No Chanda Leer or Seymore Miles, please. We almost named Samantha "Diana" before it dawned on us that we'd have "Charles and Diana."

5. **Cover yourself.** Make a backup list of equally acceptable baby names in case you change your mind after babykins debuts and you realize you've got a Butch or Herminone on your hands.

6. **Relax.** You're done now if there's no great break with family religion, tradition, heritage, or culture. If there is, read on.

7. **Spread the news.** Share your choices with the family and explain your reasons. It's always better to discuss your name choices *before* rather than *after* the birth, when everyone will be busy sobbing, scolding, and sermonizing. (Of course, don't share the name if doing so violates religious traditions.)

Did You Know?

Microbiologist Charles R. Gerba gave his oldest boy the middle name Escherichia. Gerba told his Jewish father-in-law that it was the name of an Old Testament king. What does Escherichia mean? It's a type of bacteria.

8. **Calm everyone.** If the family starts hyperventilating, have them breathe into a paper bag while you get to the root of the issue. Are they shaken because the name violates deeply held religious traditions such as the Jewish tradition of *not* naming after the living or the Catholic tradition of indeed naming after the living? Or is the objection based on a garden-variety power struggle that's unrelated to religion? Finding the cause can sometimes resolve the issue.

9. **See if you can work out a compromise.** Sometimes people *do* listen to reason. If not, stick by your guns. It's your baby.

I'm Just Wild About Harry

Stuck for boy's names? Perhaps this chart will help you.

Today's Top Trendy Names for Baby Boys

Adam	Allan	Andrew	Baylor
Brandon	Brendan	Brian	Christopher
Cody	Connor	Daniel	David
Drew	Eric	Graham	Griffin
Harley	James	Jared	Jason
Jesse	John	Jonathan	Jordan
Joseph	Justin	Marc	Matthew
Michael	Nathaniel	Nelson	Nicholas
Quentin	Robert	Shaun	Steven
Thomas	Timothy	Tye	Tyler
Vernon	Xavier	Zach	Zackariah

Where the Girls Are

Let me help you find a name for your daughter, too.

Today's Top Trendy Names for Baby Girls

Adrianna	Alexia	Allison	Amanda
Andrea	Angeline	Anna	April
Ashley	Aubrey	Bailey	Bree
Brittany	Caitlin	Carly	Cathryn
Catherine	Corrina	Crystal	Darla
Destiny	Emily	Elizabeth	Faith
Fiona	Goldi	Hailey	Hannah
Jacklyn	Jennifer	Jessica	Jillian
Juliane	Kailey	Kayla	Kyrstin
Lauren	Leah	Linda	Lisa
Madelin	Madison	Maria	Melissa
Michaela	Rebecca	Sabrina	Sadie
Samantha	Samara	Shelby	Stephanie
Tiffany	T'Aysha	Tracey	Yasmine

According to some kids hanging around my house today, here are the baby names to avoid: A. Mistake, Elvis, Diphthong, Pugsley, Fester Boyle, Demon Seed, Stimpy, and Dicky.

Act of Faith

Sometimes your in-laws will be so glad that you're having a baby that they won't care what you call him or her. Other times, however, battles will erupt over names, customs, and culture. How can we resolve these issues? Here are comedian Bill Cosby's guidelines for naming a baby:

➤ Always give your child a name that ends in a vowel so that when you yell, the name will carry. Nothing rings out like a good "o" as in "Juli-ooooooooooo." You just can't do that with James, Herman, or Meredith.

➤ If you must put some consonants in your child's name, try to put them in the middle, where a few b's or m's will work (as long as there's a vowel at the end).

Welcome, Stranger!

All faiths have their own welcoming ceremonies for babies. Christians baptize snookums; Jews hold a circumcision ceremony for male infants and, increasingly, have naming ceremonies for female babies. Baptism and circumcision are *not* spiritually identical "welcome" ceremonies, as the following chart shows:

Ceremony	Meaning
Baptism	A surrender to the power of grace
Circumcision	A covenant as a partner with God

The question isn't whether you're going to use Aunt Marguerite's antique christening gown or invite Aunt Estelle and Uncle Ruben to the bris. The question is what ceremony—if any—you're going to have to welcome your child into the family.

Baptism

Baptism means that the soul is cleansed of Original Sin.

Baptism *is not* …

➤ A *pro forma* naming ceremony.

➤ A cross between vaccination and insurance.

Baptism *is* …

➤ A sacrament that conveys a spiritual effect on the baby.

➤ A sign that the baby is a Christian.

➤ A long-term commitment to raise the baby as a Christian.

As you can tell, baptism isn't a casual act. If you don't believe in what it represents or don't want to abide by its implications, don't hold the ceremony—not even to make someone else happy.

Circumcision

All Christian babies are eligible for baptism, but only male Jewish babies can be circumcised. The ritual is usually performed on the eighth day of the baby's life. If the Jewish half of the couple is the father rather than the mother, you will likely have a difficult time finding a rabbi to perform the ceremony since the child of a Gentile woman isn't considered Jewish under traditional Jewish law (unless she has converted).

Learn the Lingo

A **mohel** (pronounced moil) is a rabbi specially trained to perform Jewish circumcisions; the ceremony is called a **bris.**

When our son was born, people argued that he should or should not be circumcised based on health reasons. But that's avoiding the central issue: In Jewish law, a circumcision is performed as a religious ritual, not a health one.

Circumcision isn't a casual act by any interpretation. As with baptism, you'd better be *really* sure you believe what it represents or can abide by its implications. Never leave issues of this magnitude to "work themselves out"; they won't.

Increasingly, naming ceremonies are becoming popular for Jewish baby girls, a symbolic parallel to a bris. Check with your rabbi if you would like to learn more about these ceremonies.

Make sure you know *exactly* what you're doing before you enter into a religious covenant on your child's behalf. Talk to as many religious leaders as you can or read more deeply on theology. Most of all, work out the issue beforehand with your spouse. Religious debates and 3:00 A.M. feedings do *not* go together well.

The Least You Need to Know

➤ Both parents must freely agree with the choice of religion for an interfaith marriage to succeed. Enforce the religious choice together.

➤ Find common ground, be a family, and celebrate religious holidays together. Have interfaith friends, spend time with the kinfolk, and respect differences.

➤ Choose your baby's name carefully because names often carry heavy religious baggage.

➤ Christian baptism means that the soul is cleansed of Original Sin; Jewish circumcision is a covenant with God. They are very different and should never be entered into casually.

Chapter 21

Home for the Holidays—But Which Holidays?

In This Chapter

➤ Why holidays cause problems for interfaith couples

➤ Major holidays of different faiths

➤ Turf wars vs. religious issues

➤ A worksheet to clarify thinking

➤ Ways to celebrate holidays in interfaith families

There were two brothers, 8 and 10 years old, who were exceedingly mischievous. Whatever went wrong in the neighborhood, they surely had a hand in it. At their wit's end, the boys' parents asked their priest to talk with the hooligans. He agreed and asked to see the younger boy alone first.

The priest sat the boy down across from his huge, impressive desk. For about five minutes, they sat and stared at each other. Finally, the priest pointed his forefinger at the boy and asked, "Where is God?"

The boy looked under the desk, in the corners of the room, all around, but said nothing.

Again, louder, the priest pointed at the boy and asked, "Where is God?"

Again the boy looked all around but said nothing. A third time, in an even louder and firmer voice, the priest leaned far across the desk, put his forefinger on the boy's nose, and boomed, "WHERE IS GOD?"

The boy panicked and ran all the way home. He dragged his older brother to their room where they usually plotted their mischief. "We are in BIG trouble," he cried.

The older boy asked, "What do you mean?"

The kid replied, "God is missing, and they think we did it!"

It's not easy raising kids, even with some outside help!

As an interfaith couple, you no doubt have heard dire warnings that religion can be divisive at holiday time. Unfortunately, that is certainly true. This chapter will help you celebrate holidays as an interfaith family.

Let's start by seeing why holidays are emotionally loaded issues in interfaith families. Then we'll discuss specific strategies for making all religious holidays as smooth and happy as possible. The chapter concludes with some general advice for making holidays fun for people of all faiths.

The December Dilemma

I found this letter in my mailbag:

> "The first time we fought over religious issues I was mortified. How could this be happening to me? I thought. I'd always regarded myself as high-minded, liberal, and cosmopolitan, and I thought of David the same way. Yet here we were nearly breaking up because he didn't want me to get a Christmas tree for our house, and suddenly I wanted one more than life itself.
>
> It was a time of self-examination for me. I realized that I was not just a default Christian. I hadn't been to church in years, I had no interest in converting anyone, but there I was, undeniably Christian, and digging in my heels about a Christmas tree. David, who hadn't been in a temple since his bar mitzvah and who regularly ate pork and shellfish, dug in his heels on the other side. How can we resolve this problem?"
>
> —Heather, age 34

Holidays are religion and family at the gut level. Christmas and Hanukkah may be the holidays we most closely associate with interfaith strife, but don't kid yourself: Easter and Passover can cause equally tense times in Jewish-Christian households. The same holiday strife affects Muslims, Hindus, and others who have married outside of their faith, too.

In large part, these religious holidays cause problems because couples haven't resolved religious differences. But even if they have, old family issues and hurts tend to resurface during holidays and place everyone under stress.

Rock Around the Clock

A generation ago, most families gathered around a large dead bird on Thanksgiving, watched a little football, and threw some plates at each other. December called for Christmas; spring was Easter. Not anymore, cupcake. The world has shifted and so have holidays. My family is a case is point.

I'm German-Jewish, and my husband is Catholic-Irish-German-Greek. On my husband's mother's side, this means the headline holidays are Christmas and Easter. On my father-in-law's side, we get Greek Christmas (Epiphany) and Greek Easter. My father-in-law remarried, and his wife is Italian-Catholic, which adds the traditional huge (and delicious) fish feast on Christmas Eve. As a result, the winter holiday season is longer than an afternoon spent waiting to renew your driver's license.

If we give equal time to both sides at holiday season, we kick off with the neutral Thanksgiving, shift into a week of Hanukkah, crash into Christmas madness, do a New Year's debauch, and mop up with Greek Christmas. After a deep breath, we spin right into Passover, Easter, and Greek Easter. That's a lot of time spent cleaning, shopping, cleaning, cooking, cleaning, and entertaining. The tension builds as people are pulled and tugged in many directions. And I'm still cleaning.

Family Matters

Couples often keep their feelings to themselves (especially about hot topics like religion) because they want to keep the peace to stay in love. Bad move.

Did You Know?

Iranian-Americans may celebrate Noruz, while Native Americans have the traditional powwows and the Green Corn Dance. Hispanic Catholics often hold fiestas during the year to honor saints.

The Party Never Ends

So many holidays, so little time. How many of the following holidays have become a part of your family traditions because of marriage?

233

Did You Know?

The first visitor of the new year is important to a Vietnamese-American family. A child or other relative is sent outside just before midnight and is invited to reenter a few minutes later. This is to make sure that the first visitor of the new year is one who brings the family good luck in the coming year.

➤ Many Chinese-Americans celebrate their New Year in January or February (the date varies), the beginning of the lunar new year.

➤ Mexican-Americans mark May 5, Cinco de Mayo, on their calendars. The holiday commemorates the Mexicans' 1867 victory over the French.

➤ Is your spouse Muslim? If so, Ramadan, celebrated in the ninth month of the lunar year, is an important holiday. It's marked by atonement and fasting from sunup to sundown.

➤ Japanese-Americans may honor their elderly relatives and friends on September 15, Respect for the Aged Day.

➤ Anyone in your new family from England? Boxing Day, celebrated on December 26, is the tradition of presenting small boxed gifts to service workers.

More, More, More!

And that's just a nibble. What about the Carnival blowout celebrated by Catholics who have come to America from Brazil, France, Haiti, Italy, and the Caribbean (as well as second- and third-generation Americans and so on)? Let us not forget that Vietnamese-Americans may celebrate Tet, their New Year, between January 21 and February 19. People make a fresh start for the new year by cleaning and painting their homes. They pay back any money they owe and try to avoid arguments.

Tiffs Over Turf

A friend shared the following memory of her first brush with interfaith holidays when she automatically assumed that she would have a Christmas tree in her house. She mistakenly assumed that a Christmas tree was an American symbol rather than a Christian one, so how could her Jewish husband object? Well, he did object to having a Christmas tree. He objected long and loud, too. Here's her story:

"I called my mother in tears because my marriage was falling apart over a Christmas tree. She pointed out that Fred had grown up Jewish, surrounded by indifferent and occasionally hostile Christians, and that a Christmas tree in his home might represent a greater threat to his identity than the traditions of his religion could ever be to mine. I saw her point and felt a bit ashamed that I had argued as though we were playing on an even field—no one had ever rammed Passover down my throat. I decided that I didn't want a tree—the cats would just knock it down anyway.

Christmas passed without a tree of my own, but I got to enjoy the family tree at my parents' home. Fred came with me to my parents' house for Christmas. He admired the tree and listened to all the family stories behind the ornaments.

We fought a lot on that vacation, but all was bliss when we returned to our co-op in Daytona, which seemed larger and less chaotic than it ever had. Slowly we figured it out: Our religious warfare, as religious warfare so often turns out to be, had been about territory—the apartment, personal space, the uncomfortable and unsettling merging of two households into one. The scales fell from our eyes, and we saw each other again for the people we were, not just the institutions we participated in."

—Val, age 26

As this story illustrates, interfaith couples may assume they're battling over different religious observances, but they may actually be arguing over turf. This is common as two people from very different backgrounds try to find common ground. The religious issue often muddies the water when couples are really battling over territory.

Sharpen Your Skills

How well interfaith couples manage during the holidays usually predicts how they deal with religious (and other) differences during the year. The skills interfaith families most need to navigate the holidays include the ability to ...

➤ Listen effectively.

➤ Express yourself honestly.

➤ Keep your cool.

➤ Negotiate fairly.

➤ See the situation from your partner's viewpoint.

➤ Compromise.

➤ Resolve conflicts creatively.

➤ Keep your sense of humor.

Don't Go There

Lack of communication often wears partners down and causes marriages to crumble. This is especially true among couples with sharp differences, such as partners from different faiths.

235

Listen Up

"If two stand together shoulder to shoulder against the fates, happy, the fates themselves cannot prevail against them, if they stand so."

—Maxwell Anderson, American dramatist

It's not surprising that the more mature people are and the stronger their sense of self, the better they deal with the stress of celebrating interfaith holidays. Couples who have formed their own sense of identity also fare better than those still strongly allied to their family of origin.

If you and your honey aren't there yet, start by openly communicating your feelings about the holidays. You can use the following worksheet to start the discussion. Try these suggestions to make the most out of your time:

➤ Make three copies of the worksheet.

➤ Take one yourself, give one to your honey, and set one aside.

➤ You and your honey should fill out the worksheet independently.

➤ Compare answers. Opening the topic of conversation can pave the way for continuing communication.

➤ Use the final copy to design your ideal holiday celebration—together.

With all the holiday madness, taking time to talk about the celebrations may seem impossible. Trust me here: it's time well spent. You'll be surprised what a little open conversation with your spouse might reveal—as I discovered a few years ago.

I always thought my husband wanted a big, fancy Christmas because that's what he had as a child; actually, he far prefers New Year's Eve, because there's no religious pressure from the past. We're free to create our own traditions—and we've fashioned a wonderful one, too. Here's how it works.

Each family member gets to pick two favorite foods and together we have a big feast on New Year's Eve. The foods don't have to go together at all, so we've had strawberry cheesecake, sauteed mushrooms, prime rib, potato pancakes, fast food fries, onion rings, spare ribs, and shrimp with pesto all at the same time. As we digest the feast, we play cards or board games. It's loads of fun, and best of all, it's a tradition that we've created ourselves that speaks to our unity as a family.

1. When I was a child, we celebrated these holidays:

   _____

   _____

2. I liked [name of holiday] most because …

   _____

3. Which childhood traditions linked to this holiday do I want to preserve?

   _____

   _____

4. Which childhood traditions linked to this holiday do I want to ditch? Why?

   _____

   _____

5. How do *I* want to celebrate this holiday?

   _____

   _____

6. Does my spouse want to celebrate this holiday? Why or why not?

   _____

   _____

7. If my spouse wants to celebrate this holiday, how would he/she observe it?

   _____

   _____

8. What makes this holiday such a touchy issue in the family?

   _____

   _____

9. What holidays do I see celebrating together with my spouse? Why?

   _____

   _____

10. What holidays do I think my spouse sees us celebrating as a family? Why?

    _____

    _____

Party Hearty

There are four ways to celebrate any religious holiday. Here they are:

1. **Follow traditional rituals.** For example, in a Catholic home, this might include decorating a Christmas tree, hanging outdoor lights and garland, attending Midnight Mass on Christmas Eve and/or Mass on Christmas Day, having an elaborate Christmas dinner, and exchanging presents on Christmas Eve or Christmas Day.

2. **Observe minimal rituals.** These families might just hang a wreath on Christmas and have a family dinner on Hanukkah, for instance.

3. **Actively do it all.** Here's a letter from a couple that has successfully melded both traditions:

   > "Sid still purchases our annual Christmas tree, and I make the Hanukkah latkes. Sid hides the Easter eggs, and I prepare our seder dinner. Now, as I plan our daughter's bat mitzvah, I find I am enjoying the traditions of this rite of passage and feeling rather content that Sid and I have overcome what could have been a huge obstacle."

   > —Melissa, 42

4. **Create nontraditional celebrations.** Interfaith families might work together in a soup kitchen or volunteer at a homeless shelter during Christmas and Hanukkah. Helping others captures the true spirit of the holiday while sidestepping the problems of "mine" or "your" holiday rituals.

Which option should you select? Here's where communication comes into play. Be honest with yourself and your partner about the importance of holiday rituals. Then you'll be ready to explore ways to share and blend rituals to create new family traditions. Start here.

1. **Decide which holidays to celebrate.** Perhaps you can celebrate them all; perhaps you can't. Make your choices—but don't close the door. Be ready to shift gears if circumstances change.

2. **Learn, learn, learn.** Don't be afraid to ask. Until recently, I didn't know the difference between Virginia ham and fresh ham. As a result, when I saw a fresh ham at my sister-in-law's Easter dinner, I had no idea what it was. The solution? I asked, "Why isn't this ham pink?" You only feel silly for a second, but then you'll never have to ask again.

3. **Make sure you correctly observe all customs.** People born into the faith or culture have the leeway to be sloppy. You don't. Adhere to the letter of the law, at least in the beginning. Later, you can have some ham on your matzo, too.

Have Your Cake and Eat It, Too?

Rebecca was raised Jewish; her husband John is Catholic. The couple decided to compromise on the issue of religion, and they now attend the Unitarian Universalist Fellowship as a family. Here's their story:

"It was important for us to have a way to worship that we could all share," John notes, adding that this compromise allows them both to keep in touch with their religious roots and to maintain the traditions of their childhood.

"The compromise gives our three children a positive religious experience, not watered down," Rebecca maintains. "This way, the kids aren't half this and half that—or all nothing," she says. Although Rebecca and John are pleased with the solution they've forged together, not everyone in their family is content with their decision.

"We're somewhat open about what we do," Rebecca says, "because even though we see it as a good thing, my parents don't. They're very upset that the kids aren't being brought up with all the Jewish traditions." Rebecca cites this example:

> "At Easter and Passover, John and I were very pleased when the Reverend laid out on a table some of the objects that the Jewish and Christian tradition have in common: an Easter egg and an egg on the seder plate. You realize that it's not such a coincidence that these two holidays fall so close together.
>
> My parents were livid at the comparison, however. 'Passover commemorates the exodus of the Israelites from Egypt and their safe flight across the Red Sea,' my mother said. 'Easter commemorates the resurrection of Jesus Christ. They are not at all the same,' she finished in a steely voice."

A friend of mine echoed the same thought: "If you are Jewish," he said, "you believe the Messiah is still coming. But if you're Christian, you believe he's already come. So you can't have it both ways—you can't really celebrate *both* Passover and Easter."

However, interfaith couples who chose to celebrate both Easter and Passover have discovered that seeking the broad spiritual meaning in any religious holidays can make it easier to find common ground. For example, in celebrating Easter and Passover jointly, your family might focus on the themes of spring's new growth, or renewal in your own life, or liberation from bondage of any kind.

All or Nothing?

ABC newswoman Cokie Roberts, raised a Christian, and her husband Steve, raised Jewish, have successfully resolved the December dilemma. "Inclusion is a much better way to go—that's the secret—though there's really no magic formula," says Steve. "It's also more fun," adds Cokie. "Your kids end up with twice as many presents."

Act of Faith

Passover (Pesach in Yiddish) celebrates the successful Jewish exodus from Egypt as told in Exodus 12:3–17. The holiday begins at sundown on the fourteenth day of Nisan (the first month of the Jewish ecclesiastical year), about the time of the vernal equinox, and lasts for eight days. Passover includes the seder, a ceremonial meal held on the first two nights. During the seder, the narrative of the exodus is retold, songs are sung, and prayers of thanks are given, read from a book called the Haggada. Observant Jews eat unleavened bread called matzo to commemorate the Jews' hasty departure from Egypt—they didn't even have time to let their bread rise.

Cokie and Steve have a very big seder every Passover and a very big Christmas. Family members host the other holidays. There is one interesting bonus to this system: Unlike couples of the same faith who often argue over whose family to celebrate with, for interfaith couples there's no contest. "One of the benefits of an interfaith marriage like ours," says Cokie, "is that it's easier to know where you'll be on holidays."

The Matzo Bunny

Some couples combine both religions, as Cokie and Steve Roberts have done. The following are some suggestions for combining Easter and Passover, if this solution works for you and your honey.

Don't Go There

Celebrating both traditions can keep people from connecting with either one, many religious leaders caution.

➤ If you're the Jewish partner, lead a seder at your spouse's church. This can help avoid "Christianizing" the Passover seder.

➤ If you're the Christian partner, discuss the history of the Last Supper. This helps all family members realize that Jesus celebrated Passover as any Jew of that time would have. This option opens the way to exploring how Judaism and Christianity are wholly separate but related.

➤ If you're the Jewish partner and you want to attend Easter Sunday services with your Christian spouse and his or her kinfolk, meet with the clergy beforehand to make sure the language won't offend your beliefs. It's not uncommon for Christian religious leaders to preach that Jews crucified Christ or that anyone who doesn't believe in Jesus' actual resurrection is excluded from salvation. Some clergy are willing to change language or add a brief statement to make Jewish partners feel more comfortable.

➤ If you're the Christian partner, share the fun of holding a family egg hunt, sporting new Easter bonnets, and watching the Easter parade.

Don't Go There

Interfaith couples must *both* make the effort to share their religious heritage. Don't throw the responsibility for this to your partner because it's easier, less stressful, or might cause strife with your parents. Don't wuss out on me here, buckaroo.

Back to the Future

Religious differences aren't the only problems we face at holidays. A number of hot spots are just built into holiday traditions, like the bike with 10,000 pieces that must be assembled on Christmas Eve. Here's how to recognize these buttons before they get pushed:

➤ **Great expectations.** Every holiday brings its own set of expectations. Your childhood Christmas celebration may have involved coming downstairs in your pj's and rattling presents; your Hanukkah party may have centered around searching for the hidden bit of matzoh. Even if you're 30 years old and are long done with pj's and party games, you may find it hard to shake those traditions.

➤ **Your side/my side.** No matter how miserable your parents may make you during the holidays, most of us are drawn toward our own side during key events, like lemmings to the cliff. Fortunately, your parents aren't members of the Borg collective, so resistance *isn't* futile.

➤ **You call this a holiday?** Celebrations vary from family to family. What one spouse considers great fun, another considers a real snooze. An afternoon spent cooking, serving, and cleaning up while the men watch football? Hey, that's *my* idea of a swell time. See my point?

We Can Work It Out

Parents often don't realize the problems their married children experience as they try to balance loyalties to their own faith as well as to their spouse's faith. If the older generation didn't experience the same stress, they may not be able to understand how difficult this problem can be to their children, especially to young couples just setting their own boundaries in the relationship.

And if they do realize it, they may not care. "I raised you Catholic, and I deserve the pleasure of spending Christmas with you!" your parents may bellow. Or, "What do you mean you're celebrating Christmas? Have you forgotten that you're a Hindu?" How about "Jews don't eat Easter ham? What kind of people are your spouse's family, anyway?" Which refrain have *you* heard since you've fallen in love with someone from another religion?

For the Families of Interfaith Couples ...

What can you do to deal with the conflicts religion and family can cause on holidays? Here are some suggestions to the "greater family" to help them understand the interfaith family at holidays times:

1. **Respect everyone's decisions.** If family members don't want to celebrate the religious holiday the way "we've always done it," don't be a sore loser. Don't pressure people to change their plans. Respect their decisions, and there's a better chance they'll respect yours.

2. **Be sensitive.** There's no denying that the holidays can be tense under normal circumstances, but they can be especially trying if the year has been difficult. Try to see things from other people's point of view, especially if your child or relative has married out of the faith and so finds your customs strange and uncomfortable.

3. **Be open.** Recognize that people of different faiths have different holiday customs. Consider making some of those customs part of your celebrations.

Family Matters

Women in particular may feel pressured to play the traditional roles at holidays to compensate for jealousy over their career success.

4. **Don't compete.** My family is Jewish, so Christmas and Easter were never headliners when I was a child. Nonetheless, when I married a non-Jewish man, my mother suddenly demanded that we appear for Christmas dinner. When I protested by saying, "We *never* had Christmas dinner," my mother responded, "We had dinner *every* night." Don't make the same mistake.

5. **Be quiet.** Remember that old saying, "If you can't say anything nice, don't say anything at all"? Sometimes, just being quiet can go a long way to smoothing over a tense situation.

6. **Don't tolerate prejudice.** That said, don't sanction intolerance. If Uncle Bonehead, Aunt Stupid, or Cousin Picklebrain says something bigoted, make it plain that the rest of the family doesn't agree. Be a good host.

For the Interfaith Couples Themselves ...

Here are some ways that you and your sweetie can make the holidays easier for each other and your "greater family":

1. **Be loyal to your mate.** Your first allegiance is to your spouse. No matter how heavy a guilt trip your relatives lay on your shoulders at holiday time, recognize that you and your spouse are a couple. By promising to love, honor, and work through the toilet seat issue, you have created your own family. Now that you're a team, work as one.

2. **Make a decision.** There are times when you can sit on the fence—but making a decision about which religious holidays to celebrate isn't one of them. With your spouse, discuss all areas of potential conflict and then create a game plan. Figure out what you're doing for each holiday, when, and why. Plan what you're going to say when the other side pitches a fit. Use the worksheet you filled out earlier to crystallize your thinking.

3. **Recognize that you can't be all things to all people.** Make your holiday decision, announce it to the relatives, and move on. I know this is a lot easier said than done (especially for someone like me who can hold a grudge until it reaches legal age), so work with me here.

4. **Tell people immediately of your plans.** Remember how angry you were when some of your wedding guests canceled at the last minute? "I'll never be such a stinker," you said. So don't be. No Scarlett O'Hara "tomorrow is another day" pronouncements on *this* issue.

   If you can't or don't want to celebrate a holiday with family or friends, don't dodge the issue. Instead, bite the bullet and tell them

Don't Go There

Under no circumstances should you let your family pit one of you against the other. Think of yourselves as the Great Wall of China: Present a solid, united front against outside assault.

Family Matters

Whatever decision you make about religious holiday celebrations is likely to upset someone. That's life.

243

Don't Go There

Always check out all invitations with your spouse before you say "yes" or "no." Try saying, "Thanks for the invitation. I'll talk it over with my beloved and get back to you." Never take it upon yourself to make a decision about the family's whereabouts on a religious holiday—even if your spouse doesn't celebrate it.

as soon as possible. In addition to getting rid of an onerous duty, early notice also allows your in-laws to make alternate plans, if they so desire.

5. **Try to involve both sides of the family in your traditions.** I'd be messing with your head if I said that it's easy to get everyone to play together nicely. Most people never learn to share their toys. Nonetheless, set aside some time for a ritual or two. It doesn't have to be something major like chopping and trimming a 200-foot blue spruce Christmas tree. Your rituals can be small and charming, like an hour of caroling or an evening of potato pancakes and applesauce.

6. **Enjoy yourself.** Try to have fun. After all, these are holidays!

The Least You Need to Know

➤ Religious holidays often cause problems because couples haven't resolved religious differences or because they are battling over power issues.

➤ Learn to communicate effectively to resolve issues. Using negotiation skills and worksheets can help.

➤ You can follow one partner's holiday rituals, observe minimal rituals, follow both spouses' holiday traditions, or create nontraditional celebrations.

➤ As part of the "greater family," make life easier for yourself as family members during the holidays by respecting everyone's decision, being open and sensitive, and resisting the urge to compete.

➤ As part of an interfaith couple, resolve holiday disputes by being loyal to your mate, making decisions, and keeping family and friends in the loop.

Baby's Religious Education

"Train up a child in the way he should go, and when he is old he will not depart from it."

—Proverbs 22:6

This is the hope that all parents have for their children, but it's not always valid where religious education is concerned. When some children of interfaith backgrounds reach maturity, they give up the religious identity in which they were raised in favor of another one. Some children will even reject religion entirely.

In this chapter, you'll discover that neither you, your children, nor the faith you have chosen will lose if the religious path of their childhood leads them to a righteous, moral life.

Play and Pray

Back in the Dark Ages when I was a child, religious education was something to be dreaded, like a root canal or an IRS audit. I remember seemingly endless afternoons of droning instruction in musty basement rooms. My friends of different religions have similar memories. Sister Mary Irene Flanagan confirms our memories.

She recalls that, in the 1960s and 1970s when she worked in the Archdiocese of Los Angeles, the walls of Catholic Sunday schools were hung with posters of children flanked on one side by an angel and the other by a devil. "I was horrified," Flanagan recalls. "Religion was used as a source of control, and the message was 'God is out to get you.'" Sister Flanagan created an entirely new program that stresses God's love for children. "We're not teaching traditional doctrine," she explains. "We're teaching attitudes and values."

Bugs and Hugs

Sister Mary Flanagan is smack dab in the middle of a revolution in religious education. Today, nearly all denominations stress that religious education can be little doses of God mixed in with big helpings of fun. Check out these examples:

Did You Know?

A person cannot make the choice to convert to Judaism until he or she reaches age 13; the choice to convert must be an adult decision and age 13 is the official "adult" age in Judaism.

➤ The "Easter Lady" (a.k.a. Maggie Wright) at Martyrs Roman Catholic Church in Manhattan Beach, California, bursts into the Sunday school program shouting, "Merry Christmas!" Not surprisingly, the kids roar with laughter. When they settle down, Ms. Wright teaches them about Easter values through performance, song, and mime.

➤ Tots at congregation Beth Hatikvah (a Reconstructionist congregation in Chatham, New Jersey) learn about Passover by pretending they are slaves crossing the Red Sea.

➤ At the weekend school at Al Farooq mosque in Atlanta, Georgia, a religious lesson focuses on being kind to animals.

"In the olden days, we used to go in and presume that we needed to introduce God to children," says Ron Cram, a professor of religious education at Columbia Theological Seminary in Atlanta. "Curriculum choices are now beginning with the assumption that the child is bringing his or her conception of who God is into the religious setting." God is still the focus of religious instruction, but the deity is overwhelmingly being revealed as loving and merciful.

These examples show that religious education for the short set is changing drastically. This shift in emphasis is a very good thing for children of interfaith marriages because it melds the differences among denominations and even religions.

This new approach to religious education among tots suggests that most children are being taught to love God, no matter what he is named and how he is worshipped. This new emphasis on caring and love makes it easier for interfaith parents to bring their own religious beliefs into the mix. This can greatly diminish the strains within an interfaith marriage as parents choose yours, mine, ours, or someone else's faith for their children.

A Fly in the Ointment

It's not difficult to select a program for your child if you and your spouse have decided to raise your children in one religion. However, the situation changes with interfaith families who are trying to raise their offspring in both faiths. (To make the task easier, I provide some suggestions in the following section.)

Recognize that not all religious-education programs welcome interfaith children and their families. Sometimes the priest, rabbi, or minister won't be comfortable with the interfaith choice. Other times, the curriculum in a church, synagogue, mosque, or temple can be offensive to interfaith children and their parents. How can you pick a program that's right for you, your spouse, and your children?

Never take a school's reputation on faith; instead, sit in on a few classes and see what is actually being taught. Get a feel for the religious community, too. Evaluate the teachers and facilities just as you would any other nursery school or private kindergarten program. Here are some questions to ask yourself during this process:

➤ What is this religion's official stance on interfaith families? (For example, you know that Muslims, Fundamentalist Christians, and Orthodox Jews don't cotton to interfaith marriages.)

➤ Will the religious leaders welcome us? How can I tell?

➤ Will the congregation make us feel comfortable?

> **Family Matters**
>
> Reform and Reconstructionist synagogues will accept a child into their educational program if either the father or mother is Jewish. Consider this if one partner is Jewish and both partners want a Jewish education for their child.

➤ Are these people whose company I enjoy? Do I feel at ease in their presence?

➤ Do I agree with the religious training that my child will receive?

Don't Go There

Religious education is a serious matter, but it doesn't have to be boring. Keep it fun at home, too.

When you feel comfortable with the religious group and think that your children will get the kind of spiritual training you and your spouse want, then you can join right up.

Put Your Mouth Where Your Money Is

Sending your kids to religious education has a number of advantages. Speaking as half of a busy two-career couple, having your kids get a healthy dose of religion outside the house removes some of the pressure to be all things to all people. But religious education that becomes a "drop and pick" adventure in carpooling is meaningless.

No matter what type of outside religious-education program you eventually select, you and your family must actively participate in the program. Home and school depend on each other. For example, if a child learns about a seder in Sunday school and doesn't have one at home, the lesson loses a lot of its effectiveness.

The following sections discuss some ways to help your child and your family get the most from the Sunday school experience.

Select the Right Approach for Your Child and Family Beliefs

The *approach* is different from the *faith*. For example, not all Sunday school programs focus on Bible stories and catechism rather than abstract concepts such as mercy and love. A Lutheran church in my area, for example, has preschoolers play games that teach the moral and ethical lessons of the faith. Decide which program best suits your family's religious orientation and your child's temperament.

If Possible, Volunteer

Be there or be square. We're all rushed for time, but interfaith families have to give religion that little extra push to make it work. Why not volunteer once a month to help out at the Sunday school? "But it's not my religion, Doc!" you yelp. "I wouldn't know what to do." Never fear; Rozakis is here. You could do any of the following:

➤ Serve snacks

➤ Read stories

➤ Bring in religious artifacts from your own home to share with the class

➤ Teach songs and dances from your own heritage, if the religious leaders agree

If you can't make the time to help, be sure to sit in on some lessons so you know what your child is being taught. If you know the material, you'll have a much easier time reinforcing it at home.

Make Religious Rituals a Part of Your Family Life

No matter how religion is taught in Sunday school, the lessons are most effective when they are reinforced at home.

Keep It Age Appropriate

When my son was on the cusp of his teen years, I decided it was time to have a talk about S-E-X. We did, and I think I got a little too technical. That night, I asked my husband to go over the material with our son to make sure he had understood what I said.

That night, my husband said to our son, "So, I hear you and Mommy talked about sex this afternoon. Do you have any questions?"

"Yes, I do," said our son. I could hear my husband sweating.

"Okay," he answered. "Ask away."

Our son said, "Why does my sister get more toys than I do?"

I'm not sure he was ready for that sex talk just yet.

Family Matters

Tap into the "Mommy network" —the parents of your child's friends—to get their impressions of specific religious-education programs in your neighborhood. I don't know what I'd do without my friends to keep me in the loop!

The moral of the story? Dole out all lessons as your kids can absorb them, especially the complex ones. For example, if your 4-year-old asks, "Why is Mommy Hindu and you are Jewish?" an appropriate answer might be: "Because Mommy and I were born that way." If your child then asks, "What am I?" you could say, "You are both Hindu and Jewish" (or whatever choice you have made).

Practice What You Preach

Actions often speak louder than words, especially when it comes to kids. I'm constantly amazed (and delighted!) at the important life lessons my kids have absorbed by watching us. If you want your kids to have a clear religious identity, have one yourself. If you want them to be spiritual, ditto. Kids can spot hypocrisy from miles away.

Religious Coming-of-Age Ceremonies

Nearly all religions have religious coming-of-age ceremonies. In America, the two most common ones are the Jewish *bar mitzvah* (*bas mitzvah* or *bat mitzvah* for a girl) and the Catholic *First Communion.*

These ceremonies are often lightning rods for problems in interfaith families because they express a family's values and goals. And as we've learned, within interfaith families, partners may not always have the same values and goals. Below are some of the problems that coming-of-age ceremonies may spark within interfaith families.

Don't Go There

Some non-Jews married to Jews welcome the chance for their children to learn Hebrew and Jewish theology, but they nix the bar/bat mitzvah because it's not part of their religious heritage. As a result, they view the ceremony as divisive to family unity.

1. **Why upset the apple cart?** For many interfaith families, the effort required to hold a coming-of-age ceremony requires too much commitment and too much acceptance on the part of extended families. After all, if it ain't broke, why fix it?

2. **It's too much hard work.** Religious coming-of-age ceremonies take a lot of effort. At the very least, someone has to drive to all those bar mitzvah/First Communion classes. When it comes time to run shuttles, many interfaith families decide the best action is inaction. The issue may continue to be unresolved until it's too late to do anything.

3. **Back off!** Within families that haven't committed to one religion or the other, coming-of-age ceremonies may renew old pressures to get off the fence and choose a religion. Jewish grandparents, for instance, may pressure you for a bar mitzvah, seeing it as the last chance they have to give a grandchild a Jewish identity and fulfill their obligations as Jews. Catholic grandparents may urge their children to hold a First Communion, seeing it as a way to make their children commit to Catholicism.

4. **Last picked.** In addition to family pressure to hold a religious coming-of-age ceremony, you and your family may feel great social pressure as well. This happened in my family with our daughter. I was a Girl Scout leader for seven years, and thanks to the chemistry between my indefatigable coleader Audrey and me, we had the "hot" troop. As a result, it was huge—over 25 girls at one point. When my daughter was in second grade, 23 out of 25 girls in the troop were having their First Communion. My daughter was one of the two girls left out.

Now, I'm not telling you to rush right out and book a restaurant for your child's First Communion party or bar mitzvah celebration. Rather, I *am* suggesting that these ceremonies are fraught with a surprisingly heavy emotional load, so buckle up. You may be astonished when your previously secular-Jewish husband suddenly announces that your son *must* have a bar mitzvah. Or when your wife who hasn't been in church since your wedding signs your daughter up for First Communion lessons. Here's a story a friend shared:

> "When I was 13 and taking Hebrew lessons in preparation for my bar mitzvah, I thought it was all a waste of time. My friend Howie and I used to sneak out of class to buy candy in the five-and-dime store next door to the temple. I didn't think I learned much Hebrew at all, but I sure did get chubby!
>
> When I married Maureen, a religious Irish Catholic, I agreed to forgo bar mitzvahs for any sons we had. We've been blessed with two fine boys. Our oldest son turned 13 this year and was so excited about being a teenager. We had a small party and bought him his own TV, but the birthday was a big letdown because it was no different from any other birthday he had ever had. I missed the excitement that came with my bar mitzvah celebration. Thanks to the rabbi's persistence, I had learned my Hebrew. On that day, I felt like I was someone very special, a member of a proud, ancient race of people. I really wish our son had become a bar mitzvah."
>
> —Glenn, age 40

Not everyone feels the same way, of course, and I certainly can't make the decision for you. However, I *can* provide you with the information you need to make an informed decision on your own. Are coming-of-age ceremonies appropriate for your children? If so, which ceremony will you and your family select? Read on to get the information you need to help with this important decision.

Bar and Bat Mitzvah

Celebrated in the child's thirteenth year, the *bar mitzvah* means that the child is obligated to take on the religious duties of an adult. The bar mitzvah ceremony dates back to the medieval period; the bas or bat mitzvah for girls is about 50 years old.

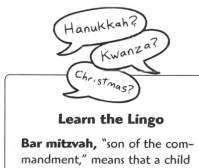

Learn the Lingo

Bar mitzvah, "son of the commandment," means that a child has become an adult in the eyes of the Jewish community.

Act of Faith

Hindu samskaras (or samskars) are the rites or practices enshrined and ordained in Hindu scriptures to guide a person toward a sense of duty and obligation during the various stages of life. Samskaras, which begin at birth and end with the cremation of the body after death, help create a religious atmosphere. The "coming-of-age" ceremonies include Namakarana (naming the child), Nishkramana (taking the child outside for the first time), Annaprasana (feeding the first solid food to the child), Mundan (cutting the child's hair for the first time, when the child is one or three years old), Karnavedha (piercing the child's ears), and Upanayana. During this last ritual (at age five or eight), the child receives three threads to remind him of the three debts he has to repay during his life: the debts to his parents, guru (teacher), and God. Three more strands are added when the young man marries to remind him of the debts he has to repay his wife. Of course, degree of adherence to the samskaras varies among Hindus.

To complete the bar or bat mitzvah rituals, the child must study Hebrew, Jewish history, and Jewish theology. It's a rigorous program that usually takes about four years to complete. The ceremony, held as part of the Sabbath service, requires the child to ...

➤ Chant the benedictions before and after the Biblical lesson is read.

➤ Read the weekly portion from the Torah or *Haftarah* (the prophetic writings) in Hebrew.

➤ Give a short speech, usually on Judaism or a personal interpretation of the Torah/Haftarah passage.

Next Year in Jerusalem

Although bar and bat mitzvah ceremonies are traditionally held in synagogues, Jewish families or interfaith families not affiliated with a congregation often hire a tutor to prepare their child. The actual service is held in a catering hall or their home. An increasing number of families travel to Israel for the ceremony. All these locations are acceptable under Jewish law. Nearly all bar and bat mitzvah ceremonies are followed by luncheons, dinners, or parties.

Many Reform congregations also hold a Confirmation ceremony to mark the child's graduation from the synagogue's religious school. Confirmations are usually held in the spring during the holiday of Shavuot, the time when Moses received the Torah on Mount Sinai. This is a group rather than individual ceremony, and children are 15 to 16 years old. The Confirmation ceremony is still relatively uncommon, however.

Recipe for Success

Interfaith families who wish to have their child become a bar or bat mitzvah should take the following steps:

➤ Make sure your child accepts Judaism as his or her faith.

➤ Find a synagogue where the entire family feels comfortable attending services. Jewish mothers shouldn't have any problems finding a rabbi willing to accept their child for religious instruction (since the child is considered Jewish under Jewish law); non-Jewish mothers will have a more difficult time unless they have converted.

➤ If you can't find a synagogue or don't wish to join one, hire a private tutor to teach your child what he or she will need to know, including Hebrew and Jewish history.

➤ Decide how to celebrate this joyous event with your family and friends. Possibilities range from a small reception at home to a huge blowout at a catering hall or hotel.

Don't Go There

Under Orthodox Jewish law, a girl would not be permitted to read from the Torah. Some Orthodox congregations allow a version of a bat mitzvah ceremony; others do not.

Did You Know?

When a child becomes a bar or bat mitzvah, a father is commanded to free his child and let him or her grow. But Judaism arms the child with knowledge to help him or her along the way: the Torah.

First Communion

The most important symbol of communion is the act of partaking of the Lord's Supper, a rite itself known as *Communion*. Children receiving First Communion must ...

➤ Be baptized members of the church.

➤ Participate regularly in parish worship with their families. Children usually study for two years, during first and second grade, although First Communion can be celebrated at any grade level.

Family Matters

A wit once said, "The reason grandparents and grandchildren get along so well is that they have a common enemy."

Parents are also required to participate in the preparation for their child's First Communion. Parents usually attend several Saturday-morning workshops with their child and work at home with the child from the booklet handed out at the first meeting.

First Communion is a group ceremony celebrated at weekend Masses on the second and third weekends in May, although this varies somewhat from church to church.

Boys usually wear suits. In the past, First Communion suits were often white to symbolize purity, but since white suits were a major expense for the family (and rarely worn again), today most boys wear dark suits. Catholic girls are still formally outfitted in white Communion dresses.

Christian Confirmation

A Christian confirmation, held when a child is 13 to 14 years old, formally marks his or her complete membership in the church. In some Catholic churches, this ceremony takes place during the sophomore year of high school. In most churches, confirmation is considered one of the first adult decisions an individual makes.

Compared to a First Communion, a Confirmation is a low-key event. The event is held in the church and most often is attended only by the immediate family. Christian children who have confirmations can expect to ...

➤ Stand in front of the church, usually in a group.

➤ Answer questions about their faith, individually or in a group.

➤ Receive the bishop's blessings.

To prepare for their Confirmation, teenagers take religious-education classes. Depending on the denomination, the church, and the child's individual circumstances, these classes can run for years or only a few months. Some churches require that parents attend classes with their children. This helps parents discuss the material and share what they've learned. Clearly, such classes are especially meaningful for interfaith families.

Planning Pays Off

When it comes to planning a coming-of-age ceremony in an interfaith family, you may find these ideas useful:

1. **Find religious advisors who share your point of view.** Since not all clergy have warm, open-minded attitudes toward interfaith families, search hard for the ones who agree with the choices you have made.

2. **Be a participant.** Even if your children are being raised in your spouse's faith, participate in their religious education, especially key coming-of-age ceremonies. *Never* sit these out.

3. **Do your homework.** Make sure you know what the ceremony involves, even if it's not your faith. Odds are, your child will ask you a question about a particular ritual. By backing your spouse's faith, you're presenting a united front and conveying the importance of a clear spiritual identity.

4. **Be aware of family concerns.** The initiation rites of all faiths have their special rituals that take time to understand, let alone accept. Christians may feel uncomfortable with the Hebrew liturgy in a synagogue; many Jews find the Christian pageantry, crucifix, and references to "Our Lord Jesus Christ" unsettling.

Act of Faith

At the Shichi-Go-San festival, Japanese parents celebrate their children's growth. On November 15, 3- and 5-year old boys and 3- and 7-year-old girls are taken to shrines, where their parents pray for their futures. Boys often wear *haori* (half-coats) and girls wear *kimono* (the women's traditional gown). Today, however, more and more children wear Western-style formal outfits, which are less expensive and easier to put on. Of course, this coming-of-age ceremony is observed and celebrated to varying degrees among Japanese, whether Buddhists or Christians.

Realize that family and friends may be off-put by the new direction your life is taking. Try to be sensitive to their feelings, but don't let them rule your decisions.

Not So Fast!

I overheard this tale of woe on the train. It involved a Catholic man and his Jewish wife.

> "When our son was 7 years old, my husband turned up at my office one day during lunch, holding our son by the hand. Without explaining why he was there, he walked me across the street to the church. The priest was standing at the door, clearly prepared to meet us—and to welcome our son to his First Communion. We had discussed this issue at length, and I had made it perfectly clear that no son of mine was going to be raised as a Catholic. My husband had arranged for our son to receive religious education for two full years—without

telling me. Our son had kept the secret as well. I grabbed my son and ran out of the church. My husband and I divorced soon after."

Every couple must decide for themselves what religious path to follow as a family. This issue can simmer for years but usually boils over when children are born. You can follow the husband's religion, the wife's religion, both religions, a completely different religion, or no religion at all. The coming-of-age ceremonies you select for your children will be determined by the spiritual path you adopt together. And that's the key word—*together.*

I know that talking about religious milestones can be difficult, even painful. Pressure from family and friends can mount. You can run and you can hide—and your family will suffer. Use the stress you experience over coming-of-age ceremonies in a positive way as a prod to encourage communication.

The following are a couple of stories from couples who have agreed on the religious training their children will receive. See if their solutions work for you.

A Pot of Gold at the End of the Rainbow

A friend shared the following story about a Hindu and Japanese Christian couple who resolved their religious differences well. The story is told from the viewpoint of their children. See if their solution works for you.

> "My parents raised us as Hindus. We celebrated Durga Puja, enjoyed Holi festival when we were in India, attended Hindu weddings, read the Mahabharata, and chanted our 'Namo Namos.' We also celebrated all the Japanese religious and cultural festivals as well as Christmas.

> Instead of focusing on one deity or one religious belief, my parents emphasized Brahman, the universal spirit of being. In retrospect, I thank my stars for being a Hindu because I believe it has such flexibility and adaptability. Being Hindu gave me confidence even as a child that I belonged to a basic, natural order of existence.

> In addition to my parents' no-pressure religious environment and being Hindu, other factors helped me assimilate my parents' religious and cultural differences. The first was being in schools with children from many faiths. Being different was commonplace, even celebrated. The second was having the opportunity to travel to India and experience my father's background. The third was learning a lot about the Hindu side of my heritage."

A Jewish-Christian couple who raised their children in both faiths said:

> "I believe we have met the challenge of an interfaith family successfully. Our children have never been confused, knowing both the history and congruency between our separate religions, yet always acknowledging their Jewish roots."

The Least You Need to Know

➤ Today, most religious education consists of little doses of God mixed in with big helpings of fun.

➤ Select the right religious-education program for your child and family's spiritual beliefs.

➤ Religious coming-of-age ceremonies include Jewish bar/bat mitzvahs and Confirmations and Christian First Communions and Confirmations.

➤ Coming-of-age ceremonies are often lightning rods for problems in interfaith families because they express differing family values and goals.

➤ Find religious advisors who share your point of view. Do your homework, participate in the ceremony, and be aware of concerns among extended family.

Part 6

Untying the Knot

Kentucky: Two men tried to pull the front off an automated teller machine by running a chain from the machine to the bumper of their pickup truck. Instead of pulling the front panel off the machine, though, they pulled the bumper off their truck. Scared, they left the scene and drove home. They also left the chain still attached to the machine, their bumper still attached to the chain, and their vehicle's license plate still attached to the bumper.

Indiana: A man walked up to a cashier at a grocery store and demanded all the money in the register. When the cashier handed him the loot, the robber fled—leaving his wallet on the counter.

Virginia: A burglar tried to break into a department store through a skylight. The police nabbed him on the roof. It seems he forgot to wait until the store was closed. His error was reported by some of the many shoppers still in the store.

Things don't always go as we plan. That's because life has a nasty way of kicking us in the face, especially when we're down. To help you deal with these curve balls, I'll wind up this guide with a discussion of some of the serious problems that confront interfaith couples when marriages dissolve through divorce or death.

Dealing with Divorce

The great American poet Robert Frost wrote a powerful little poem called "Fire and Ice." In the poem, he questions whether the world will end in fire (passion) or ice (hate). He concludes:

> "I think I know enough of hate
> To say that for destruction ice
> Is also great
> And would suffice."

Couples contemplating divorce (or those already divorced) know all about fire and ice. When a marriage is in serious trouble, passion and hate do a wicked dance of death.

This chapter opens with a survey of the ways in which the major American religions regard divorce. Then I'll give you tips for handling this painful issue. You'll get the tools you need to maintain and enrich your relationship with your former spouse (and his or her family) through the years.

In Love and War

"It's just as my parents have warned me—come the first disagreement, no matter how small, and the only thing a shikse [non-Jewish woman] knows to call you is a dirty Jew."

—*Portnoy's Complaint* by Philip Roth

Did You Know?

Clans of long ago that wanted to get rid of their kin used to burn their houses down—hence the expression "to get fired." (I do *not* endorse this method of dealing with an ex!)

Family Matters

In divorce proceedings in Middle Eastern countries, Muslim men usually assume that they are the most appropriate parent to have custody of the children. The father's opinion often prevails since he is considered superior to his wife within this culture. Be sure to consider citizenship when you marry out of your religion and culture.

Some people are ready—even eager—to pin the blame for a failed marriage on spiritual differences. Are their concerns valid or just misplaced paranoia? Unfortunately, the statistics on divorce seem to indicate a small but significant increase in divorce among interfaith couples.

However, there have been only a few studies of the direct relationship between intermarriage and divorce. A study by Harold Christensen and Kenneth Barber in Indiana showed that the divorce rate for Jewish-Christian couples was nearly six times the rate for Jewish-Jewish couples and nearly twice the overall U.S. rate. But this study is more than 15 years old, and its results may not still be valid.

A recent study found that 22 percent of Jewish spouses and about 15 percent of Christian spouses had been previously married, suggesting that remarriage and intermarriage fit together well. After someone divorces a person of their own faith, they are far more likely to marry outside their religion the second time around—about 50 percent more likely.

Logic (and personal experience) tells us that differences in religious and cultural backgrounds can enrich a marriage by adding a touch of piquancy. "Vive la différence!" as the French say. On the flip side, spiritual differences can add to the strains in any marriage, already buffeted by social, economic, and family pressures. Interfaith strain might be the straw that breaks the camel's back … and the marriage. This is especially true when the relationship was already dicey.

In America, over half of all marriages end in divorce—and the number doesn't seem to be declining. If you're involved in an interfaith marriage that's already feeling shaky, you'd better know how your religion and your honey's religion regard the issue of divorce. It's not a bad idea to have this information if you're just getting involved in an interfaith romance, too. Remember that forewarned is forearmed.

Each religion has a different response to the end of a marriage. The following sections discuss the Catholic, Protestant, and Jewish stances on divorce.

Catholic Attitudes Toward Divorce

Catholic canon, or law, views marriage as a lifelong sacrament and does not recognize divorce as a religious procedure. A marriage can sometimes be *annulled,* however, but this is often a long, arduous procedure. Since Vatican II, however, obtaining an annulment is easier than it had been in the past.

Act of Faith

Vatican II, the 21st ecumenical council recognized by the Roman Catholic Church, became the symbol of the church's openness to the modern world. Pope John XXIII announced the council on January 25, 1959, and held 178 meetings with 2,540 bishops from all parts of the world in the autumn of four successive years. The first gathering was held October 11, 1962; the last, December 8, 1965. The council issued 16 documents, most notably the constitutions on divine relevation and the pastoral constitution on the church in the modern world. In a rare departure from its deliberate policy of avoiding condemnations, the council deplored "all hatreds, persecutions, and displays of anti-Semitism at any time or from any source against the Jews."

Be aware that, since annulment has to do with the administration of the sacrament of marriage rather than with the parties involved, a marriage can be annulled without the consent of one party. This often doesn't fly well with the non-Catholic party. It may cause further resentment down the road, which can be dangerous if children are involved.

A Catholic who receives a civil divorce remains in good standing with the church unless he or she remarries without having received an annulment of the original marriage. A divorced Catholic who remarries without having obtained an annulment is

Learn the Lingo

According to Catholic canon, **annulling** a marriage means that a valid sacrament never existed. Therefore, all children born from that union are considered illegitimate.

not supposed to receive communion, but individual dioceses have been known to relax this rule.

The Church's view on the permanence of marriage extends not only to marriages between two Catholics but also to interfaith marriages involving a Catholic partner. For example, if a Jew married to another Jew gets divorced and then wishes to marry a Catholic, the Jewish partner would have to apply to the Church for an annulment of the first marriage, even though no Catholics were involved.

Protestant Attitudes Toward Divorce

In general, Protestants view divorce with sorrow and regret but not as a sin that bars a Protestant from sacramental fellowship. As a result, Protestants welcome divorced people into religious observances. Protestant clergy will often counsel couples whose marriages are in trouble but may recommend separation or even divorce when the differences seem irreconcilable. This holds true for interfaith couples as well as marriages in which both partners are Protestant.

Currently, several Protestant sects are experimenting with divorce rituals, religious ceremonies that mark the end of a marriage "in the sight of God and this company." The United Church of Christ already has such a service in its prayer book. The Evangelical Lutheran Church, the United Methodist Church, and the Presbyterian Church have used such services. These highly charged services are still in their infancy, but so far, there's been no bar for their use to mark the end of interfaith marriages as well as intrafaith ones. You may wish to consider having such a ceremony to give your divorce a sense of religious closure.

Jewish Attitudes Toward Divorce

Judaism has always accepted divorce as a fact of life, albeit an unfortunate one. In fact, Judaism recognized the concept of no-fault divorce thousands of years ago! Judaism generally maintains that it's better for a couple to divorce than to remain together in a state of constant bitterness and strife.

Under Jewish law, a man can divorce a woman for any reason or no reason. This does not mean that Judaism takes divorce lightly. Many aspects of Jewish law discourage divorce. The procedural details involved in arranging a divorce are complex and exacting. Except in certain cases of misconduct by the wife, a man who divorces his wife is required to pay her substantial sums of money, as specified in the ketubah (marriage contract). In addition, Orthodox Jewish law prohibits a man from remarrying his ex-wife after she has married another man.

To observant Jews, a civil divorce is not sufficient to dissolve a Jewish marriage. As far as Jewish law is concerned, a couple remains married until the woman receives a bill of divorce, called a *get*. If the woman remarries without obtaining a get, her second marriage is considered adulterous, and her children are considered *mamzerim* (bastards, illegitimate).

It's important to recognize that religious courts (Jewish or otherwise) have no jurisdiction in civil matters such as divorce, but secular courts are often influenced by their decisions as determiners of "community standards."

Learn the Lingo

A Jewish divorce decree is called a **get**.

Round Up the Usual Suspects

A friend shared this sad story of a marriage that he believes shattered as a result of religious differences:

Don't Go There

A rabbinical court can compel a husband to divorce his wife under certain circumstances: when he is physically repulsive because of some medical condition or other characteristic, when he violates or neglects his marital obligations (food, clothing, and sexual intercourse), or according to some views, when there is sexual incompatibility.

> "After 20 years of marriage, I asked Marie if she wanted a divorce. 'That would make your parents happy,' she replied. 'They've always hated me because I'm not Jewish.' I tried to explain that they didn't hate her at all and certainly not over religious differences. They were just scared about me losing my commitment to Judaism. She didn't buy it. She never had. She was still beautiful, and I still loved her, but she had no place in her heart for me. We decided to get a divorce right after our oldest child completed elementary school, six months away.

I spent much time reflecting on my marriage. We'd been married 20 years and had three great kids. For most of that time, I had loved her and been happy. What went wrong? I had asked Marie repeatedly, but she just shook her head. 'Mixed marriage,' my mother said sadly. 'It was bound to happen.' I couldn't believe religion had anything to do with it after all this time, I told her. She just gave me a knowing look and shrugged. 'What is it they say these days?' my mother went on. 'You just had different values.' Maybe Marie was right about my parents after all.

'Did I destroy Judaism?' I ask myself now. If asked their religion, my kids will say Jewish, but are they practicing Jews? No. Will their children be Jewish? I doubt it. Does this make me sad? Very. Should I have married Marie? I wouldn't have my children if I hadn't. Did we negotiate our differences? you ask. I don't think we ever knew what our differences were.

In an attempt to ignore the differences that were so important to our families, we overlooked all differences. We thought love was all that mattered. I suppose that makes this a pretty common 'love' story."

—Irv, 47

Did religion break up the marriage of Irv and Marie? Irv seems pretty sure that it did, but Irv may not be the most reliable witness in this situation.

Family Matters

According to the National Center for Health Statistics, most divorces occur within the first 10 years of marriage. The median duration of marriage for divorcing couples in 1995 was 7.2 years. *That's* why they call it the "seven-year itch."

I don't believe that divorce and intermarriage go hand-in-hand, despite what Irv seems to think. The differences in religious faith are often a smokescreen for other issues. For example, the key element in Irv's story is his realization that he and his wife never identified the problems in their marriage. "Did we negotiate our differences?" he wondered. "I don't think we ever knew what our differences were," Irv answered.

Pressure Points

Nonetheless, religious differences are stress points in any mixed match. Below are some ways that religion can be used as a lever to shatter a marriage. These same strategies work equally well after a divorce to make it difficult (if not impossible) for the couple to get along amicably.

1. **Using religion to work one spouse against the other.** In this scenario, family and friends use religious differences to chip away at the marriage. Ever hear lines like these? "He's not one of us." "She doesn't understand our God." "What can you expect from one of *them*?"

2. **Using religion to manipulate the spouse.** Here's what my acquaintance Mary Ellen told me:

   "My husband wants to sign our twins up for Hebrew school twice a week. These time slots interfere with their dinnertime. I am all for the children spending time learning about their Jewish heritage. However, my husband refuses to drive the carpool, and I'm exhausted after a long day at work. When I refused, he said, 'I knew this would come up. You really want the kids raised Catholic.' I really don't want one more carpool."

3. **Using religion to make the children pawns.** In this plot, the parent tries to convince the children to follow his or her religion, violating agreements made before the children were born. This is an especially ugly strategy. Ironically, it often backfires, as the child may associate religion with conflict and thus avoid all faith.

When these scenarios are played out, even the strongest marriage is likely to feel the strain. Sometimes the differences in faith are the root cause of marital problems. Other times, spiritual and cultural differences get the blame when they may not be the real cause.

Destruction at Ground Zero

A divorce is the legal dissolution of the marriage, but it doesn't have any impact on the emotional bonds that have been formed. No matter how you feel (or felt) about your ex (and his or her relatives), divorce shatters everyone's emotional landscape. The aftermath of a divorce follows a pattern. Nearly everyone involved in the situation follows these steps:

1. **Denial.** The divorcing couple is likely to think, "This can't be happening to me! This can't be happening to this family."

2. **Anger.** Unfortunately, anger over divorce is usually indiscriminate; anyone or anything within firing range is apt to be the target of errant hostility. Keep this in mind if your marriage failed because of religious differences.

Don't Go There

How long does it take a person to grieve over a divorce? No one can set a time limit on sorrow, but if you notice prolonged sadness or sharp changes in personality, it may be time to call in some professional help.

3. **Acceptance.** Finally, the individuals accept the situation and begin to make plans for the future.

As you deal with your feelings over divorce, you're also likely to bargain ("I'll be good if you can just make this go away") and grieve. Be patient and allow yourself the time you need to follow all three stages in the healing process.

Circle the Wagons

Paradoxically, divorce can have a silver lining because it allows the family to rally round, united by their common pain. Of course, adversity also allows family members to engage in covert or open hostilities. It all depends on individual agendas and family history. Unfortunately, the people least able to duck are often in firing range.

How can you help make drastic life transitions less painful for all involved? Here are some ideas:

➤ **Keep important decisions private until you're ready to alert the media.** This isn't to say that divorce should be a deep, dark secret. It *is* to say that a couple's initial decision to divorce should be kept between them until they are ready to make it public.

➤ **Remember that discretion is the better part of valor.** Of course your wife has no spiritual side. Of course your husband has never had any respect for your faith. Of course your/his/her relatives are anti-Semitic, anti-Catholic, anti-whatever-religion-you-are. Since everyone knows it, why add fuel to the fire by commenting on it? Loose lips sink more than ships; they also shatter friendships among former spouses and family members.

➤ **Be patient.** It can take years to work out a divorce. Keep the family together and try to minimize the damage.

Last Licks

All change is hard. After an eternity of doing things a specific way and interacting with your spouse and family members in set patterns, divorce pulls the rug out from under you. After any traumatic change, you'll likely find yourself adrift, bobbing on the ocean of life without any bearings. No matter how much you want to resist, the situation has changed. You have to learn new ways of dealing with your ex if you are to survive.

Try these ideas:

1. Don't expect the situation to resolve itself in a McMoment. Meaningful change comes as slowly as continental drift.

2. Ask for assistance. It's a sign of strength, not weakness.

3. Consider seeking help from someone outside the family, such as a friend, religious advisor, or professional counselor.

4. Realize that with change comes growth. It might not seem possible when the family is going through the crisis, but positive things can come from change. After the crisis, you may emerge as a stronger person.

5. Renew your faith.

Divorce is an excellent time to explore your spiritual side. Strong ties to a religious community can help you cope with most devastating changes, especially divorce.

The Least You Need to Know

➤ There is a small but significant increase in divorce among interfaith couples.

➤ The Catholic Church doesn't recognize divorce; Protestant sects and Judaism do.

➤ The aftermath of a divorce involves denial, anger, and acceptance. Allow yourself time to follow all steps and grieve.

➤ Avoid bad-mouthing your spouse, recognize possibilities for growth, and renew your faith.

Chapter 24

Christian, Jew, and Heaven Too?

> ## In This Chapter
>
> ➤ A case study
>
> ➤ Christian funeral rites and rituals
>
> ➤ Jewish funeral rites and rituals
>
> ➤ Ways to resolve religious differences about death rites

"Out, out, brief candle!
Life's but a walking shadow, a poor player,
That struts and frets his hour upon the stage,
And then is heard no more. It is a tale
Told by an idiot, full of sound and fury,
Signifying nothing."

—from *Macbeth* by William Shakespeare

The Irish have a traditional blessing: "May your relatives stay well and die quickly."
This is rarely the case, however. Life throws us many wicked curve balls, and the most
devious is death. Any death is difficult, but religious differences over belief and death
rituals can shred fragile family bonds and strain even the strongest ones.

In this chapter, you'll first read about a Jewish husband who experienced great strife when his Catholic wife died. The cause of the strife? Religious differences over burial rites. Then I'll explain Christian and Jewish death rituals to help you understand each religion's customs. This section covers some of the issues that arise when a person is close to death, the actual burial, and mourning rites. The chapter ends with suggestions for resolving some of the pressure points that can arise when one member of an interfaith marriage dies.

The Final Frontier

Death is a fact of life, but each religion views the process and aftermath from its own perspective. As a result, funeral services and burial can become bitter, agonizing issues when interfaith couples are involved. A very dear friend faced this dilemma:

> "I am a Jewish man who was married to 'Kate,' a devout Catholic. Kate had been educated completely in Catholic schools—elementary school all the way up to and including college. Kate's entire family took their faith very seriously; her aunt was a nun. Although I attended secular public schools, I consider my-self an observant Jew. Kate and I had never resolved our religious differences and certainly never talked about death. We did not have children.
>
> We were married for a decade when Kate died very suddenly. When I bought a burial plot in an ecumenical part of a local cemetery, her parents hit the roof. Why wasn't their daughter being buried in a Catholic cemetery or, at the very least, in the Catholic part of an ecumenical cemetery? I explained that many years down the road, I wanted to be buried by Kate's side and didn't want to be in a Catholic cemetery. I knew that Catholics were allowed to be buried any-where, even in Jewish cemeteries, so I thought I was being more than fair. Kate's parents weren't mollified. *I* could be buried wherever I wanted, they said, but their daughter would be buried in a Catholic cemetery. I got my way, but it was a sour victory.
>
> Several years later, I remarried, this time to a Jewish woman. Kate's family knew that I would now plan on being buried next to my second wife, in a Jewish cemetery. Kate's sister contacted me a few months after my wedding. She wanted to move her sister's body to a Catholic cemetery. The issue had clearly simmered in their family for years, and they couldn't rest easily until Kate was buried according to their beliefs. Of course, I agreed to their request."

The disagreement over burial arose over a fundamental Jewish-Catholic difference in belief. Let's examine these beliefs now.

The Christian Death Rituals

"Nothing in his life
Became him like the leaving it. He died
As one that had been studied in his death,
To throw away the dearest thing he ow'd,
As 'twere a careless trifle."

—from *Macbeth* by William Shakespeare

From a Christian perspective, death is a milestone on a much longer pilgrimage. According to Christian beliefs, God does not abandon his followers in death. The Resurrection of Christ gives Christians this hope.

As Death Approaches

When death seems near, devout Christians may want to "make their peace with God." This is accomplished through specific rites.

➤ The Catholic Church offers the sacrament of Anointing of the Sick. This includes the individual opportunity of Confession and Communion.

➤ The Protestant Church will often bring Communion to the ill, even though God will forgive a dying person even if he or she does not confess sins.

Family Matters

Catholics are encouraged to receive the sacrament of Anointing of the Sick even if they do not feel that death is near. This rite offers encouragement to help people get well soon.

After Death

Here are the Christian rituals after a death has occurred.

1. **Preparing the body.** After a Christian dies, the body is usually taken to a funeral home to be embalmed and prepared for viewing. The body of a Christian man can be dressed in any outfit he or the family desires, but it's usually a suit. Christian men who are killed while in the Armed Forces can be buried in full uniform. Police and firefighters may be dressed in their uniforms, especially if they died in the line of duty. Contact the military, police, and fire departments for specific regulations.

   The body of a Christian woman is equally well-dressed, sometimes in a new outfit or one that has special meaning. This might be a dress she had worn to an anniversary party, for example.

2. **The casket.** Christians may be buried in any type of casket they wish, from plain to very elaborate.

3. **Cremation.** Both Catholics and Protestants allow cremations as well as burial above and below the ground. In the case of an interfaith couple, neither the Catholic nor Protestant tradition has any objection to a Christian being buried in a family plot in a Jewish cemetery.

4. **Displaying the body.** The coffin may be open or closed, depending on the family's wishes.

5. **Flowers.** There is often a lavish display of flowers at a Christian funeral. In addition, Masses in memory of deceased Catholics may be arranged at parish churches. Mourners give the relatives of deceased Catholics a *Mass card* to indicate that they have made a donation to the Church to have a special Mass said. There will be a special stand at the wake to display Mass cards that have been sent.

6. **Funeral rites and officiants.** Catholics in good standing are usually given a Mass of Christian Burial in a church. As with any Mass, a priest officiates. A minister usually presides at a Protestant funeral or memorial service, but in many churches, any informed Christian may do so. The service contains prayers, scripture readings, and specific mention of the deceased (but not a eulogy).

   The funeral may be in a church or the funeral home. As previously mentioned, Catholic funerals are usually held in churches.

   After interment, the mourners return home, where family and friends share a meal. Often, friends and family will bring food to the bereaved. This meal may also be held in a restaurant.

Learn the Lingo

A **wake** is a vigil held over a corpse until burial.

7. **Burial.** Burial is usually several days after death. While burial practices vary among Christian denominations, in many cases, the family gathers in the funeral home for one or two days before the burial to pay their respects to the family and bid farewell to the deceased. The body is on display, surrounded by floral tributes. This is called the *wake*. After the wake, the body is taken for interment.

8. **Tombstones.** Christians can erect a tombstone over the grave whenever they wish. There is no set ritual.

9. **Mourning rituals.** Christianity doesn't have an established period of mourning as Judaism does. As a result, you have to treat each bereaved person individually. Some bereaved may wish to resume normal social activities within a week; others, in contrast, may wait months before reentering the social whirl.

Special times may be set aside in the church service for remembrance of the deceased. In Protestant denominations, it's customary to pay tribute to the dead during the Sunday closest to All Saint's Day (November 1). Tributes may also be offered on New Year's Eve or New Year's Day.

The Jewish Death Rituals

Since we're on such a sober topic, here's one of my favorite jokes to lighten the mood.

Seymour Schwartz was a good, deeply religious man. When Seymour passed away, he was greeted at the Pearly Gates by the Lord himself.

"Hungry, Seymour?" asked the Lord.

"I could eat," Seymour replied.

So the good Lord opened a can of tuna and reached for a chunk of fresh rye bread and they shared it. While eating this humble meal, Seymour looked down into Hell and saw the inhabitants devouring huge steaks, lobsters, pheasants, pastries, and fine wines. Curious, but deeply trusting, Seymour was quiet.

The next day the Lord again invited Seymour to join him for a meal, and again the Lord served tuna and rye bread. Once again, Seymour looked down and could see the denizens of Hell enjoying caviar, champagne, lamb, truffles, and chocolates. Still Seymour said nothing.

The following day, mealtime arrived and another can of tuna was opened. Seymour could contain himself no longer. Meekly, he said, "Lord, I am grateful to be in heaven with you as a reward for the pious, obedient life I led. But here in heaven all I get to eat is tuna and a piece of rye bread, and in the Other Place, they eat like emperors and kings! Forgive me, O Lord, but I just don't understand."

The Lord sighed, "Let's be honest, Seymour—for just two people does it pay to cook?"

In Judaism, death is considered a natural process that has meaning as part of God's plan. Observant Jews believe in an afterlife in which those who have lived a worthy life will be rewarded. Your place in the afterlife is determined by a merit system based on your actions, not by who you are or what religion you profess.

However, because Judaism is primarily focused on life here and now rather than the afterlife, Judaism does not have much dogma about the afterlife. This leaves a great deal of room for personal opinion. An Orthodox Jew may believe that the souls of the righteous dead go to a place similar to the Christian heaven, or that they are reincarnated through many lifetimes, or that they simply wait until the coming of the Messiah, when they will be resurrected. Likewise, Orthodox Jews can believe that the souls of the wicked are tormented by demons of their own creation or that wicked souls cease to exist at death.

Did You Know?

Maimonides is ranked as the outstanding Jewish philosopher of the Middle Ages; his contributions to the development of Judaism earned him the title "second Moses." His greatest work in the field of Jewish law is the *Mishneh Torah*, a 14-volume work. In addition, he created the Thirteen Articles of Faith, which many Orthodox Jews still follow. Maimonides is also famous as a physician and a writer on astronomy, logic, and mathematics.

Family Matters

Autopsies are allowed for Christians. However, Orthodox Jews generally discourage autopsies as a desecration of the body. An autopsy is permitted, however, when it may save another's life or when local law requires it. When autopsies are performed, they should be minimally intrusive.

As Death Approaches

Jews who realize that death is imminent should recite "Hear O Israel, the Lord is our God, the Lord is One." A rabbi need not be present at the death of a loved one, but family members should be. This is considered a supreme obligation in Judaism.

When death is imminent and certain and the patient is suffering, Jewish law permits a person to cease artificially prolonging life. Thus, in certain circumstances, Jewish law permits "pulling the plug" or refusing extraordinary means of prolonging life.

After Death

Jewish death rituals are very detailed and specific. Here are the main points:

1. **Preparing the body.** In preparation for the burial, the body is thoroughly cleaned and wrapped in a simple, plain, linen shroud. Traditionally, the corpse is not embalmed, and no organs or fluids may be removed. Non-Orthodox Jews may not follow these traditions, however.

2. **The casket.** In the Orthodox tradition, the casket should be free of all metal to make it easier to return to the earth according to tradition. Among the highly observant, a plain pine coffin is often used to show that all Jews are equal in death.

3. **Cremation.** Orthodox Jews do not allow cremation, although Reform and Conservative Jews may elect this option. However, even the most secular Jews may oppose cremation because they associate it with the Holocaust.

4. **Displaying the body.** The body is never displayed at Orthodox Jewish funerals because open-casket ceremonies are forbidden by Jewish law. According to Orthodox Jewish law, exposing a body is considered disrespectful because it allows not only friends but also enemies to view

the dead, mocking their helpless state. However, non-Orthodox Jews might have an open coffin, but never during the service or while the rabbi is present.

5. **Flowers.** Flowers are never sent or displayed at a Jewish funeral. People often send fruit and food baskets to the home of the deceased. In addition, people make donations to charitable organizations in the memory of the deceased.

6. **Funeral rites and officiants.** A rabbi will most likely officiate at the funeral but any knowledgeable Jew is acceptable. Funeral services are rarely scheduled at synagogues. Instead, they are held at funeral homes.

Family Matters

According to some sources, organ donation is permitted under Jewish law.

At the funeral, psalms and prayers are recited, but the heart of the service is the eulogy for the deceased. Friends and relatives are encouraged to offer their tributes and speak about the deceased's spiritual legacy.

Traditionally, close relatives of the deceased tore their clothing to show their grief. Nowadays, this is rarely done. To show this symbolically, the funeral director pins a black ribbon on the mourner's lapel and cuts it. The ribbon is placed on the left side (over the heart) of children of the deceased and on the right side of all other family members. Mourners wear the ribbon on the outside of their garments for everyone to see for 7 days and inside for the rest of the 30-day mourning period except on the Sabbath. The ribbon can be removed and pinned on any clothing. Orthodox Jews often tear their clothing rather than wear the ribbon.

7. **Burial.** The body is buried as soon as possible but never on the Sabbath (sundown Friday to sundown Saturday) or on major Jewish holidays.

The gravesite service is quite short, and mourners are invited to cover the casket with dirt. This is sometimes done literally with a shovel and wheelbarrow of soil. Other times, mourners are given small bags of soil to sprinkle on the casket. In Orthodox Judaism, the casket must be lowered and the grave completely filled.

In interfaith marriages, the non-Jewish partner might not be able to be buried with his or her Jewish mate. Cemeteries operated by Orthodox groups permit only Jews to be buried within their boundaries, but cemeteries owned a~ ated by Reform Jewish or Jewish fraternal organizations not affiliate religious denomination permit non-Jews to be buried in family Jewish symbols such as crosses are not permitted on gravesto.

Act of Faith

It is also customary in some communities to place small stones on a gravesite when visiting it. This custom has become well-known from the movie *Schindler's List,* in which the children of Holocaust survivors placed stones on the grave of Oscar Schindler. It's like leaving a calling card for the dead person to let him or her know you were there. However, the custom is not universal, even among traditional Jews, and there seems to be some doubt as to how it originated.

Learn the Lingo

Shiva is the Jewish seven-day mourning period after the burial of a loved one.

8. **Tombstones.** Orthodox Jewish law requires that a tombstone be prepared so that the deceased will not be forgotten and the grave will not be desecrated. It is customary in some communities to keep the tombstone veiled, or to delay in putting it up, until the end of the 12-month mourning period. Jews who observe this custom generally have a formal unveiling ceremony when the tombstone is revealed.

9. **Mourning rituals.** Jewish mourning rituals are designed to show respect for the dead and to comfort the living. Jewish mourning practices can be broken into several periods of decreasing intensity.

First, from the time of death to the burial, the family should be left alone and be allowed the full expression of grief. Condolence calls or visits should not be made during this time.

Second, among the Orthodox, after the burial, a relative, friend, or neighbor prepares the first meal for the mourners. The meal traditionally consists of eggs (a symbol of life) and bread. The meal is for the family only, not for visitors. After this time, condolence calls are permitted.

Third comes *shiva,* observed by parents, children, spouses, and siblings of the deceased, preferably together in the deceased's home. Shiva begins on the day of burial and continues until the morning of the seventh day after burial. Reform and Conservative Jews may sit shiva for fewer than seven days. Here's what you can expect to see:

➤ Mourners traditionally sit on low stools or the floor instead of chairs.

➤ They do not wear leather shoes, shave, cut their hair, or work.

➤ Mirrors in the house are covered (since they are a symbol of vanity).

➤ Prayer services are held where the shiva is held.

Fourth, among traditional Jews, shiva is followed by a 30-day mourning period. If a parent has died, this is followed by a year of mourning. During that time, mourners avoid parties, celebrations, theater, and concerts.

From then on, every year on the anniversary of the death, family members observe the deceased's Yahrzeit. Among the Orthodox, only sons recite Kaddish and say special prayers in synagogue; all mourners light a candle that burns for 24 hours. Among non-Orthodox Jews, all children of the deceased can say Yahrzeit.

Learn the Lingo

Kaddish is Jewish prayer said to mark yearly anniversaries of a person's death.

Holding the Bag

"If it be now, 'tis not to come; if it be not to come, it will be now; if it be not now, yet it will come—the readiness is all. Since no man, of aught he leaves, know what is't to leave, betimes, let be."

—from *Hamlet* by William Shakespeare

Hamlet realized that being mentally prepared for death is important. When it comes to interfaith couples, it's crucial to have your ducks in a row concerning your last wishes—or the survivor is sure to get shot down.

Now that you know the Christian and Jewish burial customs, you're still left with the issue of individual preferences in a mixed match. For example, how should a Jewish wife bury a Catholic spouse? What about a Lutheran man burying his Catholic wife? And so on … In short, how should interfaith couples deal with differing death rituals? Here are my suggestions:

Learn the Lingo

Yahrzeit is the yearly anniversary of the date of the deceased's death. Among Orthodox Jews, it is celebrated according to the Jewish calendar, not the Gregorian calendar.

1. **Face the music.** Only the macabre think about death. It's creepy to consider our demise. Besides, if we don't talk about it, it can't happen, right? Wrong. Dead wrong.

   There are only two certain things in this world, cupcake: death and taxes. Ignoring death won't make it go away. Recognize that, eventually, we all cash out our chips, push up daises, and take a dirt nap. No one gets out of this world alive, no matter how much health food we consume.

Act of Faith

The funeral rites of Hindus vary considerably, but commonly the corpse is cremated and the ashes (or a portion of them) are thrown into the Ganges or some other sacred river. Traditionally, the leader of the ceremony sprinkles the body with holy water and repeats: "Depart (ye evil spirits), slink away from here; the Fathers (ancestors) have made for him this place of rest, distinguished by days (ahobhir), waters (adbhir), and bright lights (aktubhih)." The practice of *suttee* (widows immolating themselves on their husband's corpses) is no longer practiced.

Family Matters

Be aware that people for whom religion never seemed important may suddenly become very religious when it appears that the end is near. Respect their wishes.

2. **Figure out how you want to depart.** Decide what would make you happy at the end of your life. Your death and burial might have a religious component, or they might not.

   For example, I've decided that when I die, I want anything usable (eyes, kidneys, heart, liver, lungs, and so on) to be donated. The rest gets cremated and put into an urn. I've already picked the urn out: It's like a tissue box—a subtle but effective allusion to my constant allergies. I want my remains (in this cute box) put smack dab in the middle of a table just loaded with desserts. I'm thinking an ice-cream sundae bar, several cheesecakes, chocolate cakes, and a load of cookies—in short, all my favorites. I want my friends to stop by for dessert, say something nice about me, and take home the extras in a doggie bag. I don't want a religious component at all.

3. **Have your honey share his or her last wishes.** Now you have to open up a dialogue with your spouse to find out his or her last wishes. Even if you don't want all the bells and whistles that faith provides, your honey might. But you'll never know if you don't talk about it together.

4. **Get the rules.** Decide whether what you and your honey want done with the remains is possible. For example, recall that some Jewish cemeteries do not allow anyone who is not Jewish to be buried in their grounds. If an interfaith couple wants a Jewish burial, I advise them to make their burial arrangements far in advance of anticipated need. Planning ahead helps ensure that you and your honey get the final resting place you want. It also makes the event much easier on those left behind who have to make the plans.

5. **Discuss it.** Overcome your queasiness and tell your spouse and children exactly what you want done. My beloved hubby and sweet kids know all about my last plans. Now you do, too.

6. **Recognize and acknowledge religious-based points of conflict.** There's great room for problems when it comes to religious burial rites. Take the issue of displaying the body. Catholic mourners may be comforted at the last sight of a dead person looking peaceful and at rest. In contrast, Jews are likely to find the Christian custom of "viewing" the dead body in an open coffin repulsive—even nauseating.

   Similarly, Christian partners may take comfort from buying an expensive burnished coffin lined with rich satin. They are likely to see the coffin as a sign that they have done their best by ushering out their beloved in rich style. The coffin and flowers show their love for the deceased. Jews, raised on a tradition of simple burials, are likely to find such a display ostentatious and unseemly.

   Likewise, a Christian might find the Jewish custom of burying the deceased quickly very upsetting, and interpret it as not allowing people time to mourn. Christians may also see the plain pine coffins as a sign of disrespect.

   Will you be able to carry out the wishes of a deceased spouse if they contradict your own beliefs? And if you do, will you feel estranged from your partner at the very end of your lives together? These are key issues to consider and discuss with your family and perhaps your religious advisor.

7. **Put it in writing.** It's not enough just to talk about it; write your last wishes down and get your spouse to do the same. If nothing else, you'll protect your honey from the inevitable criticism or smoldering resentment from your side of the family if you make these decisions yourself.

8. **Get everyone in the loop.** Don't wait until you're coffin shoppin' to let the family in on the news that your Lutheran husband has decided he wants to be buried according to Jewish rites. If you anticipate a crisis developing, make sure you and your spouse share your plans with everyone involved.

Don't Go There

Never criticize someone's religious preferences, especially when death rituals are involved.

Funerals are never pleasant events, but they don't have to resemble nuclear meltdowns.

It's important to be sensitive to your partner's spiritual needs all during your relationship together. If you're able to do this, making funeral plans should be smooth.

The Least You Need to Know

➤ Each religion views death and its aftermath from its own perspective.

➤ Learn as much as you can about the funeral customs of each religion.

➤ Recognize your own mortality, decide how you want to be buried, and make your wishes known to your spouse and children. Have your spouse do the same.

➤ Recognize and acknowledge religious-based points of conflict and put your wishes in writing.

Glossary

abrazo   Among people from Hispanic backgrounds, it is good manners for friends to embrace and simultaneously pat each other on the back. This action is called the abrazo.

adherents   People who follow a certain creed, sect, or religion.

Advent Christian Church   First organized in 1860 in Salem, Massachusetts, the Advent Christian Church preached a doctrine of "conditional immortality," according to which the dead remain in an unconscious state until the resurrection, which would take place at the second coming after the millennium.

Allah   The Arabic name for God. Refers to the same God worshipped by Jews and Christians.

Amish   A very conservative Christian faith group. Many of their beliefs are identical to those of Fundamentalist and other Evangelical churches, including baptism and a literal interpretation of the Bible. Differences include their determination to remain aloof from the world; their rejection of the military and warfare; their lack of a central authority (each district is self-governing); and the fact that they usually do not seek converts.

Anglican Church   In England, the Church of England is also called the Anglican (English) Church; in America, it's called the Episcopal church.

annulling   According to Catholic Canon law, annulling a marriage means that a valid sacrament never existed. Therefore, all children born from that union are considered illegitimate.

Ashkenazic Jew   Ashkenazic Jews are descended from Jews who emigrated from Germany and Eastern Europe in the mid-1800s. Some speak Yiddish, a language based on German and Hebrew.

atheists   Those who profess skepticism, disbelief, or irreligion, including people opposed to all religion.

Baha'i   Founded by Baha'Ullah ("glory of God") in Iran in 1844, Baha'i teaches that the revealed religions of the world are in agreement.

Baptism   Immersion or sprinkling with water, part of the conversion to Christianity.

Baptist   Baptists are members of a Christian sect who believe that the New Testament is God's authority for all matters of faith and conduct.

Bar Mitzvah   Literally "son of the commandment," it means that a child has become an adult in the eyes of the Jewish community.

Bhagavad-Gita   The Hindu holy book.

body language   A form of nonverbal communication. Body language includes such gestures and movements as nodding, crossing your arms and legs, tapping your foot, jiggling your leg, and looking someone in the eye.

Brahman   In Hinduism, the spiritual source of the universe.

Buddha   Means "the awakened" or "the enlightened" one. It commonly refers to Siddhartha Gotama, who became enlightened around 500 B.C.E.

Buddhism   A doctrine begun by Siddhartha Gotama, the Buddha, who became enlightened around 500 B.C.E. Buddha's teachings are based on the Four Noble Truths: that life is impermanent and produces suffering (or *dukkha*); that suffering is caused by ignorance of reality and the craving, attachment, and grasping that result; that suffering can be ended by overcoming ignorance and attachment; and that the way to end suffering is the Eightfold Path.

cantor   is a trained musician who leads the worship services at a larger synagogue. Cantors are also teachers of religion.

castes   Hindu society is divided into social strata called *castes*. Traditionally, observant Hindus would never date or marry outside their caste, much less their religion.

Catholicism   The largest body of Christians in the world, Catholics believe that Jesus Christ established the Church under the leadership of Peter, His disciple. Catholics accept the seven sacraments: baptism, confirmation, holy matrimony, holy orders, sacrament of the sick, reconciliation (confession), and Eucharist (communion).

Chanukah   Also **Hanukkah.** The annual Jewish festival celebrated on eight successive days in December. Also known as "the Festival of Lights," Chanukah commemorates the rededication of the Temple of Jerusalem by Judas Maccabee in 165 B.C.E. after it had been profaned by Antiochus, King of Syria and overlord of Palestine.

chiansam   An Asian woman's form-fitting outfit with high slits up the sides of the skirt.

Christianity   The most widely distributed of the world's religions, Christianity is based on the acts and sayings of Jesus Christ as related by his followers and apostles. Christians believe that by his death on the cross, Jesus Christ made a covenant for the redemption of humanity.

chuppah (or huppa)   A Jewish wedding canopy. It symbolizes the home.

Church of God of the Abrahamic Faith   Also called the Church of God General Conference. Members believe the Bible is the supreme standard, resulting in a literal interpretation.

circumcision   Cutting off the foreskin of the penis.

Conservative Judaism   Formally organized as the United Synagogue of Conservative Judaism in 1913, Conservative Judaism maintains that the truths found in Jewish scriptures and other Jewish writings come from God, but were transmitted by humans and contain a human component. Conservative Jews follow Jewish laws, but believe that the Law should change and adapt, absorbing aspects of the predominant culture while remaining true to Judaism's values.

convenant   An agreement or a contract.

conversion   The formal process of changing religious beliefs.

dharma   In Hinduism, a code of moral and religious conduct followed by the devout.

diocese   An ecclesiastical district under the jurisdiction of a bishop.

Druze   The Druze (or Druse) are members of a Middle Eastern sect who live mainly in mountainous regions of Lebanon and southern Syria. The Druze believe that at various times God has been divinely incarnated in a living person; His final incarnation was in the person of al-Hakim (985–1021).

Eastern Orthodoxy   The general term for the various Christian communions of the Middle East and Eastern Europe, of which three groups remain today: the Oriental Orthodox (Armenian church, Coptic church of Alexandria, Ethiopian church, and Syrian church, Syrian church in India), the Orthodox church (Turkey), and the Eastern Rite churches.

Eightfold Path   In Buddhism, the way to end suffering. It consists of right views, right intention, right speech, right action, right livelihood, right effort, right-mindedness, and right contemplation.

Episcopalian   An offshoot of the Roman Catholic Church, the episcopal church was begun by King Henry VIII of Great Britain in 1534. The church believes in many of the same rites as the Roman Catholics, but permits divorce.

epistle   A letter.

Eucharist   Communion, the sacramental offering and consumption of bread and wine representing the body and blood of Christ.

evangelical Fundamental Christians often prefer to call themselves evangelical Christians—*evangelical* referring to a belief in the Gospel, the Christian message of the New Testament—because *fundamentalist* is often used in a derogatory way.

Five Pillars of Islam The essential religious duties required of every adult Muslim who is mentally able. They constitute the core practices of the Islamic faith.

fundamentalist Fundamentalist Christians take their name from their belief that the Bible truly is the Word of God and that it is to be interpreted literally. They believe that to reach God, it takes an admission of need (that is, a recognition that one has sinned and thus has a need to be forgiven by God), coupled with the belief that it was Jesus' death on the cross that provided payment for sin. Followers also believe that Jesus took the punishment for all sin and that deliverance from that punishment (and a place in Heaven) will come if the individual lives by faith in Christ.

G-d To observant Jews, God's name is considered too sacred to write out. Instead, it is written G-d.

gentile A non-Jew.

get A Jewish divorce decree.

goy The most commonly used word for a non-Jew is *goy*. The word, which means "nation," refers to the fact that goyim are members of nations other than the Children of Israel. There is nothing inherently insulting about the word "goy," although it has adopted a slight disparaging edge.

hamula "Kinship group." Since Arab society emphasizes the group over the individual, people see themselves as extensions of the hamula.

Hanukkah *See* Chanukah.

Hinduism Hinduism is rooted in the belief that the individual should connect their selves (*Atman*) with Brahman (or Godhead), the spiritual source of the universe.

Holy Spirit The spirit of God.

imam A prayer leader.

Islam In Arabic, the word *Islam* means "surrender" or "submission" to the will of God.

Jainism A dualistic, ascetic religion founded in the sixth century B.C.E. by a Hindu reformer as a revolt against the caste system and the vague world spirit of Hinduism.

Jehovah The name of the God of the Hebrew people incorrectly translated from the Hebrew text.

Jehovah's Witness Established in 1870 in Pennsylvania, Jehovah's Witnesses believe in the second coming of Christ and consider each Witness (member) a minister. The religion teaches that Christ began His invisible reign as king in 1914. They believe that soon the forces of good (led by Christ) will defeat the forces of evil (led by Satan) at the battle of Armageddon. Thereafter, Christ will rule the world for a thousand years.

Jesus Christ   In Christian theology, the Savior.

Judaism   The monotheistic religion of the Jews, based on the teachings and commentaries of the rabbis as found in the Talmud.

Kaddish   Jewish prayer said to mark yearly anniversaries of a person's death.

karma   In Hinduism and Buddism, an action that brings inevitable results, either in this life or in a reincarnation; in Hinduism, one of the means of reaching Brahman.

ketubah   A Jewish marriage contract.

kibbutz   A cooperative farm in Israel.

Koran   Also **Qur'an**. The holy book of Islam. Muslims regard the Koran as God's direct speech to Muhammad, mediated by Gabriel (the angel of revelation). As a result, the Qur'an is considered infallible.

kosher   Refers to a series of dietary laws followed by all Orthodox Jews and some Conservative and Reform Jews.

Latter-Day Saints (Mormons)   Established by Joseph Smith in the early 1800s, the Mormon religion follows many basic tenets of Christianity, but diverges in three key points: a belief in the prenatal existence of human souls; a conviction that the Trinity is three separate individuals; the belief that humans can attain the status of godhood.

Lent   The 40-day period of penance preceding Easter. It begins on Ash Wednesday and concludes at midnight on Holy Saturday (the day before Easter Sunday).

liturgy   A form of public worship; ritual.

Lutheran   A sixteenth-century movement headed by Martin Luther. According to Lutheran doctrine, everyone is a sinner due to original sin and is in bondage to the powers of evil. Salvation is God's gift, not dependent on worthiness or merit.

mass   A service in which Roman Catholics celebrate their faith, the Mass consists of several parts of which the longest and most important are the liturgy of the Word and the Eucharist liturgy, during which Holy Communion is distributed. Within this structure, music, pageantry, and other elements are varied to suit the occasion.

matzoth   An unleavened bread eaten by Jews during the holiday of Passover.

Mennonites   Named after Menno Simons (1496–1561), a Dutch Anabaptist leader, the Mennonites are an evangelical Protestant sect that practices baptism of believers only, restricts marriage to members of the denomination, and is noted for simplicity of living and plain dress. The Mennonites reject most of the developments of modern society.

Menorah   A seven-branched candelabrum, can be found in synagogues and is used on Chanukah.

Messiah   The Greek word for "Christ," or the anointed one.

Methodist   A branch of Protestantism that believes in personal salvation through faith, and Christian perfection.

Mezuzah   A small case attached to the doorposts of traditional Jewish homes. It serves as a reminder of God, not as a good-luck charm. Jews touch the mezuzah and then kiss their fingers to express love and respect for God.

minaret   A tower on a mosque.

mizvoth   In Judaism, the commandments by which individuals interact with one another and with God.

mohel   A rabbi specially trained to perform Jewish circumcisions; the ceremony is called a *bris*.

moksha   In Hinduism, means "liberation"—liberation from the temporal world through self-discovery, the union of the self with the Godhead, Atman-Brahman.

monotheism   A doctrine or belief that there is only one God.

Mormon   See **Latter Day Saints**.

mosque   The Muslim house of worship.

muezzin   In Islam, the crier who calls worshippers to prayer, from a mosque, on public announcement systems.

Muhammad   The founding prophet of Islam.

Muslim   A follower of Islam, means "one who surrenders to God."

nirvana   In Buddhism, nirvana is freedom from the endless cycle of reincarnations, each with its own form of suffering.

Orthodox Christian   See **Eastern Orthodox**.

Orthodox Judaism   The Orthodox movements all believe that the Torah is true and has come down intact and unchanged. Men and women do not sit together at prayer and the service is nearly all in Hebrew. Orthodox Jews follow traditional customs, such as lighting the Sabbath candles, limiting their activities on the Sabbath, and observing special food laws. These customs are rare among American Reform Jews.

Passover   Passover (Pesach) is an eight-day holiday that celebrates the Jewish Exodus from Egypt after generations of slavery. It refers to the fact that God "passed over" the houses of the Jews when he was slaying the firstborn of Egypt.

Pentecostal   A denomination that stresses Scripture and the teachings of the Holy Spirit.

Pope   The spiritual leader of the Roman Catholic church.

pre-Cana   Refers to Christ's presence at a wedding in Cana of Galilee. The term is used to refer to Catholic pre-marital counseling.

predestination   The belief that God has foreordained ("predestined") salvation for the elect, His chosen people.

Presbyterian   The Presbyterians emerged from the Protestant Reformation of the 1500s. In the beginning, the religion stressed the authority of Scripture and predestination; the former remains, but the latter is no longer a central element.

priests   Catholic men ordained to serve as religious clergy. Catholic women bound to a religious order are called *nuns* or *sisters;* their male counterparts are called *monks, friars,* or *brothers.*

privacy   Privacy is discretion; *secrecy* is concealment. The first is open; the second, closed.

proselytize   To try to convert others to your religious beliefs.

Protestantism   One of the three major divisions of Christianity, the others being Roman Catholicism and Orthodoxy. Protestantism began as a movement to reform the Western Christian church in the sixteenth century, resulting in the Protestant Reformation, which severed the reformed churches from the Roman Catholic church. The declared aim of the original reformers was to keep the Christian faith as it had been at the beginning, while keeping what they thought valuable from the Roman Catholic traditions that had developed during the intervening centuries.

Qur'an (or Koran)   See **Koran.**

rabbi   A rabbi is a Jewish religious leader. The word "rabbi" means *teacher.*

Ramadan   The holy month during which Muslims fast from daybreak to sunset by refraining from eating, drinking, and sexual intercourse.

reconstructionist movement   In Judaism, an offshoot of the Conservative movement. Reconstructive Jews believe that Judaism is an evolving religious civilization. They don't believe in a personified deity that is active in history or that God chose the Jewish people.

Reform Judaism   Reform Jews believe that the Bible was written by separate sources, not by God. Reform Jews retain much of the values and ethics of Judaism, along with some of the practices and the culture. Men and women pray side by side and much of the service is in English. The religious service is shorter than that found in Conservative or Orthodox congregations.

religion   Can be defined as a way of life or belief based on a person's ultimate relation to the universe or God. As such, religion is often an integral part of a person's identity.

rhythm method   A method of birth control that involves abstaining from intercourse during the times of the female cycle when fertilization is most likely.

Roman Catholic Church   The Catholic Church is called "Roman" because its spiritual leader, the Pope, is based in Rome.

Roman Catholicism   The largest body of Christians in the world belongs to the Roman Catholic Church. Catholics believe that Jesus Christ established the Church under the leadership of Peter, his disciple. Catholics accept the seven sacraments.

Rosh Hashanah   The Jewish New Year, culminating in Yom Kippur. It's a time of introspection, when observant Jews look back at the mistakes of the past year and plan changes to make in the new year. People don't fast, but they do spend the day praying in the synagogue. Apples dipped in honey are often eaten to symbolize a sweet new year.

sacraments   The Church teaches that the seven sacraments were instituted by Christ and given to the church to administer. The vehicles of grace that they convey, the sacraments are necessary for salvation.

Saktism   A form of worship dedicated to the female consorts of Vishnu and Siva.

samsara   The Hindu word for reincarnation.

seder   A special meal held on the first night of Passover (on the first two nights for more observant Jews). The ritual meal involves special foods served in a set order, prayers, and songs.

Sephardic Jews   Sephardic Jews are descended from Spaniards. Some speak Ladino, which was based on Spanish and Hebrew.

Seventh Day Adventist   Seventh-Day Adventists believe Christ will return to earth soon, even though the exact time cannot be determined; that the Bible is the sole religious authority; that grace alone is sufficient for salvation; that the wicked will be destroyed at the Second Coming; that the just (including the living and the resurrected dead) will be granted everlasting life.

Shaygetz   The male equivalent of a shikse (see **shikse**).

Shi'ite Muslim   One who belongs to the partisan sect of Islam. About 16 percent of all Muslims belong to the Shi'ite sect.

Shikse   from the Hebrew word meaning "abomination," is a pejorative term for a non-Jewish woman. *Shaygetz* is the male equivalent.

Shiva   The Jewish seven-day mourning period following the burial of a loved one.

shul   The Yiddish term for "synagogue" used by the Orthodox and Chasidim.

Sikh   Means *disciple*, one who seeks the truth.

Sikhism   Founded by Guru Nanak in the early sixteenth century, the Sikh religion is a combination of Hindu and Islamic beliefs. The religion advocates a search for eternal truth, rejects the Hindu caste system, and stresses the equality of all men and women. Sikhs believe in reincarnation but reject the notion of divine incarnation.

Star of David (Magen David)   This six-pointed star is the symbol most commonly associated with Judaism today. It appears on Israel's flag as well as many other items.

Sunna   In Islam, the Sunna is known through the *Hadith*, the body of traditions based on what Muhammad did or said. Unlike the Qur'an, the Hadith is considered fallible because it has come down through the oral tradition.

Sunnite Muslim   One who belongs to the traditionalist sect of Islam. Most Muslims (83 percent) identify themselves as Sunnites.

synagogue   The center of the Jewish religious community: a place of prayer, study and education, social and charitable work, and a social center.

Tipitaka   The Buddhist holy books, oral beliefs written down after Buddha's death.

Torah   The Pentateuch, the first of three Jewish divisions of the Old Testament; often used to refer to the Old Testament itself.

triangulation   Occurs when a third party gets sucked into helping two people communicate with each other.

Unitarian   Unitarians deny the doctrine of the Trinity, believing instead that God exists in one person only.

United Church of Christ   A Protestant denomination, the United Church of Christ was organized in Cleveland, Ohio, in 1957 when the General Council of the Congregational Christian Churches and the Evangelical and Reformed Churches combined.

values   Your *values* are your moral touchstones, the ideals and customs that spark emotional responses.

Vedas   The Hindu holy books.

wake   A vigil held over a corpse until burial.

ward   The Mormon ward are the congregants, similar to a Protestant, Jewish, or Catholic congregation.

Yahweh   In Judaism, the single God who created the universe and continues to govern it.

yarmulke   A skullcap worn by Jewish men as they pray, and by non-Jewish men in a synagogue as a sign of respect.

Yom Kippur   Yom Kippur, the Day of Atonement, is the most important holiday of the Jewish year. On Yom Kippur, observant Jews atone for the sins of the past year by demonstrating repentance and making amends. Most of the holiday is spent praying in the synagogue. Services end at nightfall, with the blowing of the *shofar*, the ram's horn. The holiday takes place in the fall.

Resources on Interfaith Relationships

I'm often asked, "Where can I find a book on ...?" Below is information about some of the resources I used in writing *The Complete Idiot's Guide to Interfaith Relationships*. I also included some material I didn't access but that looked interesting and useful. In some cases, these materials had not yet been published; in others, they repeated information I already had. Nonetheless, these sources might contain facts that you haven't yet discovered. The information is arranged by religion and topic.

Amish and Memmonites

Consult the following sources for futher information about the religious beliefs of the Amish and Memmonites, especially their stance on interfaith marriages.

Web Sites and Mail Order

"Mennonite Connections on the WWW" has a number of Amish links at http://www.personal.umich.edu/~bpl/mennocon.html#amish.

The Plain People is a Web site maintained by the Pennsylvania Dutch Country Welcome Center that describes the Amish, the Mennonites, the Brethren, and the other "Plain People" near Lancaster, PA. The site's address is http://padutch. welcome. com/amish.html.

The National Committee For Amish Religious Freedom promotes religious freedom for the Amish. See http://holycrosslivonia.org/amish/.

The Mennonite Information Center supplies information on both Amish and Mennonites. Their address is 2209 Millstream Road, Lancaster, PA 17602-1494, USA.

Books and Videos

Folsom, Jan. *The Amish: Images of a Tradition*. Stackpole Books, 1995.

Good, Merle & Phillis Good. *20 Most Asked Questions About the Amish and Mennonites*. Good Books, 1995.

Hostetler, John A. *Amish Roots: A Treasury of History, Wisdom, and Lore*. Johns Hopkins University Press, 1992.

Kraybill, Donald B. *The Amish and the State*. Johns Hopkins University Press, 1993.

Kraybill, Donald B. & Steven M. Nolt. *Amish Enterprise: From Plows to Profits*. Johns Hopkins University Press, 1995.

Kraybill, Donald B. & Marc Alan Olshan. *The Amish Struggle With Modernity*. University Press of New England, 1994.

Niemeyer, Lucian. *Old Order Amish: Their Enduring Way of Life*. Johns Hopkins University Press, 1996.

Nolt, Steven M. *A History of the Amish*. Good Books, 1992.

Smucker, Donovan E. *Sociology of Canadian Mennonites, Hutterites and Amish: A Bibliography With Annotations*. Wilfrid Laurier University Press, 1977.

Multicultural Peoples: The Amish (Multicultural Peoples of North America Video Series). Baker & Taylor Video, 1993.

Christianity

Consult the following sources for further information about Christian religious beliefs, especially their stance on interfaith marriages.

Books

Book of Common Worship. Westminster/John Knox Press, 1993.

Christian Marriage (Supplemental Liturgical Resource 3). Westminster Press, 1986.

Henesy, Michael and Rosemary Gallagher. *How to Survive Being Married to a Catholic*. Liguori Publications, 1997.

Office of Ecumenical and Interfaith Relations. *Interfaith Marriage: A Resource by Presbyterian Christians*. Presbyterian Church, 1992.

Islam

Consult the following sources for further information about Muslim religious beliefs, especially their stance on interfaith marriages.

Web Sites and Mail Order

Islamic Educational Center of Seattle at http://www.ershad.org . This Web site is dedicated to providing a better forum for understanding the religion of Islam and its heritage.

Ghazwa Islamic Web at http://home.beseen.com/belief/khizar_al_khan/index.htm includes Islamic articles, an online book store, discussion forum, and links to Islamic sites.

Arabic.com provides news and views from the Muslim world.

Books and Videos

Abd al Ati, Hammudah. *The Family Structure in Islam.* American Trust Publications, 1977.

Anway, Carol Anderson. *Daughters of Another Path: Experiences of American Women Choosing Islam.* Yawna Publications, 1995.

Chalfonte, Jessica. *I Am Muslim* (Religions of the World [Rosen Publishing Group]). Powerkids Press, 1997.

Cragg, Kenneth (ed.). *Common Prayer: A Muslim-Christian Spiritual Anthology.* Oneworld Publications Ltd., 1999.

Hughes, Thomas Patrick. *A Dictionary of Islam: Being a Cyclopaedia of the Doctrines, Rites, Ceremonies and Customs, Together With the Technical and Theological Terms, of the Muslim Religion.* Kazi Publications, 1995.

Hubbard, Benjamin J. (ed.). *The Abraham Connection: A Jew, Christian and Muslim in Dialogue* (Church and the World, Vol 6). Cross Cultural Pubns/Crossroads, 1994.

Jones-Bey, Hassaun Ali. *Better Than a Thousand Months: An American Muslim Family Celebration.* Ibn Musa, 1997.

Kose, Ali. *Conversion to Islam.* Kegan Paul International, 1996.

Lang, Jeffrey. *Even Angels Ask: A Journey to Islam in America.* Amana Publications, 1997.

Poston, Larry A. and Carl F., Jr. Ellis (Contributor). *The Changing Face of Islam in America: Understanding and Reaching Your Muslim Neighbor.* Christian Publications Inc. 1996.

Wasserstrom, Steven M. *Between Muslim and Jew.* Princeton University Press, 1995.

Wormser, Richard. *American Islam: Growing Up Muslim in America.* Walker & Co, 1994.

Judaism

Consult the following sources for further information about Jewish religious beliefs, especially their stance on interfaith marriages.

Web Sites and Mail Order

The site http://www.interfaithfamily.com/article/issue7/sampleif.htm features a sample of a Jewish-Catholic wedding ceremony with both a priest and rabbi officiating.

Read "Thoughts on my Interfaith Wedding" by Rabbi Tirzah Firestone at http://www.interfaithfamily.com/article/issue7/firestone. htm.

The site http://www.tlc-services.com/Ceremonies.html provides services that help you plan an interfaith wedding and also provides priests, rabbis, and others to officiate wherever you want to get married.

Access a mail order service offering a wide variety of Judaic materials at 1-800-JUDAISM.

Commission on Reform Jewish Outreach. *What Is Reform Jewish Outreach*? Union of American Hebrew Congregations and Central Conference of American Rabbis, 838 Fifth Avenue, NY NY 10021, 1991. [Non-Orthodox]

Bibles

Tanakh: A New Translation of the Holy Scriptures. Jewish Publication Society.

The Pentateuch and Haftorahs. Soncino Press.

The Stone Tanach. Mesorah Publications.

Books

Belin, David. *Why Choose Judaism: New Dimensions of Jewish Outreach.* UAHC Press #381900, 1985. [Non-Orthodox.] Explores the uniqueness of Judaism and its special roles in America today. Designed for partners in an interfaith relationship.

Biale, Rachel. *Women and Jewish Law.* Schocken Books.

Cohen, A. *Everyman's Talmud.* Schocken Books.

Donin, Rabbi Hayim Halevy. *To Be a Jew.* Basic Books.

Dovetail: A Newsletter by and for Jewish-Christian Families. Boulder, CO: Dovetail Publishing. Order from 3014A Folsom Street, Boulder, CO, 80304.

Eban, Abba. *Heritage: Civilization and the Jews.* Summit Books.

Forster, Brenda and Tabachnik, Joseph. *Jews by Choice: A Study of Converts to Reform and Conservative Judaism.* K'tav, 1991.

Gruzen, Lee. *Raising Your Jewish/Christian Child.* Newmarket Press, 1990.

Himelstein, Shmuel. *The Jewish Primer.* Facts on File.

Jacobs, Sidney J. and Betty J. Jacobs. *Clues About Jews for People Who Aren't.* Jacobs Ladder Publications, 1985.

Kemelman, Harry. *Conversations with Rabbi Small.* Ballantine Books, 1987.

King, Andrea. *If I'm Jewish and You're Christian, What Are the Kids?* UAHC Press, 1994.

Lerner, Devon. *Celebrating Interfaith Marriages: Creating Your Jewish/Christian Ceremony.* Owl Books, 1999.

Linzer, Norman, Irving N. Levitz, David J. Schnall (Ed.). *Crisis and Continuity: The Jewish Family in the 21st Century.* K'tav Publishing House, 1995.

Litvin, Baruch. *Jewish Identity: Modern Responsa and Opinions on the Registration of Children of Mixed Marriages.* Feldheim, 1970.

Mayer, Egon. *Love and Tradition: Marriage Between Jews and Christians.* Schocken Books, 1987.

Neusner, Jacob. *The Mishnah—a New Translation.* Yale University Press.

Pasternak, Velvel. *The Jewish Fake Book.* Tara Publications. (A fake book has only the melody line, chords, and lyrics, rather than a complete piano arrangement.)

Petsonk, Judy and Jim Remsen. *The Intermarriage Handbook: A Guide for Jews and Christians.* Quill/William Morrow, 1988. (This book explains basis of each other's culture, and guidelines on how to proceed.)

Prager, Dennis and Joseph Telushkin. *The Nine Questions People Ask About Judaism.* Simon & Schuster.

Reuben, Steven Carr. *Raising Jewish Children in a Contemporary World: The Modern Parent's Guide to Creating a Jewish Home.* Prima, 1992.

Romanoff, Lena. *Your People, My People—Finding Acceptance and Fulfillment as a Jew By Choice.* Jewish Publication Society, 1990. Focuses on conversion, but gives insights on intermarriage and how to make conversion work. (Non-Orthodox)

Sacks, David G. *Welcoming the Intermarried In Your Jewish Family.* Jewish Outreach Institute (33 W 42nd Street), New York, NY, 1995.

Seltzer, Sanford. *Jews and Non-Jews: Falling in Love.* UAHC Press #164050. Informal guide on intermarriage for couples and their families. (Non-Orthodox)

———. *Jews and Non-Jews: Getting Married: A Look At Interfaith Marriage and its Consequences for Jewish Survival.* UAHC Press #164055, 1984. Discussion for couples contemplating intermarriage from the Reform Jewish perspective.

Siegel, Richard et. al. *The First Jewish Catalog.* Jewish Publication Society.

Silverstein, Alan. *It All Begins with a Date: Jewish Concerns about Intermarriage*. Jason Aronson, 1995.

————. *Preserving Jewishness in Your Family: After Intermarriage Has Occurred*. Jason Aronson, 1995.

General Interfaith Issues

The following resources provide information ongeneral interfaith problems.

Web Sites and Mail Order

InterfaithFamily.com offers support for interfaith families. The site includes a webzine, articles, discussion boards, and an online shop.

Books

Augustin, Barbara and David E. Kennard. *Marriage Across Frontiers*. Multilingual Matters, 1989.

Cohen, Paul and Rachel Cohen. *Mixed Blessings: Overcoming the Stumbling Blocks in an Interfaith Marriage*. Viking Penguin.

Crester, Gary and Joseph J. Leon (ed.). *Intermarriage in the United States: Marriage and Family Review;* Volume Five, Number One. Haworth Press, 1982.

Crohn, Joel. *Mixed Matches: How to Create Successful Interracial, Interethnic, and Interfaith Relationships*. Fawcette Columbine, 1995.

Dovetail, a journal for Jewish/Christian families. One-Year subscription: $24.99. For information call 1-800-530-1596.

Glaser, Gabrielle. *Strangers to the Tribe. Portraits of Interfaith Marriages*. Houghton Mifflin, 1997.

Goodman-Malamuth, Leslie and Robin Margolis. *Between Two Worlds: Choices for Grown Children of Jewish-Christian Parents*. Pocket Books, 1992.

Gruzen, Lee F. *Raising Your Jewish Christian Child: Wise Choices for Interfaith Parents*. Dodd, Mead, and Company, 1987.

———— *Raising Your Jewish Christian Child: How Interfaith Parents Can Give Children the Best of Both Their Heritages*. Newmarket Press, 1990.

Hawxhurst, Joan C. (ed.) *Interfaith Wedding Ceremonies: Samples and Sources*. Dovetail Publishing, 1997.

———— *Interfaith Family Guidebook: Practical Advice for Jewish and Christian Partners*. Dovetail Publishing, 1998.

Ho, Man Keung. *Building a Successful Intermarriage Between Religions, Social Classes, Ethnic Groups or Races.* Abbey Press, 1984.

Jacobs, Sidney J. and Betty J. Jacobs. *122 Clues for Jews Whose Children Intermarry.* Jacobs Ladder Publications, 1988.

Johnson, Walton and Michael Warren. *Inside the Mixed Marriage: Accounts of Changing Attitudes, Patterns and Perceptions of Cross-Cultural and Interracial Marriages,* 1994.

The Journal of Marriage & the Family, November 1993, Vol 55, Issue 4.

King, Andrea. *If I'm Jewish and You're Christian, What are the Kids? A Parenting Guide for Interfaith Families.* Union of American Hebrew Congregations, 1993.

Lerner, Devon A. *Celebrating Interfaith Marriages: Creating Your Jewish/Christian Ceremony,* 1999.

Packard, Gwen. *Coping in an Interfaith Family.* Rosen, 1993.

Petsonk, Judy and Jim Remsen. *The Intermarriage Handbook: A Guide for Jews and Christians.* Quill.

Reuben, Steven Carr. *But How Will You Raise the Children?: A Guide To Interfaith Marriage.* Pocket Books, 1987.

——. *Making Interfaith Marriage Work.* Prima, 1994.

Richardson, Brenda Lane. *Guess Who's Coming to Dinner: Celebrating Interethnic, Interfaith, and Interracial Relationships.* Wildcat Canyon Press, 2000.

Romano, Dugan. *Intercultural Marriage: Promises & Pitfalls.* Intercultural Press, 1997.

Rosenbaum, Mary Helene and Rosenbaum, Stanley Ned. *Celebrating Our Differences: Living Two Faiths in One Marriage.* Ragged Edge Press, 1994.

Rosenberg, Roy A.; Meehan, Peter; and Payne, John Wade. *Happily Intermarried: Authoritative Advice for a Joyous Jewish-Christian Marriage.* New York: Collier Books, 1989.

Schaper, Donna. *Raising Interfaith Children: Spiritual Orphans or Spiritual Heirs?* Crossroads Publications Company, 1999.

Silverstein, Alan. *Dual Faith Parenting, Second Thoughts on a Popular Trend.* The Federation of Jewish Men's Clubs, Inc., 1993.

Smith, Reger C. *Two Cultures One Marriage: Pre-Marital Counseling for Mixed Marriages.* Andrews University Press, 1996.

Spickard, Paul R. *Mixed Blood: Intermarriage and Ethnic Identity in Twentieth-Century America.* University of Wisconsin Press, 1991.

Index

305

THE COMPLETE IDIOT'S GUIDE TO

Arts & Sciences | Business & Personal Finance | Computers & the Internet | Family & Home | Hobbies & Crafts | Language Reference | Health & Fitness | Personal Enrichment | Sports & Recreation | Teens

IDIOTSGUIDES.COM
Introducing a new and different Web Site

Millions of people love to learn through *The Complete Idiot's Guide*® books. Discover the same pleasure online in **idiotsguides.com** – part of The Learning Network.

Idiotsguides.com is a new and different website, where you can:

- Explore and download more than 150 fascinating and useful mini-guides—FREE! Print out or send to a friend.

- Share your own knowledge and experience as a mini-guide contributor.

- Join discussions with authors and exchange ideas with other lifelong learners.

- Read sample chapters from a vast library of *Complete Idiot's Guide*® books.

- Find out how to become an author.

- Check out upcoming book promotions and author signings.

- Purchase books through your favorite online retailer.

Learning for Fun. Learning for Life.

IDIOTSGUIDES.COM • LEARNINGNETWORK.COM

Copyright ©2000 Macmillan USA, Inc.